The evolution of retail systems

The evolution of retail systems, c.1800–1914

edited by
John Benson and Gareth Shaw

Leicester University Press
Leicester, London and New York

© Editors and contributors 1992

First published in Great Britain in 1992 by Leicester University Press
(a division of Pinter Publishers Limited)

Editorial offices
Fielding Johnson Building, University of Leicester,
Leicester, LE1 7RH, England

Trade and other enquiries
25 Floral Street, London, WC2E 9DS

British Library Cataloguing in Publication Data
A CIP catalogue record for this book is available from the
British Library

ISBN 0 7185 1335 5

For enquiries in North America please
contact PO Box 197, Irvington, NY 10533.

Library of Congress Cataloging-in-Publication Data
The Evolution of retail systems, c.1800–1914/edited by John Benson
 and Gareth Shaw.
    p. cm.
  Includes bibliographical references and index.
  ISBN 0-7185-1335-5
  1. Retail trade—History. I. Benson, John, 1945– . II. Shaw,
Gareth.
HF5429.E89 1992
381'.1'09—dc20
                                     91-39132
                                       CIP

Typeset by DP Photosetting, Aylesbury, Bucks
Printed and bound in Great Britain by
Biddles Ltd of Guildford and Kings Lynn

Contents

Notes on contributors

John Benson is Professor of history at Wolverhampton Polytechnic.

Dietrich Denecke is lecturer in geography at the University of Gottingen, Germany.

Martin Phillips is lecturer in geography at Coventry Polytechnic.

Martin Purvis is lecturer in geography at the University of Leeds.

Gareth Shaw is senior lecturer in geography at the University of Exeter.

List of figures

List of tables

Acknowledgements

The authors wish to acknowledge the Nuffield Foundation for providing funds to hold a conference on the evolution of retail systems. This enabled the contributors to test out their ideas and discuss at some length the general issues concerning the history of retailing. We are particularly grateful for the contributions of Michael Winstanley, Trevor Wild, Jeff Porter, John Jones, Andrew Alexander, Jane Southern and Diane Collins. In addition, we would like to thank Judy Gorton and Jane Skinner for all their efforts and patience in wordprocessing the text, and Terry Bacon for drawing the diagrams.

Chapter 1

The study of retail development

Gareth Shaw

1.1 Introduction

In the foreword to his book on *The Wheels of Commerce*, Braudel (1985) writes that 'Between "material life" (in the sense of an extremely elementary economy) and "economic life", the contact surface is not continuous, but takes the form of thousands of humble points of intersection: markets, stalls, shops.' The purpose of this book is to explore and examine these different 'humble points', especially their evolution during the period of industrialisation in the nineteenth and early twentieth centuries. We start by reviewing the various perspectives presented on the history of retailing and retail change, in an attempt to demonstrate both the need for closer academic co-operation and more comparative studies. Braudel (1985, p.21) tried to 'grasp regularities and mechanisms, to write a sort of general economic history', which in a sense marks one of the aims of this book, to present a general history of retailing, set within a comparative framework.

1.2 Perspectives on retail change

A common complaint heralding almost any publication on the history of retailing is that it is a much neglected field of study. The claim is that most large-scale historical studies have bypassed retailing and the distribution system for seemingly more promising fields of study in manufacturing, or social and demographic change. Thus, Jefferys (1954, preface) claimed that the 'study by the British . . . of the art of shopkeeping has been surprisingly neglected'. This he thought was because most British economic historians held the 'false belief that distribution is a sterile, unproductive activity' to study. Similar sentiments are expressed by Porter and Livesay (1971, p.1), whose work on marketing in nineteenth-century America attempted 'to redress part of the historical imbalance reflected in the many shelves groaning with the weight of volumes dealing with the means by which Americans have produced manufactured goods'.

A closer inspection of the studies researching the history of retailing reveals two interesting and significant features. The first is that the statements about retailing being a neglected theme tend not to diminish over time, thus giving the impression that even now there is little in the way of any long-term research being established which can build on previous studies. These views are explained by a second factor, which is the extremely fragmented nature of existing research on the history of retailing. The study of retailing and the distribution system in general remains a kaleidoscope of unrelated perspectives, with very few comparative studies. Although workers drawn from the fields of economic history, geography, business studies, economics and marketing have all presented, at one time or another, their views of retail change, they have made little or no reference to one another's work. This seems particularly surprising as the potential for multi-disciplinary work was given early recognition when, in 1958, a conference on marketing history held in Chicago stressed the need both for comparative studies and the establishment of a unified research centre (Myers and Smalley, 1959).

At this conference the group gathered together included anthropologists, economic historians, geographers, business historians, business consultants and market researchers, and we can safely assume that each subject represented had – and has – different aims and methodologies. Thus, for those interested in marketing and business studies, the interest in retail history forms part of the search for a better understanding of contemporary retail institutions, motives that may be very different from those of the historian or geographer (Savitt, 1989). It is such diversity of aims that produces not only different perspectives on the history of retailing, but also, very often, isolation within, and more particularly between, the various subject areas.

This also raises the question of whether such diverse views can be brought together, and if so whether they can provide any meaningful framework within which to examine retail change. Before embarking on such an exercise it is necessary to get some perspective on these different approaches, at least in general if not in detail. Consideration needs to be given to examining those attempts at constructing evolutionary and explanatory frameworks or models of retail change. Within this context some of the most promising studies are to be found within the fields of economics and business history. Unfortunately, many of the studies have been specific and based very strongly on events in the USA, thereby adding a further complexity to our general understanding of retail systems. That even such nationalist approaches take very different forms may be illustrated by examining three major studies of marketing in North America. For example Hower (1943), in his study of department store evolution, recognises the appearance of 'alternating movements' in the history of retail trade. One movement was towards the specialisation of the functions performed, or the goods handled by individual retailers. The alternative movement was away from such specialisation toward the integration of related activities under one management or through the diversification of products handled by a single firm. Before 1800 there was little retail specialisation in North America, but such a trend became the dominant feature between 1800 and 1860 according to Hower, who quotes many contemporary views to reinforce his thesis. Accordingly, the movement towards retail specialisation progressed so rapidly along the eastern seaboard of America that in 1855 a Philadelphia publication stressed that 'The tendency . . . is to simplification, and in many cases only a single class of articles is kept by the merchant' (Hower, 1943, p.73).

   This may be compared with the work of the American economist, Nystrom (1930) who identified five main periods of retail change: the prehistoric Indian trade, the trading post era, the period of the general store, speciality retailing and the rise of large-scale retail institutions. Though far less historically specific than Hower's work, Nystrom was essentially chasing the same goal, to provide a descriptive framework of retail development. In both studies the emphasis is on the predominant form of retailing, and as such they very often lose sight of the survival of the more traditional types of retail structure, as well as regional variations.
   A broader view of retail change in North America is provided by Porter and Livesay (1971) who present an evolutionary overview of the distribution system, focussing on the changing channels of distribution. Within this perspective the critical nature of change depends on the interplay between producers, merchants and retailers. This interplay, they argue, produced three distinct phases in the development of America's distribution system. The first, before 1815, was characterised by the 'all-purpose merchant', who dealt in a wide range of goods, buying and selling items at wholesale and retail, as well as acting as importers and exporters. This was followed between 1815 and 1870 by the 'age of the wholesaler', with merchants becoming more specialised as the economy expanded and became more complex. After 1870 Porter and Livesay (1971) argue that the domination of the independent merchant was strongly challenged by the rise of modern manufacturing corporations. Once again emphasis is on the dominant form with little attention being given to the variations around this.
   In addition to such views the fields of business history and marketing also produced a range of more general evolutionary frameworks aimed at summarising changes in retail organisation. As Table 1.1 shows, such perspectives range from place-specific models, such as the 'general–specific–general cycle' through to broader-based interpretations exemplified by McNair's 'wheel of retailing'. McNair's model in particular has formed the focus of much debate in marketing as

Table 1.1 Major theories of retail institutional change

Theory	Basic characteristics
General – specific – general cycle or retail accordion	Retail institutions widen (general) and narrow (specific) their range of goods over time. First noted by Hower (1943) and extended by Hollander (1966).
Retail life cycle	Based on product life cycle, retail cycle maintains institutions evolve through anthropomorphic stages of 'birth', 'growth', 'maturity' and 'decline' (Davidson, 1970).
Economic natural selection	Environmental factors determine introduction, acceptance and survival of retail institutions through process of 'natural selection' (Alchain, 1950; Gist, 1968).
Wheel of retailing	See text for characteristics

the credibility of such theories of retail change has been tested (Hollander, 1966). This model contends that new retail institutions begin as cut-price, low-cost operations which subsequently 'trade-up' (Brown, 1988, p.16). McNair (1931 and 1958) maintained that North American department stores and multiple retailers evolved through three stages. First, they start by developing cut-price operations, second become high-cost modes of distribution, and the third stage sees the appearance of new, low-cost retailers. Similar observations have also been made in other countries, such as Germany, where Nieschlag (1954) claimed that the retail system was characterised by marked periodic appearances of dynamic and low-cost retailers. Certainly the evidence collected on the rise of British department stores would support some parts of these changes, though not all organisations followed the same evolutionary pathways.

These so-called theories of retail change centre to a large extent on providing a descriptive framework for the behaviour of the firm or at best a sector of the retail trade, such as multiple retailers or department stores. Such perspectives also relate to economic views of retail competition, the most relevant of which to historical studies is that provided by Schumpeter (1939). His work introduced the concept of repetitive or innovative competition, in which new retail organisations successfully competed in established markets.

Unfortunately, few empirical studies of a historical nature have been undertaken to help establish either the usefulness or validity of such theoretical perspectives. For example, Mason and Mayer (1984), and Kotler (1986) present these retail theories as major principles in marketing, but without any long-term, historical background to demonstrate their worth. In this respect Shaw's (1978) study of Hull remains one of the few attempts to link the ideas of retail competition and structural change to a historical perspective of the growth of multiple retailers. Savitt (1989, p.336) goes further in his criticism of these theories of retail change and urges that they 'should not be confused with a history of American retailing'. He claims that they are nothing more than artefacts of the history of retailing rather than its substance and that they are too narrowly focussed on one type of retail institution to be of much general use.

We can recognise therefore within the fields of business history, economics and retail marketing two main perspectives on retail change. One involves the somewhat narrowly based and largely untested theories concerned with retail organisational change, while the other approach is more closely related to describing structural changes based on historical trends. This latter group of ideas also attempts to provide explanations for retail change, which is best highlighted in the rather undervalued work of Bucklin (1972). His model of structural changes in the retail system firmly linked variations in retail operations with changes in consumer demand, with strong support being given to the idea that retail change was most influenced by differences in the levels of consumer income. The 'model' itself as originally outlined by Bucklin is demand-led, although adaptations by Shaw and Wild (1979) introduced a broader link between levels of industrialisation, urbanisation and stages of retail development in Britain. As Figure 1.1 shows, this adapted model suggests that the British retail system moved through a recognisable sequence of changes, from stages dominated by markets to periods when shops became more important. It should be stressed, however, that the model emphasises retail development in terms of changes in average retail operating costs, rather than

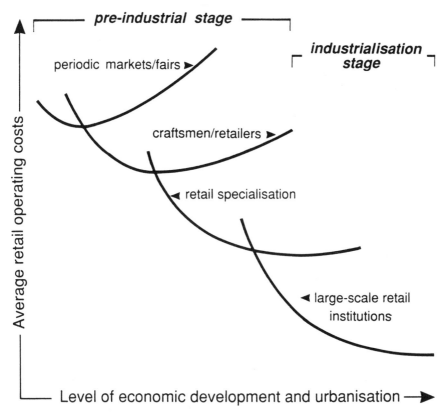

Figure 1.1 The idealised relationship between economic development and retail change in Britain

explicitly pointing to a period totally dominated by a particular form of retailing.

Bucklin's work and its adaptations in Britain are potentially more significant since they can serve as bridgeheads between many of the different disciplines involved in researching retail change. This role may be demonstrated by examining the contributions of economic historians and geographers to the debate. In both areas of study, economic and social variables have received considerable attention. The view is clearly expressed by Alexander (1970, p.1) in his study of English retailing, in which he states that 'economic and social variables . . . determine the kind of distribution system which is necessary and possible for any given society'.

Economic historians, especially those working within Britain, have made few attempts to present any detailed, structural perspectives of retail change. In the British context progress has been conditioned by a series of interrelated events. The first of these was the publication of a highly influential book, by Jefferys (1954), which sought to present a comprehensive and compelling view of the rise of modern large-scale retailing. He argued that, even by the mid-nineteenth century, 'the wholesale and retail trades of Britain . . . were examples of those trades that still bore the marks of the old system rather than of the new', and that major changes only occurred during the second part of the century (Jefferys, 1954, p.1). His book had two effects. The first was to act as something of a deterrent to further large-scale studies of British retailing. The second, during the 1970s and early 1980s, was to stimulate a debate over the timing of the growth of fixed-shop retailing. In fact, the issue of when shops became the predominant form of retailing became the focal point for the handful of studies produced by British academics (see Shaw, 1985, for a review).

The debate itself produced little innovative work in respect of any general perspectives on the evolution of retail systems. It did, however, remove the idea that rapid urban and industrial development, of the type encountered in nineteenth-century Britain, destroyed the more traditional retail forms of the market trader and the pedlar. Eventually the debate refocussed attention on the importance of taking a broad view of the retail distribution system, rather than merely limiting the examination of change to that of shop versus market stall (Shaw, 1985). Historical studies serve to challenge the so-called models of retail change on a number of different fronts. The first, as already mentioned, is the idea that new, dominant forms of retailing entirely sweep away older traditional systems. Evidence from Europe and North America completely contradicts this view, and shows the 'models' to be insensitive to a number of critical factors. First, they ignore that the pace of retail change and the degree to which new retail forms gain a stronghold varies by retail sector, type and size of settlement, and by region. Second, no account is taken of the resistance of existing, traditional retailers to new selling practices. All the models assume that economic factors predominate, but historical evidence shows time and again that the growth of new retail types is tempered by legal and political constraints imposed by traditional retailers. Davies (1966, p.64), for example, shows how even during the sixteenth century the freemen involved in the London food trades were 'constantly complaining about their privileges being infringed by foreigners (people from outside London) in selling food in the City'. The conflict of interests grew as more retailers entered the system from the seventeenth century onwards, though the need to be a freeman to enter the retail trade in Britain – the requirements of which were only legally removed by the 1835 Municipal Corporation Act – never acted as an effective barrier. By the nineteenth century the reaction to change and new forms of retail competition was just as pronounced though, as we shall see, was met in different ways in the case studies of Britain, Germany and Canada.

1.3 A synthetic approach to the history of retailing

The patchiness of research concerned with retail change has prompted the call by Hollander (1983) for a synthetic approach to the history of retailing. In Hollander's view such an approach would bring together the various individuals, institutions, events, trends and themes which are at present examined by different disciplines. He repeats the message of the Chicago conference more than fifty years ago, but now, as then, the multi-disciplinary pathway is paved with many problems, not least because of an absence of common goals and methodology.

Only Savitt (1989) has set out with the clear intention of attempting to follow a synthetic approach, but even this is limited to a small-scale study of retail change in New England during the early colonial period. His research has focussed on the identification of commercial and mercantile institutions, with the related functional analysis of retail types. Despite the limitations imposed by its temporal and spatial scales the study illustrates the main structural developments in retailing, through differentiating establishments by: type of product sold; sources of supply and customers; store location; and the functions of stores. Using these criteria, Savitt has been able to construct a descriptive, functional framework of the region's distribution system as shown in Table 1.2

Table 1.2 Retail development in New England: early colonial to 1796

Establishment type	Source of products	Location of customers	Primary functional orientation
Merchants	Import	Local/Regional	Wholesaling/retailing
Artisans (leather, pottery, etc.)	Local	Local	Production/retailing
Retail specialists (books and paper)	Import	Local/Regional	Retailing/production
General stores	Import/ Domestic	Regional	Retailing/ wholesaling/financing

Source: modified from Savitt, 1989

The type of analysis undertaken by Savitt highlights the importance of examining the system of retail distribution as well as the form of the retail unit. It is, however, a far cry from developing either a theory of retail change or, for that matter, a comprehensive history of retailing. Like Bucklin's work, it provides a template which may be useful for other studies. Other potentially useful templates come from the work of retail geographers. Of particular note are the studies by Berry (1963) and Simmons (1964) researching twentieth-century North American cities. Both stressed the importance of understanding the factors that produced retail change and focussed particular attention on the role of socio-economic forces. Simmons went further and offered a generalised model of urban retail change which identified two broad groups of factors, one of which may be termed modifying forces, in the sense that they provide the general background and stimulus for changes in the distribution system. These include changes in production and transport technology, trends in the national economy, and the growth of urbanisation. These interact through economic, social and ecological links with a series of controlling factors that produce changes in the number, organisation, structure, and location of retail units within a particular city (Figure 1.2). Shaw (1985) has attempted to utilise this model to explore changes in food supply within nineteenth-century cities, and to show how previous research has concentrated merely on the controlling factors, with little reference to the other forces. In this respect Simmons' model provides a convincing explanatory framework for the changes outlined in Bucklin's demand-led model of the different phases of retailing.

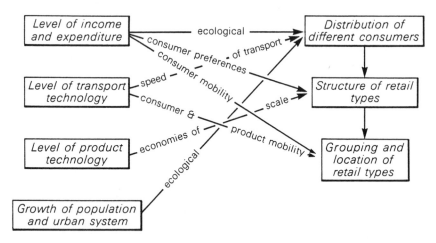

Figure 1.2 A generalised model of urban retail change (modified from Simmons, 1964)

The development of a synthetic or comprehensive perspective on the evolution of retail systems may therefore make use of three dominant models or frameworks. A generalised model of the type outlined by Simmons helps our understanding of the factors behind retail change and their interactions. This in turn leads to Bucklin's stage model, which allows us to conceptualise the different phases through which retail systems may evolve. Finally, the theories of retail institutional change give an insight into when and how particular types of retailer emerge.

Unfortunately, as we have seen, there is a considerable gap between these explanatory and descriptive frameworks and much of the history of retailing. In general a great deal of our knowledge about the long-term history of retail change remains fragmented along the lines of individual businesses, particular retail sectors and individual countries. It is the aim of this book to remove some of these demarcation lines in an attempt to provide a comparative study of the history of retailing.

1.4 Comparative studies of retail evolution

There have been very few comparative studies of retail change and certainly none that tackle the subject in any detailed historical perspective. Work on retail developments during the twentieth century has spawned some cross-cultural studies within Europe (Jefferys and Knee, 1962, Dawson, 1982) but these have paid only the smallest interest to any long term trends of historical aspects. Thus, Jefferys and Knee (1962. p.8) claim that 'historical evidence on changes in the numbers engaged in the distributive trades is somewhat scattered and not very reliable' for many

European countries. They nevertheless attempt to draw a general picture of the factors affecting retail change in different European economies, although most of their historical interests are confined to the period after 1930. Within these constraints they suggest, for example, strong relationships between the role of different types of independent retailer and regional economies, as shown in Table 1.3.

Table 1.3 The role of independent retailers in European economies during the early twentieth century

Type of retailer	Type of economy	Role in economy
Itinerant/market stall operator	Agrarian economies, e.g. S. Italy, Spain, Portugal, Greece	Important link between producer and consumer in agricultural communities
	Urbanised economies, e.g. parts of Germany and France	Acts as a channel of distribution for agricultural products to reach urban areas
Small independent	Developed urban economies, e.g. Britain and Belgium	Marginal role; often retailing seen as just a supplement to family income
Medium-sized independent	All European economies	The mainstay of retailing, and in urban areas form most important group of specialist retailers

Source: modified from Jefferys and Knee, 1962

At a more detailed and impressive scale of analysis and understanding is the work of Braudel ((1985), which seeks to present a comparative view of commerce (in all its forms) between the fifteenth and eighteenth centuries. The approach is, as the author states, 'the comparative method particularly recommended by Marc Bloch . . . using the perspectives of the long term' (Braudel, 1985, p.21). Retail markets and shops are unfortunately only given limited attention by Braudel (1985, p.68), who describes how 'shops of all categories came to conquer and devour the towns' during the seventeenth century and, more especially, the eighteenth century. This widespread and early growth of shops was, he claims, observed by contemporaries throughout Europe; for example, Rome in 1622 had an estimated 5,578 shops for about 114,000 inhabitants, while in Basle the number of shopkeepers increased by 40 per cent between the sixteenth and eighteenth centuries (Bennassar, 1967; Maversberg, 1963). Braudel attributes this 'boom in shopkeeping' to three main groups of factors. Population increase and long-term upward economic trends led to the establishment of shops; while their popularity spread because of 'long opening hours, advertising bargains' and through word of mouth. But the third, and the principal, factor according to him, was that shops provided credit. At this early stage of shop growth in seventeenth- and eighteenth-century Europe, it would seem that 'the shopkeeper, a capitalist in a very small way, lived between those who owed him money and those to whom he owed it' (Braudel, 1982, p.73).

Braudel's work gives us, therefore, a very limited starting point from which to develop more detailed comparative studies, and allows us to recognise in a very broad sense the apparent universal appeal of shops. It does, however, fall outside our immediate period of interest, as does the work on European retail systems in the inter- and post-war periods. Considerable gaps in our knowledge exist therefore during the industrialisation period of the nineteenth and early twentieth centuries. Moreover, comparisons of retail change in European economies with that in North America are limited to the studies by Hall, Knapp and Winsten (1961), and Padberg and Thorpe (1974). The former is the most wide ranging, but is somewhat constrained for our purposes as it sought to make a detailed statistical comparison of retail efficiency in Canada, the United States and Britain. It attempted to do so by making 'a direct international comparison based on the extrapolation of the experience within one country into conditions of the others' (Hall, Knapp and Winsten, 1961, p.131). Environmental differences were measured using levels of per capita income, population density, rates of population growth, and age of settlement. Sadly, in spite of all its statistical information the study tells us little about retail change relative to these environmental factors.

A more promising, though smaller-scale, study is the work of Padberg and Thorpe (1972, p.1) whose paper represented 'the first stage of an international comparison of developments in food distribution and manufacturing'. This research traced the evolution of food distribution from 1850 to 1970 and in doing so presented a simple stage-like model for both Britain and the USA (Figure 1.3). Within this rather simplistic framework the first period, covering the second half of the nineteenth century, was supposedly characterised by 'traditional' food distribution networks. In the USA the traditional stage of distinct wholesale and retail units lasted until 1910. In Britain, by comparison, although the stage appeared to have ended at roughly the same time as in America, it was superimposed by stage two at an early date (Figure 1.3). Despite these differences, Padberg and Thorpe (1974, p.13) thought that on the whole the early stages of development were roughly similar, though in Britain there 'would appear to be a finer grain of change'. We may disagree with such findings and even criticise the general nature of the study, but at the same time the comparative perspective provides a welcome approach.

There are a number of potential difficulties in adopting a comparative approach to retail change, including the major problem of finding common terms to describe different retail organisations. In the work on contemporary retail systems these difficulties have been overcome by imposing rigid definitions of what constitutes a department store or a multiple retailer. Thus, Jefferys and Knee (1962) in their study of European retail systems put forward definitions which they could apply to different countries.

In historical studies the situation becomes far more complex, not least because the established organisations that Jefferys and Knee were examining were still in a state of flux during the nineteenth century. In their book, and indeed in Jefferys' (1954) earlier work on the evolution of multiples, the definition of a multiple-shop organisation was one that possessed ten or more retail establishments. Clearly, this

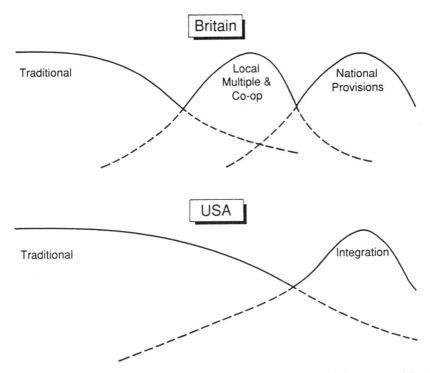

Figure 1.3 Suggested changes in food distribution systems in Britain and the USA (modified from Padberg and Thorpe, 1972)

definition begs the question of how we treat those organisations with between two and nine branch shops. Alexander (1970, p.103) was happy to term all retailers with more than two shops as multiples; but as Jefferys (1954) points out, his definition had an economic basis to it, the argument being that organisational economies of scale applied to those firms with ten or more shops.

Similar problems afflict the study of department stores, in that throughout their growth some early developments failed to match all the definitional requirements. Jefferys (1954, p.326) attempted to solve this by adopting the term 'part department store' which refers to 'a large firm that had more than one retail department' but had not reached the status of a full department store.

Such is the situation of studies of nineteenth-century retailing in Britain. These problems are greatly enhanced, however, when consideration is given to other European countries such as Germany. For example, many of the statistics on German retailing in the nineteenth century are based on firm size as measured by number of employees, with large firms being those with fifty or more (Schmoller, 1923). Obviously, such measures include both multiples and department stores and as such make direct comparisons with Britain almost impossible. Fortunately, there are other sources available in Germany, though in the case of department stores definitions even varied between different German states.

Clearly there are definitional problems both within and between different countries that tend to hinder direct comparisons of numerical growth. However, it is possible to take a more pragmatic approach to these difficulties and examine, for example, the growth of large-scale retailers in a general context. Of course with regard to developments such as department stores and multiples it is necessary to identify their main features, which revolve as much around organisational form as size criteria. To this end a department store is 'a retail institution organised around different merchandise departments' with some central operating functions (Hower, 1943, p.68). Similarly, in the case of multiples a central feature 'was the application of mass, standardized techniques to the problems of buying and selling' through the operation of a number of shops (Jefferys, 1954, p.27). In both developments size is obviously important though difficult to measure in the context of changing retail institutions, and different national perspectives.

Unfortunately, these problems of definition and terminology are not restricted to large-scale retailers, since it is just as difficult to identify the ubiquitous 'shopkeeper' in nineteenth-century Britain. The distinctions between wholesale and retail markets are also problematic, as is the identification of itinerant retailers.

1.5 The scope and aims of the book

It can be seen from this brief review that our knowledge about the degree and types of difference between retail systems is surprisingly limited. Even more limited is our understanding of whether such differences are significant, how they emerged and when. Within this context the aim of this book is to demonstrate, by comparative studies, just how different societies have evolved differing distribution systems. At the same time emphasis is also given to contributions that bring together a diversity of academic approaches which lead to considerations of historical and geographical variations.

The book is organised around three different themes, namely: the economic and social context of retailing (Part One), fairs, markets, pedlars and small-scale fixed shops (Part Two) and large-scale retailing (Part Three). Each of these themes is explored within the context of three economic, social and geographical environments, represented by case studies of Britain, Germany and Canada. The authors are conscious of the fact that these three examples do not represent the full range of national backgrounds, although they are strongly indicative of variations between different industrialising economies. As each individual study indicates, levels of knowledge based on past research are very unequal, with Britain having received far more attention than either Germany or Canada. Such variations are reflected in parts of this book, where, because of the greater amount of information available on British retailing, extra space has been allocated; for example a special chapter has been included on British co-operatives.

Part One starts by examining the background of environmental factors conditioning the processes of retail change in the European economies (Chapter 2) and the North American scene, as represented by Canada (Chapter 3). The time period under consideration is approximately 1800 to 1914, which encompasses not only a period of rapid social and economic change in all three countries, but also covers significant, some would argue revolutionary, developments in retailing. The end of our period was selected, first because of convenience – since it avoids the disruptions of the First World War – and second since it roughly delimits the start of a new wave of retail innovations during the inter-war period.

Parts Two and Three, which form the main focus of the text, explore in some detail the evolutionary trends in different forms of retailing, as well as giving attention to the interaction between the traditional retail system and the new ways of selling practised by large-scale retailers. Each of the three countries is given separate attention to facilitate in-depth study, with common threads and contrasts being highlighted in short summaries at the start of each of these two main parts. Finally, Chapter 11 presents a more wide-ranging discussion of the evolution of retail systems in Britain, Germany and Canada.

References

Alexander, D., 1970, *Retailing in England during the Industrial Revolution*, Athlone Press, London

Alchain, A.A., 1950, Uncertainty, Evolution and Economic Theory, *Journal of Political Economy*, 58: 211–21

Bennassar, B., 1967, *Valladolid au siècle d'or* quoted in Braudel, 1982

Berry, B.J.L., 1963, *Commercial Structure and Commercial Blight*, Department of Geography, University of Chicago

Braudel, F., 1985, *Civilization and Capitalism, 15th–18th Century: The Wheels of Commerce*, Fontana, London

Brown, S., 1988, The wheel of the wheel of retailing, *International Journal of Retailing*, 3 (1): 16–37

Bucklin, L.P., 1972, *Competition and Evolution in the Distributive Trades*, Prentice-Hall, Englewood Cliffs

Davidson, W.R., 1970, Changes in distributive institutions, *Journal of Marketing*, 34: 7–10

Davies, D., 1966, *A History of Shopping*, Routledge and Kegan Paul, London

Dawson, J., 1982, *Commercial Distribution in Europe*, Croom Helm, London

Gist, R.R., 1968, *Retailing: Concepts and Decisions*, Wiley, New York

Hall, M., Knapp, J. and Winsten, C., 1961, *Distribution in Great Britain and North America: A Study in Structure and Productivity*, Oxford University Press

Hollander, S.C., 1966, Notes on the retail accordion, *Journal of Retailing*, 42: 29–40

Hollander, S.C., 1983, Who and what is important in retailing and marketing history, in S.C. Hollander and R. Savitt (eds.), *Proceedings of the First North American Workshop on Historical Research in Marketing*, Michigan State University, East Lansing

Hower, R.M., 1943, *History of Macy's of New York 1858–1919: Chapters in the Evolution of the Department Store*, Harvard University Press, Cambridge, Mass.

Jefferys, J.B., 1954, *Retail Trading in Britain, 1850–1950*, Cambridge University Press

Jefferys, J.B. and Knee, D., 1962, *Retailing in Europe: Present Structure and Future Trends*, Macmillan, London

Kotler, P., 1986, *Principles of Marketing*, Prentice-Hall, Englewood Cliffs

Mason, B.J. and Mayer, M.L., 1984, *Modern Retailing: Theory and Practice*, Business Publications, Plano

Maversberg, H., 1963, *Wirtschafts – und Sozialgeschichte zentraleuropäischer Städte in neverer Zeit*, quoted in Braudel, 1985

McNair, M.P., 1931, Trends in large scale retailing, *Harvard Business Review*, 10: 30–9

McNair, M.P., 1958, Significant Trends and Developments in the Post-War Period, in A.B.

Smith (ed.) *Competitive Distribution in a Free High Level Economy and its Implications for the University*, University of Pittsburg Press

Myers, K.M. and Smalley, O.A., 1959, 'Marketing history and economic development: a report and commentary on two recent conferences concerning the need for a history of marketing in the United States', *Business History Review*, 33: 387–401

Nieschlag, R., 1954, *Die Dynamik der Betriebsformen in Handel*, Rheinisch-Westfalisches Institute für Wirtschaftforchung, Essen

Nystrom, P., 1930, *The Economics of Retailing: Retail Institutions and Trends*, Roland Press, New York

Padberg, D.I. and Thorpe, D., 1974, Channels of grocery distribution: changing stages in evolution – a comparison of USA and UK, *Journal of Agricultural Economics*, 25: 1–2

Porter, G. and Livesay, M.C., 1971, *Merchants and Manufacturers: Studies in the Changing Structure of Nineteenth-Century Marketing*, Johns Hopkins Press, Baltimore

Savitt, R., 1989, Looking back to see ahead: writing the history of American retailing, *Journal of Retailing* 65 (3): 326–55

Schmoller, G., 1923, *Grundriss der Allgemeinen Volkswirtschaftslehre* (2 vols) München

Schumpeter, J.A., 1939, *Business Cycles*, Wiley, New York

Shaw, G., 1978, *Processes and Patterns in the Geography of Retail Change, with special reference to Kingston upon Hull, 1880–1950*, University of Hull Press

Shaw, G., 1985, Changes in consumer demand and food supply in nineteenth-century British cities, *Journal of Historical Geography* 11 (3): 280–96

Shaw, G. and Wild, M.T., 1979, Retail patterns in the Victorian city, *Transactions of the Institute of British Geographers*, NS 4: 279–91

Simmons, J.W., 1964, *The Changing Pattern of Retail Location*, Department of Geography, University of Chicago

Part I: The economic and social context of retail evolution

Chapter 2
The European scene: Britain and Germany
Gareth Shaw

2.1 Economic growth, urbanisation and developments in transportation

Most commentators who have sought to explain the changing nature of retailing in Britain and Germany have done so within the context of economic advancement (Alexander, 1970, p.1; Gellately, 1974, pp.12–13). Industrialisation, the factory system and the processes of mass production, in the words of Roscher (1901), were the allies of the retail trade; at least in the sense that they allowed it to be expanded and transformed. In both Britain and Germany the nineteenth century saw impressive, if at times erratic, economic expansion. From the point of view of the evolution of retail systems, general economic growth worked its changes through five main areas, namely: population growth and concentration, transportation, improved living standards, a rise in factory produced consumer goods, and changes in lifestyles. These are the variables identified by Simmons (1964) in his attempts to model contemporary retail change (see Chapter 1), and will form the focus of this chapter.

One obvious factor affecting the retail system was the growth and urbanisation of population that took place almost continually between 1800 and 1914. In Britain population increased from around 10 million in 1801 to over 20 million by 1851, and reached 40 million by 1911. A similar expansion in the retail market was afforded in Germany, where population grew from 25 million in 1817 to just over 40 million by 1870 and to almost 61 million by 1913. However, as Alexander (1970, p.4) indicates, retail demand is not only a function of population growth, but also the degree of occupational specialisation (self-sufficiency) and population distribution.

In both countries urbanisation was a particularly potent force, as more and more people sought a better way of life in towns; a process which saw the 'representative man turn town dweller' (Court, 1954, p.232). The urbanisation of population occurred in a series of stages and varied regionally, with some of the earliest growth being associated with industrial centres. In England and Wales the first half of the nineteenth century witnessed the dramatic development of industrial towns compared with other urban areas. Thus, while the modal class of all urban areas remained in the population group 2,000–4,999 between 1801 and 1851, that for industrial towns had changed to between 20,000 and 49,999 by 1851 (Shaw, 1989, p.61). During this period of rapid growth many of these industrial centres expanded their service economy, especially retailing, to cater for the increased demand for food. Accurate large-scale population data are difficult to obtain for Germany during the early nineteenth century, although by 1861 those provinces with above average industrial employment can be identified as Prussian Saxony, Silesia, Rhineland and Westphalia (Tipton, 1976, p.28). In Germany, even by the mid-nineteenth century, regional differences in economic performance appear more extreme than in Britain, though the differences between town and country with regard to retailing were probably much less so. Certainly, in many German towns there appears to be a tendency towards a longer survival of the producer–retailer and close links with the surrounding rural area. The large urban centres did however provide strong contrasts, although by mid-century Germany had only four cities with populations over 100,000, compared with 10 such British cities. In general therefore, while the population upsurge of the industrial revolution in Britain started between 1800 and 1840, within Germany the corresponding phase only came after 1870 (Mellor, 1978, p.103).

During the period after 1871 Germany experienced a more rapid and widespread process of urbanisation, resulting in the growth of very large cities. In 1910, for example, there were 16 cities with populations over 250,000 and 7 in excess of 500,000. It was such concentrations of purchasing power that enabled German retailing to develop large, capital-intensive firms in the period after 1890, and more particularly during the early twentieth century. A feature that both countries shared was the dominance of one large consumer market in respect of their two capital cities, Berlin and London. In 1871 Berlin's population stood at 826,000, but by 1900 it had grown to 1.8 million, providing a large attracting force for the owners of department stores. London was even more dominant in Britain, with 1.1 million people as early as 1801, rising to 2.6 million in 1851 and increasing to 4.2 million by 1891. As Mathias (1967, p.5) points out, 'In this teeming metropolis well over a tenth of the population of England and Wales had their being'. Not only did London contain the largest concentration of consumer demand, it was also the wealthiest. In 1812 more than half of Britain's middle-class income was concentrated in London, a lead that the capital held over other urban areas throughout the nineteenth century (Rubinstein, 1986, p.201). For example, while the 28 largest provincial cities with populations over 100,000 in 1879–80 were assessed for tax purposes at £78.1 million, ten London boroughs were assessed for £87.7 million. There was not only more business income in the capital, but its middle classes were individually richer than their provincial counterparts (Badcock, 1984, p.103).

Berlin's influence as a retail centre was greatly enhanced with the development of railways, especially its radial rail network constructed during the mid-1840s. For example, by 1846 Berlin had rail connections with Hamburg, Stettin, Frankfurt, Breslau, Leipzig, Magdeburg, and Anhalt, giving good links with all the major domestic industrial areas (Tipton, 1976, p.103). During this first phase of rail developments the merchants of Berlin claimed that the expansion of their market area and the increase in the regions of food supply had 'eliminated all hindrances to the city's growth' (Dietrich, 1952, p.127). By the turn of the century railways were an integral part of the city's food supply system carrying, for example, some 72 per cent of the 600,000 quarts of milk consumed by Berliners (Board of Trade, 1908, p.33). This example highlights the importance of improved transport systems, not only in aiding urban growth, but also in acting as a conditioning factor in the evolution of retail distribution.

The role of improvements in transportation within the distribution system operates along a number of different levels, each of which can be observed in Britain and Germany. At a broad level the retail market of both countries was rapidly extended by new transportation systems, which throughout the nineteenth century transformed the geography of market areas. Shaw (1985) has demonstrated how food supply areas were transformed by changes in transport and corresponding developments in marketing (Figure 2.1). This represents a simplified view of the expansion of supply areas, from local and regional procurement through to international commodity trading, together with the necessary increased organisation of marketing networks.

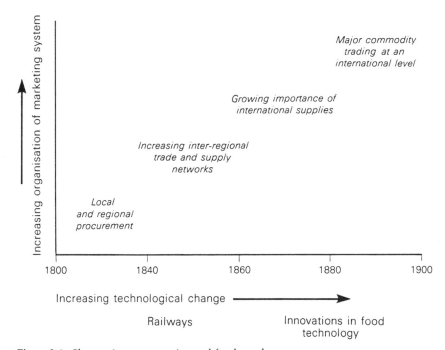

Figure 2.1 Changes in transportation and food supply areas

In Britain, London led the way in establishing extensive food supply areas, a feature that existed well before the nineteenth century, though it was increasing its market pull during that period. Indeed, according to Defoe (Cole, 1927, p.27), 'every Part of the Island is engaged in some degree or other of that Supply'. Alexander (1974, pp.14–16) has demonstrated how the increased market for fresh fish, for example, depended on the coming of the railways, especially during the 1840s when rail companies began to organise the carriage of fish. Thus, the Manchester market expanded rapidly at this time when fresh fish began to arrive from Hull, pushing down prices from 6d–1shilling/pound to 1½–2d/pound and increasing the volume sold in the market from 3 tons to 80 tons per week. Similar trends could be observed in Birmingham, while in London Mayhew (1851, p.62) believed 'the fish season of the poor never, or rarely, knows an interruption'. A similar picture was emerging in other basic foodstuffs such as cheese and butter, with the large cities drawing on such markets as the Netherlands, Germany, Ireland and France even before the railways. However, as Fussell (1966, pp.285–6) has shown, the railways were a boon to traders in butter and cheese, though they also introduced intense competition from imports.

In Germany also, transport improvements were breaking down local and regional self-sufficiency, despite the regulations of outmoded medieval municipal laws that had attempted to encourage dependency on local food supplies (Gellately, 1974, p.19). Local economic relations were strongly controlled to ensure self-sufficiency as far as possible, although by the early nineteenth century such ideas had largely disappeared as foreign produce (tea, tobacco, sugar and citrus fruits) were sold by most grocers. The railways not only intensified this trend by lowering food prices, for example the wholesale prices of wheat, rye and barley all declined after 1870, but also widened the range of consumer goods available as a national market began to evolve.

During the 1870s and 1880s both countries witnessed the increasing importance of international supply areas, made possible by further improvements in transport and also by innovations in food technology and organisational changes in marketing (see Figure 2.1). In Britain changes in fiscal policy at first drastically cut duties on imported livestock and meat and then finally abolished them in 1846, along with those for oil, lard, butter and cheese (Mathias, 1967, p.10). These policies acted as a stimulus for food imports, as did a series of innovations in food technology after 1870. Of particular importance was the development of chilling and freezing techniques which aided the long-distance transportation of meat. These technological breakthroughs paved the way for large-scale imports of meat to the UK from distant supply areas such as South America, Australia and New Zealand. As Capie and Perren (1980) have shown, the importance of imported meat grew rapidly after 1880; before that date it accounted for only 25 per cent of UK meat consumption, compared with 41 per cent by 1900.

Changes in transport also had the effect of increasing consumer mobility, and certainly the developments of a dense rural rail network in parts of Germany showed the 'country cousins' what the city had to offer (Gellately, 1974, p.20). These rail connections put regional and local market centres well within the reach of many rural dwellers as may be seen in Figure 2.2. This map shows the dense railway network of part of Lower Saxony, which was typical of many rural areas, as branch lines extended their influence into small market centres by 1914. The very large urban centres of Hannover, Braünschweig and Kässel all became within reach by rail even from some of the smallest of settlements.

In larger cities, new urban transportation systems made it increasingly possible for the middle classes to have greater levels of choice in their shopping from the 1880s onwards. Urban transportation grew rapidly in Germany after 1880, from 1.8

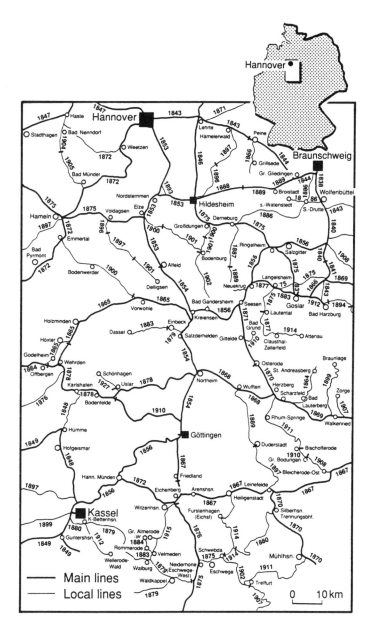

Figure 2.2 The expansion of rural rail networks in Lower Saxony, Germany

billion passenger-kilometres in 1889 to 11.8 billion by 1913 (Gellately, 1974, p.20). It was moreover intensive developments in local transport that led to the rapid growth of Berlin after 1880. The horse-drawn trams and buses introduced in the 1840s brought some improvements but much of the population was tightly concentrated around the central area. It was only through the development of commuter railways that the pressures could be released, as occurred with the completion of the Ringbahn in 1877 and the Stadtbann in 1882 (Tipton, 1976, p.105). Both of these lines connected with the central retail core and they both encouraged suburban development, especially for working-class people after 1891 when fares were lowered. Steam trams, although introduced into the new suburbs after 1886, had a more limited early impact on central Berlin where they were initially excluded because of police regulations.

In British cities railways exerted an important influence on the internal structure of central retail areas from the 1840s onwards. Apart from increasing general accessibility to city centres, railways had two other significant controls over the emergence of central shopping areas. First, they forced up land values through differentiating site accessibility and what Kellet (1969) terms 'railway land hunger'. To illustrate the scale of this demand for strategic parcels of land, Kellet has calculated that railways occupied 5.4 per cent of land in central London and 9 per cent in Liverpool by 1900. Their second control was through the physical constraint they placed on the spatial expansion of many city centres, the boundaries of which often coincided with railway lines. In Manchester, for example, this situation had already arisen by the 1880s when the central core was ringed by a series of railway lines, owned by companies that had fought bitterly to obtain access to the city centre during the 1840s and 1850s. Progress in urban tramways during the 1880s also helped create accessible central shopping areas in British cities, as well as shaping new suburban shopping streets along the main tram routes, a feature highlighted by Shaw's (1978) work on Hull. The increasing demands placed on urban transport systems during the late nineteenth century required considerable investment, resulting in an estimated expenditure by railway and tramway companies of some £5 million per annum between 1877 and 1902 in London alone (Royal Commission on London Traffic, 1905, p.6). However, in spite of such large investments the provision of tramways in London fell considerably short of that in other cities, as Table 2.1 shows.

Table 2.1 The provision of tramway systems in selected cities, 1902

City	Population per mile of tramway
New York	5,800
Manchester and Salford	9,138
Hamburg	11,082
Berlin	11,685
Liverpool	13,368
Glasgow	14,216
London	19,571

Source: Royal Commission on London Traffic, 1905

2.2 The nature of consumer demand

Economic growth, urbanisation and improvements in transportation systems all provided an environment necessary to induce a growth and transformation of Britain and Germany's retail systems. Such forces worked not only through permitting larger supply areas to be tapped or more factory-produced consumer goods to be available, but also because of changes in demand. At the most generalised level of study such changes may be simply accounted for by discussing a growth in the number of consumers and their geographical concentrations. Such an approach, however, completely ignores the nature of consumer demand and its changes during a period of unparalleled industrial growth in the two countries.

The characteristics of consumer demand and its changing nature may be examined, as Baudet and van der Meulen (1982) have shown, in three different ways. One involves the historical development of changes in the standard of living; a traditional historical approach that has very much focussed on either providing average national estimates or, more specifically, charted the progress of the working classes. A great deal of the early work on the standard of living debate was specifically concerned with establishing whether conditions, with respect to dietary well-being, had improved for the masses, a theme that lies somewhat outside our immediate interest. Of greater importance in this chapter are the questions about levels of food consumption and consumer preferences during a period of retail change in Britain and Germany.

The emphasis on preferences also stresses consumer lifestyles and, more specifically, the adaptation of consumers to changes in their material environment. This identifies the second major approach to historical patterns of consumption. During the late nineteenth and early twentieth centuries the rise of new ways of selling and of new consumer goods altered material life for all households in Britain and Germany. As Baudet and van der Meulen (1982, p.4) state, this approach 'brings us face to face with the phenomena of adjustment: the adjustment of demand to supply'. In the period covered by this book (1800 to 1914) demand was being changed by improved incomes and greater consumer mobility, while supply was being conditioned by mass produced new products sold through a rapidly changing distribution system. The process of adjustment is however far more than a mere economic one, since it also involves a growing closer relationship between consumer products and consumers. Consumption took on meanings of lifestyle for a far greater number of people than ever before. Mass production was met by mass consumption though, as we shall see, the processes of consumer demand were far more subtle than that. To some contemporary commentators consumption had moved to a new plane; Veblen (1912, p.xiii), for example, introduced the phrase 'conspicuous consumption' to describe 'expenditure made not for comfort or use, but for purely honorific purposes'. These aspects will be given particular attention in this chapter, partly because they are somewhat neglected in historical studies of retailing and also because they link closely with the growth of large-scale retail organisations. Furthermore, 'the advent of mass consumption represents a pivotal historical movement', which altered the patterns of personal and social consciousness as well as having profound material effects (Williams, 1982, p.3). In Britain and Germany, as in other industrialising economies, the personification of these new patterns of consumer behaviour were the department stores – the palaces of the new consumer age.

The third main approach to consumption has been at a macro-economic level through the examination of the link between business cycles and consumer demand. This will not form part of any substantive analysis in this chapter, though the ideas of long waves of economic development and phases of innovations can be utilised within the context of new consumer products. The remainder of this chapter will therefore focus on the changing nature of consumer demand and consumption, with particular attention being given to the growth of consumerism.

2.3 Consumer demand and food consumption

One important factor in considering the expansion of the retail system in Britain and Germany is to measure the increase in consumption in terms of retailed goods. In this section emphasis is placed on assessing the changing demand for food and its

Table 2.2 Per capita consumption of food and drink in nineteenth-century Britain

	Bread[1] (lbs/day)	Meat[2] (lbs/year)	Tea[3] (lbs/year)	Sugar (lbs/year)
1800			1.48	15.32
1820			1.22	17.74
1825	1.60			
1831–40		86.8		
1835	1.50			
1840			1.22	15.20
1841–50		82.5		
1846	1.25			
1851	1.60			
1851–60		87.3		
1860			2.67	34.14
1861–70		90.0		
1870–74		108.3		
1875–79		111.0		
1880			4.57	60.28
1880–84		109.8		
1985–89		111.7		
1890–94		122.4		
1900			6.07	85.53

Notes:
[1] Excludes Ireland, while other columns refer to United Kingdom. Based on R. N. Salaman, *The History and Social Influence of the Potato* (London, 1949)
[2] Taken from R. Perren, *The Meat Trade in Britain 1840–1914* (London, 1978)
[3] Data for tea and sugar taken from B. R. Mitchell and P. Deane, *Abstract of British Historical Statistics* (Cambridge, 1962)

relationship with retail change. Without getting embroiled too much in the standard of living debate, it is possible to identify a number of broad changes in the consumption of certain basic foodstuffs.

In the absence of any complete statistical coverage, the available evidence from Britain seems to suggest that up to the mid-1840s there was no general increase in per capita levels of basic food consumption (Table 2.2). Some caution is required in interpreting these data as they are based on a range of estimates, and only cover selected items. Furthermore, as Rule (1986, pp.46–62) demonstrates very well, improvements in the food consumption of the working classes were at best slight during the early nineteenth century, and varied enormously, by class of worker, regionally, as well as between town and country. For example, evidence from 1849/ 50 suggests that meat consumption by farm labourers and their families in southern England remained at very low levels throughout the first half of the nineteenth century. Thus, the proportion of expenditure by Kentish labourers on meat declined by 20 per cent between 1793 and 1812 (Rule, 1986, p.54). In contrast coal miners when enjoying 'good wages' were among the largest consumers of meat. Similarly, town dwellers had generally higher levels of per capita meat consumption than their rural counterparts. Even in towns, however, the consumption of meat by some of the 'elite' of the working classes fell short of the average per capita levels shown in Table 2.2. In Sheffield, for example, a cutler in 1855, one of the better-off artisans, was estimated to have an annual consumption of 81 lbs of meat, compared with a national average of 87.3 lbs/head between 1851 and 1860.

General attempts to measure the growth of private consumption in Britain during the first part of the nineteenth century conclude that it rose (at constant 1791 prices) only slowly from £8.7 per head in 1801 to £17.6 in 1841, or by 2.5 per cent per annum. By comparison, consumption had risen to £24.5 by 1851 or at an annual rate of 3.9 per cent (Williams, 1966, p.586). As with the data in Table 2.2, such average figures cover a wide range of consumption levels, with the greatest benefits falling to a small but rapidly expanding group of skilled workers and an even smaller number of owners, managers and professionals – what we might term the middle classes. As Alexander (1970, p.34) argues, this high consumption class, though still a small segment of the population, 'was probably getting richer and its modest growth is suggested by the rise in the number of domestic servants as a proportion of the occupied population'. In addition to the growth of the professional middle classes and the skilled artisans, there was also during the 1830s the spread of a so-called rentier class in country towns, who brought with them new wealth for investments and also high levels of personal consumption. The impact of all three of these high-level consumer groups was most felt in the expansion of fixed shop retailing, especially in the fashionable resorts and country towns.

The evidence from Germany is even more fragmented than that for Britain, although it would seem that similar trends were in existence. Teuteberg (1982), for example, has presented a three-stage model of food consumption, although the evidence is very largely based on national trends and gives only a general picture. In the first, or pre-industrial, stage which dates back to the late eighteenth century, average household expenditure on food ranged from 50 to 70 per cent; with the largest amounts being spent on vegetables. The second stage, which Teuteberg terms a transitional one, occurred between the late eighteenth century and the first part of the nineteenth century. This involved for key workers an improvement in food supply, especially for those concentrated in areas passing through proto-industrialisation to industrial concentration. In more traditional rural economies relationships between retail distribution and consumers were often more strictly controlled as both master artisans (many of whom were producer–retailers) and merchants 'shared a common desire to preserve a local monopoly' (Gellately, 1974, p.19). As a consequence regional patterns of food consumption varied greatly in Germany, a fact reflected in the very great differences in shop provision.

Regional differences in the types and amounts of food consumed were also a marked feature of consumer demand in Britain, especially during the first half of the nineteenth century (Rule, 1981). Furthermore, at this time, supply side variables were extremely important in conditioning local and regional patterns of food consumption. Most of our direct, contemporary evidence comes from surveys of lower-paid rural consumers. The most widespread of these was that undertaken by Smith (1864), which picked out Cornwall, Devon, Somerset, Dorset, Wiltshire, Staffordshire, Oxford, Berkshire, and Hertfordshire as 'counties where carbohydrate and protein consumption was seriously below average' (Rule, 1986, p.47). In the poorer south-western counties almost a third of the families never or rarely tasted butchers' meat, while fish hardly ever comprised part of rural diets outside Cornwall.

Another dimension of regional variations in demand was the English food riots started in the eighteenth century but continued through to the early nineteenth century (Stevenson, 1979). These were not only about what the rioters saw as the creation of artificial scarcity and price rises by jobbers and middlemen, but were also a direct reflection of failures in the distribution system. Indeed, many of the riots occurred in areas of food production, like Devon and Cornwall, when local people perceived that prices were being driven up by merchants removing supplies from the district for more distant wealthier urban markets. As Rule (1986, p.351) remarks the 'geography of food rioting suggests which consuming communities were most vulnerable to the effects of scarcity and high prices', especially in the market for grain. The importance of transport networks and nodes to the occurrence of food rioting has already been noted by Stevenson (1979); although riots were also frequent in early industrial and mining settlements which had a great dependency on local food supply areas. This latter situation may have been brought about more by the poor performance of local harvests and the frequent control over local supplies by a small number of traders.

If, as we have suggested, the period before the 1840s in Britain was characterised by only relatively small general increases in per capita levels of consumption and strong regional variations, the events after this time conspired to present a whole new picture of consumer demand. From the mid-1840s to around 1873 a fairly dramatic rise in per capita levels of consumption occurred in a range of food commodities. This was followed, between 1873 and 1896 by a period of falling prices and cheaper imported foods associated with significant changes in food technology. Patterns of consumption, at least viewed at a national level, showed the signs of such developments. Thus, tea consumption rose from 3.5 lbs per head in 1870 to 6.2 lbs by 1910, similarly, the amount of sugar consumed rose from 45 lbs to 87 lbs per head over the same period. Equally the per capita consumption of butter and margarine and ham and bacon showed threefold and sixfold increases respectively between 1870 and 1910. Similar trends were witnessed in Germany with a doubling of real per capita incomes between 1871 and 1913, together with a 43 per cent growth in the production per capita of consumer goods (Bry, 1960, pp.21–3). In addition, over the same period, Bry (1960, p.67) has shown how the wholesale prices of cattle and vegetables declined in part as a response to improvements in agriculture, but also because of the increasing importance of food imports. In Germany the decline in wholesale prices was also indicative of structural changes in the economy and trade cycles producing a depression between 1873 and 1896 and did affect the economy, but for the consumer more goods were available. Thus, measures of per capita consumption of vegetables, meat and luxury items, such as tobacco, cognac and wine, all show great increases after the early 1870s. As Pierenkemper (1987, p.71) remarks, 'the phase from the end of the 1870s up to the First World War can be described with some justification as a period of distinct improvement in the standard of living'. However, while real wages rose markedly, the years between 1875 and around 1880 saw a period of suffering for large sections of the population because of short-term falls in income.

Despite these short-lived falls in real wages, overall levels of food consumption were increasing in Germany, with per capita levels of fresh meat, for example, growing from 165.7 lbs/head in 1894 to 178.2 lbs at the turn of the century in Berlin (Board of Trade, 1908, p.33). As in Britain such figures masked social as well as geographical variations. In Germany, for example, it was the middle classes that consumed large quantities of fresh meat and meat products, despite improvements in working-class households. Similarly, even by the early years of the twentieth century strong regional patterns of food consumption existed. Thus, in the Board of Trade's survey (1908) of some 5046 German households, the highest consumption of beef was in Münich with the lowest in the north German city of Brünswick. By contrast, consumption of pork was recorded at its highest in the Westphalian town of Bochum and lowest at Dusseldorf. Such patterns were conditioned by geographical situation, local agricultural conditions and tastes. For example, there was strong and long held prejudice in south Germany against the consumption of mutton.

The availability of not only greater quantities of food but also new food products was aided in no small part by changes in the food processing industry. In Britain many large-scale multiples became directly involved in acquiring food processing plants during the early twentieth century, while there was also a rise in major food processors. The increase in sugar consumption for example was facilitated by the abolition of duties in 1874 and at the same time changes in sugar refining led to the growth of a large-scale refinery industry, with the development of firms such as Henry Tate and Abram Lyle, established in the early 1860s (Murray, 1983). At the other end of the spectrum home-produced foodstuffs, such as cheese, were also influenced by the importation of new factory processing techniques, in this case from America. The visible success of this American factory-made cheese in British shops, especially in many of the big multiple grocers, convinced British traders and farmers of the need for change (Fussell, 1966, p.291). Thus, in 1869 the Derbyshire and Midland Agricultural Societies were both concerned about foreign competition and established in 1870 an experimental factory cheesemaking plant, and by 1874 there were at least six factories in Derbyshire alone. It was these types of development, through a whole range of foodstuffs, that increased supplies and created a mass market during the 1870s.

In both countries contemporary commentators had started to focus attention on the changing nature of food consumption and its relationship with income through a number of surveys (Shaw, 1985, provides a summary of those in Britain, while Desai, 1968, gives German material). These surveys serve to highlight two main features of food consumption. The first is that the pattern of urban working-class demand was characterised by regular and frequent purchases of food in fairly small quantities. Secondly, the character of family expenditure on food had started to change in a number of significant ways during the latter part of the nineteenth century. As we have seen the range of foodstuffs increased and in addition the location of consumer demand started to change as population suburbanised.

For the low-income families basic foods continued to account for a major part of the family income compared with higher-income groups, although the latter spent more on meat. In a survey of 852 household accounts based on families living in Berlin and 27 other German cities in 1907, for those earning 600–1,200 marks per year 11.4 per cent of their income went on meat compared with 13.7 per cent for families with incomes of 1,200–1,600 marks (Desai, 1968, pp.22–3). From those few surveys that sought information on the frequency of purchase, a picture of frequent, small-scale food shopping trips among working-class households emerges. Higgs (1893), for example, in a detailed study of one London working-class family of five, calculated that they made an average of 46 purchases per week in the years between 1891 and 1893. As Booth (1902, p.131) observed the poor 'go to the shop as an ordinary housewife to her canisters', such was the precarious family budgets even in the early twentieth century. These small purchases, often on credit, bound the poor to the small shopkeepers who acquired power and status in working-class areas by accommodating such purchases of food (Hosgood, 1989, p.441).

In these circumstances it was only for the financially secure working classes, skilled workers and the lower middle classes, that the multiples, and to a lesser extent the co-operative stores, brought new opportunities in the period before 1914. The impact of the rapid and strong growth of these retail institutions in Britain, compared with their German counterparts, may partly explain the lower food costs found in England and Wales during the early twentieth centurey. Thus, the Board of Trade's (1908, p.xiv) survey found that for a range of foodstuffs the 'English working man would have to spend almost 219 pence in Germany to purchase the same goods that he could have bought for 185 pence in England'. In general,

Table 2.3 A comparison of retail prices for selected food items in England and Wales, and Germany, 1905

Item (quantity)		England/Wales	Germany
Sugar	(1 lb)	2d	$2\frac{1}{4}$d – $2\frac{1}{2}$d
Butter	(1 lb)	1s $1\frac{1}{4}$d	1s 1d – 1s $2\frac{3}{4}$d
Potatoes	(7 lb)	$2\frac{1}{2}$d – $3\frac{1}{2}$d	$2\frac{1}{4}$d – 3d
Beef	(1 lb)	$7\frac{1}{2}$d – $8\frac{1}{2}$d (British)	$7\frac{3}{4}$ – $8\frac{3}{4}$d
		5d – 6d (foreign)	

Source: Board of Trade, 1908

therefore, factors combined to produce prices for general 'foodstuffs that were 18 per cent higher in Germany than England' (Table 2.3).

2.4 The rise of consumerism: Britain

The origins of consumer culture in the United States are based, according to social historians (Fox and Lears, 1983, p.xi), on the activities of the urban elites during the last two decades of the nineteenth century. This group of consumers were seen to react to three developments from the 1880s onwards: the maturation of the national marketplace, the rise of a commercial media and the emergence of a new stratum of professionals. Similarly, in France the rise of consumerism has been closely examined through the work of Miller (1981) and at a more comprehensive level by Williams (1982). Unfortunately, Britain and Germany have received far less attention, although the common threads that can be recognised between consumerism in late-nineteenth-century France and North America are strongly suggestive that similar general trends were occurring in other industrial economies. Research on Britain has to date focussed more on the coming of a consumer revolution in the eighteenth century, characterised by 'an eruption of new prosperity' such that more people were 'able to enjoy the pleasures of buying consumer goods' (McKendrick, Brewer and Plumb, 1982, p.9).

What these studies have in common is the identification of significant changes in conditions of supply and demand that produced consumer growth, at first among an elite group, however large or small that may be, and then ultimately through to a wider section of the population. The consumer boom in eighteenth-century England certainly had ramifications on the retail structure, as Davies (1966) points out, but was significantly overshadowed by the events during the late nineteenth century. It was from the 1880s onwards that British and German society witnessed the real growth of modern consumerism. In both cases the underlying factor was the availability of mass produced factory goods fed through a more commercially aware and aggressive retail system, as represented by the rise of department stores and multiple shop organisations.

The factories and the new shops, though extremely significant, were however only the vehicles of this consumer revolution since it was the influences on consumer behaviour of mass advertising, price competition, fashion magazines, informed opinion and credit buying that fuelled the new consumer society. These influences and the ability to react to them worked initially on a growing urban elite, the factory owners, merchants, managers and professionals who had increasing amounts of wealth. Unlike in previous societies, such as the 'closed world of courtly consumption' in France, described by Williams (1982, Ch. 2), the desire and response to increased consumption was, in the late nineteenth and early twentieth centuries, more quickly taken up by the lower-middle-class and upper-working-class groups.

These influences on consumer attitudes and the creation of a consumer society may be viewed under three main headings: new consumer goods and production methods, media influences, and the changing impact of consumer credit. Of course each of these combined and linked with the rise of new retailing methods which forms the focus of Part Three of this book. Moreover, each of these influences could be seen as major research areas in themselves, although for the purposes of this book a small number of illustrations for each one will suffice.

In terms of new products and production methods, mention can be made of factory-made furniture replacing craft-based production, the advent of machine-made, mass produced shoes, new textile materials such as artificial silk later to be called rayon, factory-made clothing (especially for men), mass produced carpets and, towards the very end of our period, electrical consumer goods. Each of these produced marked reactions in both the retail distribution system and in consumer buying. Obviously, these changes came at different times although most occurred after 1880, with the exception of ready-made footwear through firms such as Clarks which began a progressive marketing policy from the 1840s onwards (Sutton, 1964). Some of the major changes were taking place in the clothing industry in the late nineteenth century, producing what some commentators feel was a 'clothing revolution' (Hudson, 1978, p.76). The first stages of this revolution consisted of factory-produced clothing being made available at prices affordable by the great mass of lower-middle-class and working-class people. This was brought about by firms such as Barrans in Leeds, which introduced the latest technology into their factory during the 1870s, and later power-driven sewing machines. By 1900, as Hudson (1978, pp.77–8) points out, the Leeds clothing industry was split into two main parts. One section comprised individuals or small firms making directly for the customer or wholesalers, while the second was made up of large wholesale clothiers producing clothes under factory conditions for sale direct to shops. During the 1880s firms such as Hepworths and Blackburns opened their own shops and started selling ready-made men's and boys' clothes direct to the customer. The production and distribution methods for the first time brought well-produced clothes within the range of many working-class people, thereby transforming their consumption patterns (Redmayne, 1951).

In terms of female customers clothing had already acquired marked fashion importance for an increasing number during the mid-nineteenth century (Cunnington, 1937). Not only did styles change, but also new fabrics and materials came into the stores. For the well-off such trends can be traced back at least to the second part of the eighteenth century, but they became much more significant and prominent by the 1850s. Adburgham (1981, p.91), for example, has described the advent of crinoline in women's fashion and the impact it had on both shops and consumers. By the late 1870s and the 1880s fashion had become strongly influenced by a series of distinctive 'movements', one of which was the so-called aesthetic movement. This was in turn a reaction against the rather brash products associated with machine-made finishes. Liberty, as a leading shop for the promotion of aestheticism, introduced soft oriental fabrics, a trend quickly followed by some of London's innovative department stores, such as Whiteleys (Adburgham, 1981, pp.173–7).

Other fashion trends were associated with fabrics such as silk, which became an increasingly popular material, and was actively promoted by the British Silk Association which held its first national exhibition in 1890. The material was also strongly favoured in the Victorian cult of mourning, and every large clothing and department store had its specialised mourning department. Within this context the firm of Courtaulds established their initial enterprise by producing special stiff black crepe, a silk material used for mourning garments (Hudson, 1978, p.61). By the 1890s the 'crepe boom' and its associated fashions was coming to an end, being replaced by a movement towards using natural woollens, following trends in Germany based on Jaeger's health culture. In addition newer materials were also being introduced, such as artificial silk, later known as rayon, the patent rights for which were acquired by Courtaulds (Hudson, 1978, pp.62–3).

What made these new fashion trends different from those of previous periods was the way in which manufacturers and retailers promoted them to a wider group of consumers (Plumb, 1983). The adoption and pace of fashion change may have been set by a small elite, but retailers, especially the more popular department stores, made sure that other consumers could share in such fashions (Miller, 1987, pp.138–9). Cheaper factory-made clothes and store economies of scale brought prices well within range of the middle classes and the elite of the working classes. Ideas about what was fashionable and why were strongly promoted by a growing media industry. Indeed, the whole influence of advertising was a potent force in shaping the rise of consumerism, a fact carefully explored by Wilson (1983) in a North American context. Wilson (1983, p.41) argues that for 'Victorian Americans of the upper and middle classes, the activity of reading served as a haven of revered cultural values'. However, by the late nineteenth century the impact of mass-market magazines rose to cultural prominence and these, Wilson argues, formed part of a 'consumerist' trend. In Britain similar forces can be identified, as newspapers and more especially weekly magazines became taken up with advertising and an overall belief in material consumption (Forty, 1986; Leiss, 1983).

The promotion of fashions and new consumer products was brought about in a number of different ways, with high-class fashion magazines representing some of the earliest developments in the late eighteenth and early nineteenth centuries (Adburgham, 1981, p.29; McKendrick, Brewer and Plumb, 1983, p.47). After 1850, however, fashion magazines not only increased in number (to the ten or so published in London were added at least another six) but also widened their circulation. Many of these brought the new fashions direct to the consumer through the inclusion of paper patterns for dresses to be made at home (Adburgham, 1981, p.115). The mid-nineteenth century also witnessed improved printing processes that enabled cheaper, mass produced bill posters to be produced. This fact, together with a take-off in retail competition led to a much greater use of wall posters, which in turn were promoted by a growing number of advertising contractors. The Billposters Association was established in 1862, and by 1885 there were at least 522 bill poster firms operating in some 447 towns (Fraser, 1981, p.135). By the late nineteenth century many food and drink manufacturers had established effective national advertising campaigns and the posters of such firms as Bovril, Cadbury, Rowntrees, and Oxo became familiar icons in high streets throughout Britain.

Consumers were also influenced by the growing number of department stores issuing mail order catalogues, and the many trade advertisements placed in directories, journals and newspapers. All these had an impact on shaping consumer demand, especially from the 1880s onwards when advertising agencies, like the Central London Agency, extended their functions. Such agencies, and there were several hundred operating in London alone by 1900, saw it as their role to find new markets and extend existing ones. Newspapers took on more prominent roles under the use of these professional agencies and in turn developed new ways of selling products, the most significant of which was the *Daily Mail*'s launch of the Ideal Home Exhibition in 1908 (Fraser, 1981, pp.138–9).

Faced with new products, increased pressures to buy and a wealth of different stores, consumers often found their household budgets under pressure. Despite general increases in real incomes all levels of society found that at certain times they had insufficient funds to purchase a particular product. To enable supply to match demand in such circumstances retailers and manufacturers had developed a range of credit facilities. These were not new to the second half of the nineteenth century as records of the instalment selling of consumer high-cost goods date from at least the early eighteenth century (BPP 1970–1, p.40). However, it was after 1850 that hire purchase was applied in selling a range of goods to the middle and working classes, especially pianos and sewing machines by the Singer Sewing Machine Company in the early 1860s. During the 1870s this whole system of credit selling was referred to colloquially as the 'hire-system' for furniture and the 'two-year system' for sewing machines (BPP 1970–1, p.41). This system of credit selling grew rapidly during the 1880s and by 1891 there were an estimated one million hire-purchase agreements in existence, with the majority being financed either by manufacturers or retailers. The first specialised financing of consumer goods was the Civil Service Mutual Furnishing Association founded in 1877 to help civil servants purchase furniture (BPP 1970–1, p.42).

During the late nineteenth century the hire-purchase system was mainly used by the middle classes to buy fairly costly consumer durables. Among the working classes, however, other forms of credit buying were available for food, clothing and household items. Credit was offered by the small shopkeeper, and even co-operative stores were forced on occasions into giving credit when their customers were in economic distress, with 82 per cent of societies admitting to this in 1911 (Johnson, 1985, p.133). The predominant form of credit for many better-off working-class consumers was either through so-called 'check clubs', institutions which started as self-help movements, or the 'Scotch Drapery' system. This latter was the older form and was typified by a trader operating a central warehouse from which itinerant salesmen sold clothing and household goods on credit by doorstep selling (BPP 1970–1, p.47). The other form of credit was to expand rapidly through such organisations as the Provident Clothing and Supply Company established in 1881. It was through such companies that many lower-income families were able to benefit from the availability of cheaper machine-made clothing, especially for men and children. It was therefore the combination of new products, a growth in consumer awareness, large-scale selling techniques, aided when necessary by a widening of consumer credit facilities, that helped create a broadly based consumer society from the 1880s onwards.

References

Adburgham, A., 1981, *Shops and Shopping, 1800–1914* (second edition), George Allen and Unwin, London

Alexander, D., 1970, *Retailing in England during the Industrial Revolution*, Athlone Press, London

Badcock, B., 1984, *Unfairly Structured Cities*, Blackwell, Oxford

Baudet, H., and van der Meulen, H., 1982, *Consumer Behaviour and Economic Growth in the Modern Economy*, Croom Helm, London

Board of Trade (1908) *Cost of Living in German Towns*, Col. 4032, London

Booth, C., 1902, *Life and Labour of the People in London*, Macmillan, London

British Parliament Papers, 1970–1 IX, Report on Consumer Credit

Bry, G., 1960, *Wages in Germany, 1871–1945*, National Bureau of Economic Research, Princeton

Capie, F. and Perren, R., 1980, The British market for meat, 1850–1914, *Agricultural History* 54: 502–15

Cole, G.D.H., 1927, *The Life of William Cobbett*, Collins, London

Court, W.H.B., 1954, *Concise Economic History of Britain from 1750 to Recent Times*, Cambridge University Press

Cunnington, C.W., 1937, *English Women's Clothing in the Nineteenth Century*, Faber and Faber, London

Davies, D., 1966, *A History of Shopping*, Routledge, London

Desai, A.V., 1968, *Real Wages in Germany*, Clarendon Press, Oxford

Dietrich, R., 1952, Von der Residenzstadt zur Weltstadt, *Jahrbuch für die Geschichte Mittelund Ostdeutschlands*, 1: 121–32

Forty, A., 1986, *Objects of Desire*, Thames and Hudson, London

Fox, R.W. and Lears, T.J.J. (eds.), 1983, *The Culture of Consumption: Critical Essays in American History, 1880–1980*, Pantheon Books, New York

Fraser, W.H. 1981, *The Coming of the Mass Market, 1850–1914*, Macmillan, London

Fussell, G.E., 1966, *The English Dairy Farmer, 1500–1900*, Frank Cass, London

Gellately, R., 1974, *The Politics of Economic Despair: Shopkeepers and German Politics 1890–1914*, Sage, London

Higgs, H., 1893, Workmen's budgets, *Journal Royal Statistical Society* 56, 255–85

Hosgood, C.P., 1989, The 'pigmies of commerce' and the working-class community: small shopkeepers in England, 1870–1914, *Journal of Social History* 22 (3): 439–59

Hudson, K., 1978, *Food, Clothes and Shelter: Twentieth Century Industrial Archaeology*, John Baker, London

Johnson, P., 1985, *Saving and Spending: The Working-class Economy in Britain, 1870–1939*, Oxford University Press

Kellet, J.R., 1969, *The Impact of Railways on Victorian Cities*, Routledge, London

Leiss, W., 1983, The icons of the marketplace, *Theory, Culture and Society*, 1, 3, 10–21

Mathias, P., 1967, *Retailing Revolution*, Longman, London

Mayhew, H., 1851, *London Labour and the London Poor*, Penguin, Harmondsworth (1985 edition)

McKendrick, N., Brewer, J., and Plumb, J.H., 1983, *The Birth of a Consumer Society: the Commercialization of Eighteenth-century England*, Hutchinson, London

Mellor, R.E.M., 1978, *The Two Germanies: A Modern Geography*, Harper and Row, London

Miller, M.B., 1981, *The Bon Marché: Bourgeois Culture and the Department Store, 1869–1920*, Princeton University Press

Miller, D., 1987, *Material Culture and Mass Consumption*, Blackwell, London

Murray, A., 1983, A staple consumer industry on Merseyside: sugar refining in the late nineteenth century and the emergence of Henry Tate and Company, in B.L. Anderson and P.J.M. Stoney (eds.), *Commerce, Industry and Transport: studies in economic change on Merseyside*, Liverpool University Press

Pierenkemper, T., 1987, The standard of living and employment in Germany, 1850–1980: an overview, *The Journal of European Economic History*, 16 (1): 51–73

Plumb, J., 1983, Commercialization and Society, in N. McKendrick, J. Brewer, and J.

Plumb (eds.), *The Birth of a Consumer Society: The Commercialization of Eighteenth-century England*, Hutchinson, London

Redmayne, R. (ed.), 1951, *Ideals in Industry: Being the Story of Montague Burton Ltd., 1900–1950*, 2nd edition, Montague Burton Ltd., Leeds

Roscher, 1901; quoted in Gellately, R., *The Politics of Economic Despair*, Sage, London, p.13

Royal Commission on London Traffic, 1905, Report to the Royal Commission on London Traffic, Vol. VII, HMSO, London, cd 2743

Rubinstein, W.D., 1986, The Victorian middle classes: wealth, occupation and geography, in P. Thorne and A. Sutcliffe (eds.) *Essays in Social History*, Vol. 2, Clarendon Press, Oxford.

Rule, J.G., 1981, Regional variations in food consumption among agricultural labourers, 1790–1860, in W. Minchinton (ed.) *Agricultural Improvements: Medieval and Modern*, Exeter University Press, pp.112–37

Rule, J.G., 1986, *The Labouring Classes in Early Industrial England, 1750–1850*, Longman, London

Shaw, G., 1978, *Processes & Patterns in the Geography of Retail Change, with special reference to Kingston upon Hull, 1880–1950*, University of Hull Press

Shaw, G., 1985, Changes in consumer demand and food supply in nineteenth-century British cities, *Journal of Historical Geography* 11 (3): 280–96

Shaw, G., 1989, Industrialization, urban growth and the city economy, in R. Lawton (ed.) *The Rise and Fall of Great Cities: Aspects of Urbanization in the Western World*, Belhaven Press, London, Ch. 5

Simmons, J.W., 1964, *The Changing Pattern of Retail Location*, Department of Geography, University of Chicago

Smith, E., 1864, *Sixth Report of the Medical Officer of the Committee of Council on Health*, British Parliamentary Papers, 28

Stevenson, J., 1979, *Popular Disturbances in England 1700–1870*, Longman, London, Ch. 5

Sutton, G.B., 1964, The marketing of ready made footwear in the nineteenth century, *Business History*, 6: 93–112

Teuteberg, H., 1982, German food consumption after 1850, in H. Baudet and H. van der Meulen (eds.) *Consumer Behaviour and Economic Growth in the Modern Economy*, Croom Helm, London, Ch. 8

Tipton, F.B., 1976, *Regional Variations in the Economic Development of Germany During the Nineteenth Century*, Wesleyan University Press, Middletown, Connecticut

Veblen, T., 1912, *The Theory of the Leisure Class* (new edition) reprint Viking Press, New York

Williams, J.E., 1966, The British standard of living, 1750–1850, *Economic History Review*, 19: 580–92

Williams, R.H., 1982, *Dream Worlds Mass Consumption in Late Nineteenth-Century France*, University of California Press, Berkeley

Wilson, C.P., 1983, The rhetoric of consumption: mass-market magazines and the demise of the gentle reader, 1880–1920, in R.W. Fox and T.J.J. Lears (eds.) *The Culture of Consumption: Critical Essays in American History, 1880–1980*, Pantheon Books, New York, Ch. 2

Chapter 3
The North American scene: Canada
John Benson

3.1 Introduction

Canada industrialised late, and industrialised unevenly. This was most important. For although it is never easy to disentangle the relationship between retailing and broader economic and social change, it is clear that the timing and nature of Canada's industrialisation exercised a profound effect upon the ways in which the country's retail system evolved between 1800 and 1914.

It is not the aim of this chapter to provide a potted economic and social history of Canada in the years between 1800 and the outbreak of the First World War. That would be both boring and unproductive. The objective here is more modest but, it is hoped, more valuable. It is to delineate some of the major shifts in the demand for, and the supply of, consumer goods and services, and so to facilitate a sustained discussion of the ways in which the retail system of Canada developed during these years of increasingly rapid economic and social change.

It is well known that consumer demand grew rapidly in Canada during the second half of the nineteenth century (Santink, 1990, pp.3–4, 40, 51). It was stimulated in three ways: by the growth, and urbanisation, of the population; by a rise in levels of disposable income; and by the improvements that took place in personal mobility.

3.2 Population growth and urbanisation

The growth, and urbanisation, of the population proved of considerable significance. Of course the population of Canada was tiny compared with its size, and tiny too compared with the populations of many other industrialising countries. For whereas Canada is 40 times as large as either Great Britain or the Federal Republic of Germany, its population has always been many times smaller. In 1851 there were 2.4 million Canadians compared with almost 21 million Britons; and even in 1911, when there were 7.2 million people living in Canada, there were more than 40 million clustering in tiny, overcrowded Britain (Deane and Cole, 1969, p.8).

Nonetheless, the population of Canada was growing apace. The number of people living in this part of North America increased from just 100,000 in 1783, to 1.4 million in 1831, 2.4 million in 1851, 4.8 million in 1891, and 7.2 million in 1911. The most rapid advances occurred in the 1850s and the 1900s, decades during which the number of Canadians grew by just below, and just above, 33 per cent (Urquhart and Buckley, 1965, p.14; Innis, 1935, p.97).

However it must be remembered that the demographic development of Canada was remarkably unbalanced. For although Table 3.1 shows that the majority of the Canadian population lived in the two central provinces of Ontario and Quebec, it reveals too that during the final third of the period the western provinces enjoyed rates of growth that were a great deal higher than those in the centre (or the east) of the country. Between 1871 and 1911 the number of people living in the Maritime provinces of Nova Scotia, New Brunswick and Prince Edward Island rose by nearly a quarter, the population of Ontario grew by over a half, while the number of Quebecois increased by more than two-thirds. Yet during the same years, British Columbia's population increased by 875 per cent, while the number of people living in the prairie provinces of Alberta, Manitoba and Saskatchewan multiplied by 1,800 per cent. 'Between 1901 and 1911,' it has been pointed out, 'more than 60 per cent of the total increase in Canadian population was absorbed west of the Ontario border' (Ostry and Zaidi, 1979, p.58). The result was that between 1871 and 1911 the proportion of the population living in Quebec fell by an eighth; the proportion living in Ontario dropped by a fifth; while the proportion living in the Maritime provinces declined by nearly two-thirds. Thus the proportion of the Canadian population to be found in the centre and east of the country declined from 95 per cent in 1871 to barely 75 per cent 40 years later.

Demographic development was unbalanced too in that urban growth occurred primarily in just three provinces: British Columbia, Quebec and Ontario.

Table 3.1 The population of Canada, 1851–1911

Year	Canada	Maritimes[1]		Quebec		Ontario		Prairies[1]		British Columbia	
	mill.[2]	mill.	%[2]	mill.	%	mill.	%	mill.	%	mill.	%
1851	2.44	0.53	22	0.90	37	0.95	39			0.06	2
1861	3.23	0.66	21	1.11	34	1.40	43	0.01	0	0.05	2
1871	3.69	0.77	21	1.19	32	1.62	44	0.07	2	0.04	
1881	4.33	0.87	20	1.36	31	1.93	47	0.12	1	0.05	1
1891	4.83	0.88	18	1.49	31	2.11	44	0.25	5	0.10	2
1901	5.37	0.89	17	1.65	31	2.18	41	0.47	8	0.18	3
1911	7.21	0.94	13	2.01	28	2.53	35	1.33	19	0.39	5

Notes:
[1] Maritimes: Prince Edward Island, Nova Scotia and New Brunswick.
Prairies: North-West Territories (from 1905 Alberta, Manitoba, Saskatchewan and Yukon).
[2] mill. millions
% percentage of Canadian population.

Source: Urquhart and Buckley, 1965, p. 14; Innis, 1935, p. 97

Nationally, the proportion of the population classified officially as urban (in that they lived in settlements of a thousand or more) stood at 20 per cent in 1871, 32 per cent in 1891, 38 per cent in 1901, and 45 per cent in 1911 (Urquhart and Buckley, 1965, p.14; Porter, 1965, p.18; Ostry and Zaidi, 1979, p.65). However it is clear that (even using this most undemanding definition of what constituted an urban settlement) the degree of urbanisation varied widely between regions; at the end of the period more than half the inhabitants of Ontario and British Columbia could be defined as urban dwellers, compared with fewer than a third in the Maritimes, and barely a quarter in the Prairies (Artibise, 1982, p.265).

The imbalance was more striking still in the case of the larger, more truly 'urban' settlements. In 1911 Canada had 26 cities with 15,000 or more inhabitants – and of these 16 were to be found either in Quebec or in Ontario. British Columbia had two such cities: Vancouver and Victoria; the prairie provinces and the Maritime provinces each had four: Calgary, Edmonton, Regina and Winnipeg; and Glace Bay, Halifax, Saint John and Sydney. Quebec had give of these cities: Hull, Three Rivers, Montreal, Quebec and Sherbrooke; while Ontario's eleven largest centres included Berlin, Fort William, Guelph, Hamilton, Kingston, Ottawa, Toronto and Windsor (Census of Canada, 1911, VI, pp.8–9). Some of these cities grew very large indeed. Hamilton's population increased from fewer than 1,500 in 1834, to nearly 10,000 in 1848, 32,000 in 1876, and practically 82,000 in 1911 (Weaver, 1982, p.265). The population of Montreal grew from under 10,000 in 1800, to 25,000 in 1819, 58,000 in 1851, 131,000 in 1871, and 491,000 in 1911 (Pentland, 1959, p.456; Innis, 1935, p.277; Careless, 1989, p.127); while the population of Toronto expanded from 9,000 in 1834, to 30,000 in 1851, 56,000 in 1871, 208,000 in 1901, and 376,000 in 1901 (Pentland, 1959, p.456; Kealey, 1980, p.99; Drummond, 1987, p.168).

Demographic development was unbalanced still further in that the ethnic (and gender) composition of the population changed much more in some parts of the country than in others. Nationally, it must be said, the ethnic composition altered relatively little: between 1871 and 1911 the number of Canadians of French and British (including Irish) descent declined from over 90 per cent to under 85 per cent, while the number of Canadians of (non-British and non-French) European extraction increased from just under 7 per cent to just over 13 per cent (Urquhart and Buckley, 1965, p.18). Regionally, however, the ethnic composition sometimes changed much more dramatically. By 1911 the proportion of the population that had been born in continental Europe varied widely: from 0.8 per cent in the Maritimes, to 2.1 per cent in Quebec, 3.5 per cent in Ontario, 10.2 per cent in British Columbia, and 13.3 per cent in the Prairies (Census, 1911, II, p.445). In Saskatchewan, more than a third of the population had been born either in Scandinavia or in central and eastern Europe (and unmarried men in their early twenties outnumbered eligible women by a ratio of four to one) (Archer, 1980, p.358; Rasmussen *et al.*, p.13).

This increase in non-English-speaking, continental European immigration reinforced the tendency towards residential and social segregation that was so marked a feature of large-scale urbanisation. Not of course that such segregation was unknown when towns and cities were small. It is true, as John Weaver points out, that in the early and middle years of the century residential segregation 'lacked the clear patterns evident in cities during the age of mass transit', but as he goes on to explain there were already clearly visible divisions that were determined primarily by elevation and/or natural drainage (Weaver, 1982, pp.32, 60). However it is well known that it was the industrial city of the late nineteenth century that 'carried forward the trend toward income and ethnic segregation. The environmentally obnoxious traits of the manufacturing boom – plant size, noise, fumes, rail traffic – deterred men of means from dwelling close to their place of employment' (Weaver, 1982, p.99). Every large city spawned its combination of low- and high-status neighbourhoods: Vancouver had its East End and its West End, Hamilton its Corktown and its Westdale, Winnipeg its North End and its River Heights, Toronto its Cabbagetown and its Rosedale.

It is not difficult to appreciate the intrinsic importance of such demographic change. Nor is it difficult to recognise the intimacy of the relationship between demographic change and retail development. Indeed, as will be seen in subsequent chapters, it was the expansion of population, and its concentration into urban areas, that provided a crucial basis for the growth, and redistribution, of consumer demand that took place in Canada during the late nineteenth and early twentieth centuries.

3.3 The growth of purchasing power

Consumer demand was stimulated too by a rise in the level of disposable incomes. Of course the fact that incomes generally tended to rise does not mean that the improvement was either uniform or uninterrupted. Incomes were checked – and demand curtailed – by a wide range of factors: from personal failings like laziness and irresponsibility; to social barriers such as poor health and large family size; to economic impediments in the form of casual work and seasonal and/or cyclical unemployment.

The economic impediments were particularly severe. The winter slowdown was a perennial problem. The Dominion was notorious, after all, for being an 'eight months country' (Struthers, 1984, NP; *Labour Gazette*, Feb. 1902, March 1903, Sept. 1904). It has been estimated that towards the end of the period some 10 per cent of Toronto workers, and up to 25 per cent of those in Montreal, found themselves unemployed every winter (Copp, 1974; Piva, 1979). Embittered no doubt by the prairie climate, one Winnipeg worker complained at the turn of the century that 'The problem of the day for the majority of workingmen, who strive to make a living in this northwestern country, is to be found in the one word – winter' (*Voice*, 22 May 1897; also Makahonuk, 1982, p.108). Equally deleterious, though less predictable, was the business cycle, that fluctuating pattern whereby economic growth, rather than proceeding smoothly, was punctuated by a series of depressions and recoveries. The major national depressions were those of 1836–7, 1849, the late 1850s, the mid-1870s, the early 1890s, 1907–8, and 1913–15. The downturn of the 1870s was by far the most serious; it had grave consequences for Ontario manufacturing and for the prosperity of the industrial communities that were beginning to emerge in older commercial centres such as Montreal (Acheson, 1971, pp.1, 5; Cross, 1900, p.6; Wells, 1982; Bliss, 1987, pp.150, 179, 158–9, 189, 249–52, 373).

Nonetheless, incomes generally did begin to rise. Self-sufficiency and self-employment gave way gradually to wage labour. However the transition was less clear-cut than is sometimes supposed. For it is important to realise that the self-sufficiency of pioneer society has often been exaggerated (Fowke, 1962) and that the census returns are misleading in so far as they suggest a precipitous decline in seasonal and part-time activities such as begging and petty crime, gardening and allotment-holding, and hunting, trapping and fishing. Indeed I have argued elsewhere that small-scale, working-class entrepreneurial activity 'remained an important component of Canadian economic life until well into the twentieth century' (Benson, 1988, p.67; also Benson, 1990; Spry, 1968).

Yet there seems to be no doubt that, as industrialisation and urbanisation began to take hold, so the population came to rely increasingly upon wage labour. It is now more than 30 years since H. C. Pentland showed how this critical change occurred around the middle of the nineteenth century.

By the 1850's, three events combined . . . The first was the fading into the far interior of the frontier of readily available land. The second was an influx of Irish peasants who were prepared to remain permanently in the unskilled labour market. The third was the coming of a substantial body of British artisans who were similarly prepared, though for quite different reasons, to remain in wage employment (Pentland, 1959, p.459; cf. Greer, 1985).

It is only much more recently that scholars such as Bettina Bradbury have begun to investigate in more detail the transition from self-employment to wage labour. She concludes from her study of late-nineteenth-century Montreal that,

As new laws and restructured urban spaces curtailed access to subsistence, the ways in which married working-class women could contribute to the family's survival were narrowed and altered. Where once she could make or save some money raising animals, making butter, selling eggs or vegetables, now her contribution lay in sharing her living and cooking space with other individuals and families, taking in boarders, or going out to work occasionally for wages herself (Bradbury, 1984, p.46).

It was not simply that industrialisation and urbanisation brought with them an increase in the number of workers who were working for wages. They brought with them too a realignment in the occupational structure of the wage-earning workforce. It is clear from the census returns that towards the end of the nineteenth century there was a decline in the proportion of the workforce engaged in poorly paid agricultural pursuits, and an increase in the proportion employed in more highly paid non-agricultural activities. The census suggests that the percentage of the working population employed in these latter activities increased from 52 per cent (715,000 people) in 1881, to 60 per cent (1.07 million) in 1901, and 66 per cent (1.8 million) in 1911 (Urquhart and Buckley, 1965, p.59).

There can be no doubt that the movement from self-sufficiency and self-employment to wage labour, and within wage labour from poorly paid to more highly paid occupations, had a significant impact upon the purchasing power of Canadian consumers. Unfortunately, however, such a claim is easier to make than it is to substantiate. For there still exists no detailed investigation of the long-run movement of wages, incomes and prices in Canada during the nineteenth and early twentieth centuries. All that can be done therefore is to describe, in very broad terms, the ways in which consumer purchasing power developed during this period of rapid economic and social change.

There have been no detailed studies of middle-class purchasing power. However it seems, as might be expected, that the middle class proved successful at maintaining, if not extending, its share of the nation's wealth (Darroch, 1983, p.54). There have been a small number of studies of working-class purchasing power. These suggest that workers' real wages increased little, if at all, during the first 65 years of the period (Russell, 1983), and began to improve only in the late 1860s. It has been calculated, for example, that between 1865 and 1870 the real wages of skilled tradesmen such as carpenters, masons and blacksmiths increased by between 40 and 85 per cent (Weaver, 1982, pp.68–9). Thereafter working-class purchasing power began to increase much more consistently. It has been estimated that the real earnings of industrial workers in Ontario grew by 74 per cent between 1870 and 1910 (Drummond, 1987, p.427), and it has been suggested that in major cities across the country real hourly wage rates increased by 16 per cent between 1901 and 1914 (Bertram and Percy, 1979, p.307).

The close relationship between income growth, income distribution and retail change will be examined in subsequent chapters. All that needs to be emphasised for the moment is that it was the rise in working-class purchasing power which, along with population growth and urbanisation, provided the basis for the expansion of consumer demand which so stimulated Canadian retailing in the years after 1870.

3.4 Improvements in personal mobility

Consumer demand was stimulated too by improvements in personal mobility. There were certain, limited, advances in private transport. The first bicycle reached Canada from England in the late 1870s, and for several decades cycling remained a form of leisure rather than a means of day-to-day travel. Nonetheless by the mid 1890s Toronto alone had over 90 cycle shops and its inhabitants had bought more than 18,000 bicycles (Drummond, 1987, p.265). 'No more remarkable development has been witnessed in our day', remarked the *Manitoba Free Press* in 1899, than 'the growth in the use of the bicycle. It has furnished a new means of locomotion, has solved for a great many people the old problem of rapid transit in the cities.' (Artibise, 1975, p.166; also Drummond, 1987, p.266).

In fact, advances in public transport were of still greater importance. The final decades of the nineteenth century saw both the construction of an inter-city electric railway network and the electrification of the existing intra-urban street railway system. Electric railways were extended, as 'radials' or 'interurbans', to serve suburban areas and to connect urban centres with one another. The first such railway was built in 1887 and ran just seven miles from St Catharines to Thorold in south-west Ontario. Even in 1914 there were only two inter-urban railways in western Canada, one running south from Vancouver, the other running north from Winnipeg to Selkirk (Blake, 1971, NP; Due, 1966, pp.5, 8). However by the end of the period Ontario alone had nearly 400 (of the nation's 559) miles of track, with lines stretching up and down the St Clair River and running out from cities such as Toronto, Hamilton and London (Drummond, 1987, p.262; Due, 1966, pp.6, 22, 24).

The first horse-driven street railway was opened in Toronto in 1861. The first electrically powered system was opened in St Catharines in 1887, and over the next few years electrified systems were established in Montreal, Ottawa, Toronto, Hamilton, Winnipeg, Brandon, Calgary, Vancouver and other major cities. By 1912 the Winnipeg Street Railway had 75 miles of track and carried over 50 million passengers a year (Manitoba, 1913, NP; Artibise, 1979, p.272). By 1915 the province of Ontario had 13 street railways, the largest being those in Ottawa and London (each of which had 25 miles of track), the Hamilton Street Railway (which, with two associated lines, had 34 miles of track), and the Toronto Street Railway (which ran 62 miles of track) (Drummond, 1987, p.272; Glazebrook, 1938, Vol. 2, pp.241–3). 'More efficient and cheaper to operate than its predecessors – omnibuses, stage coaches, and horsecars – the electric streetcar meant lower fares and a greatly expanded ridership in most places where it was introduced' (Doucet, 1982, p.356). The street railways had a significant impact upon consumer demand: shoppers used them to get to the shops, and shopkeepers advertised the routes by which their premises could be reached. Thus, despite complaints that the Winnipeg Street Railway was slow, irregular and overcrowded, retailers were convinced that 'the routing of cars past . . . [their] place of business is of paramount importance to the solution of the traffic problem' (Feustel, 1913, NP).

It can be seen then that opportunities for intra-urban mobility and for short-distance inter-urban mobility increased substantially towards the end of the nineteenth century. Indeed it will be clear by now that it was in the years immediately before, and immediately after, the turn of the century that the developments discussed so far in this chapter began to have their effect. It was during these years that the growth and urbanisation of the population, the spread of prosperity, and the enhancement of personal mobility tended, both individually and collectively, to increase consumer demand for the goods and services that retailing provided.

3.5 The growth of manufacturing and processing

Of course this growth in consumer demand could be satisfied only if the supply of goods and services increased to meet it. Indeed this is exactly what happened. For although there is some debate as to precisely when, and where, Canada industrialised, it is now generally agreed that the process began some time during the 1870s, and that it was well under way by the following decade (Bercuson, 1987, p.5; Palmer, 1983, pp.61, 66). In all events, industrialisation increased the supply of consumer goods and services in two main ways: by the expansion, mechanisation and diversification of processing and manufacturing; and by the expansion and increasing sophistication of transport and communications.

The secondary sector of the economy grew prodigiously during the late nineteenth and early twentieth centuries. Between 1872 and 1911 the manufacturing workforce increased by 180 per cent, and manufacturing production by 430 per cent (Urquhart and Buckley, 1965, pp.23, 59, 141, 173). These increases in production and productivity were made possible, to a great extent, by the introduction of new factory methods of production. Factory production came first to the towns and cities of central Canada, and by the time of Confederation there were factory complexes operating both in large cities such as Montreal, Toronto and Hamilton and in smaller centres such as Galt, Kingston, Dundas, Ottawa and St Catharines. These factories were producing clothing, footwear, tobacco and metal products for sale on a provincial, and even a national, scale (Langdon, 1972, pp.82-3, 99, 109, 119-21, 398; Bradbury, 1984, pp.73, 85). Outside central Canada, factory production was much slower to take root. But take root it did. By the end of the period Winnipeg had become the fourth largest manufacturing centre in the country (Bercuson, 1974, pp.1-4) while, in the Maritimes, factories had been built in cities such as Halifax, Saint John, Moncton and St John's (Acheson, 1971, pp.62, 65; Sacouman, 1977, p.77).

The application of factory methods made possible the mass production of a growing variety of standardised, packaged and branded products (Burns, 1985, p.v). For example, lumber companies mechanised the processing of the timber that the new furniture factories used in large quantities. By the middle of the century the Toronto firm of Jacques and Hay was already manufacturing 10,000 bedsteads and 75,000 chairs a year. Firms like this employed travelling salesmen, published illustrated catalogues and advertised aggressively. For example, London manufacturer George Moorhead claimed in 1868 to have 'the Largest, Cheapest and Best of every description of FURNITURE in Western Canada.' He explained that 'For years past his aim has been, by constantly adding to and extending his premises, and the introduction of first-class machinery, to lessen the cost of manufacturing, and enable him successfully to compete with any other house in the trade' (Koltun, 1979, p.131; also Nelles, 1970).

The application of mechanisation, refrigeration and the new factory methods made it possible to develop food processing and preparation on an equally large scale. The second half of the nineteenth century saw fish merchants and fishing companies acquiring steam-powered vessels to catch, and steam-powered factories to process, the fish on which their businesses depended (Sanger, 1973, pp.14, 22; Reid, 1975). The second half of the century saw too the canning of fruit and vegetables, and the mass production of items such as butter, cheese and bacon. Between 1870 and 1910 the amount of cheese produced domestically in Ontario declined by over 90 per cent, while the value of that produced in factories increased by more than 75 per cent (Drummond, 1987, pp.128-30, 415; Canada Farmer, 1 August 1865). By the end of the century the pork-packing factory of William Davies employed 300 workers in Ontario, and processed nearly half a million pigs a year – enough to make it the largest firm of its kind throughout the whole of the British Empire (Drummond, 1987, p.128).

The late nineteenth and early twentieth centuries saw too the mass production of bread, biscuits and confectionary. When the Toronto-based Canada Bread Company was formed in 1911, its bakeries were capable of producing 600,000 loaves a week, an output that the firm's directors expected to be able to increase to 2 million a week within just two years (Davies, 1987, pp.43-4). In Halifax the long-established firm of Moirs had introduced steam technology and achieved a good measure of vertical and horizontal integration as early as the 1860s. By the turn of the century the firm was the largest bread producer in the city, delivering, it seems, more than 11,000 loaves to its customers on Saturdays alone. Moreover it had managed to obtain a substantial market for its biscuits in Cuba and Puerto Rico, and was making a determined, and successful, bid to share in the opportunities created by the opening up of the Canadian west. 'We are now', claimed Moirs in 1911, 'shipping the products of our factories throughout the whole of the Dominion as far as the Pacific Coast' (McKay, 1978, p.85; also pp.80–4).

3.6 Improvements in transport and communications

The tertiary sector of the economy also expanded rapidly during the late nineteenth and early twentieth centuries. Between 1891 and 1911 alone there was a doubling of the number of people employed in the service industries of transport and communications, trade and finance, and professional and personal services. Indeed by the end of the period there were three times as many clerical workers as there were fishermen and trappers; and there were nearly five times as many people working in trade and finance as there were employed in an industry as archetypically Canadian as logging (Census, 1911, VI, pp.2–7; Urquhart and Buckley, 1965, p.59). The expansion of transport and communications was of particular importance to the development of retailing, and during the final 20 years of the period the number of workers employed in these two industries grew from 61,000 (4 per cent of the recorded workforce) to 159,000 (6 per cent of the recorded workforce) (Urquhart and Buckley, 1965, p.59).

The transport industry changed very greatly. It has been seen already that opportunities for intra-urban and short-distance inter-urban personal mobility improved quite markedly towards the end of the nineteenth century. So too did facilities for the long-distance movement of raw materials, and for the distribution, on a nation-wide scale, of the processed and manufactured goods that were produced as Canada began to industrialise. It is true that canal building had begun much earlier, in the 1820s, and that by the middle of the century a through route for shipping had been established from the mouth of the St Lawrence as far west as Sault Ste Marie (Glazebrook, 1938, pp.72–6). But here again it was the end of the century that witnessed the decisive transition, for the volume of freight carried on the canals grew from barely 3 million tons in 1886 to 37 million tons in 1914 (Urquhart and Buckley, 1965, p.543).

Yet of all developments anywhere in the economy, none has been celebrated more than the construction of the railway network. Railway mileage increased from just 16 miles in 1836, to 66 miles in 1850, 4,000 miles in 1874, 13,000 miles in 1890, and more than 21,000 miles in 1906. By the time that the First World War broke out, more than 2 billion dollars had been invested in the industry, and there were well over 45,000 miles of track in operation (Urquhart and Buckley, 1965, pp.528, 532, 537–8; Easterbrook and Aitken, 1961, p.401). As Robert Babcock has pointed out, throughout most of North America the railways 'served as advance agents of industrialisation' (Babcock, 1979, p.4). Certainly the volume of freight being carried increased hugely: from 5.7 million tons (including 0.1 million tons of manufactured goods) in 1876, to 24.3 million tons (and 3.4 million tons) in 1896, to 58 million tons (and 11.2 million tons) in 1906 (Urquhart and Buckley, 1965, pp.528–9). Whatever the doubts cast upon the impact of the railways by the efforts of econometric historians armed with counterfactual arguments, it is difficult to escape the conclusion that in Canada at least the expansion of the railway network proved of crucial significance to the economy in general, and to retailing in particular.

The improvement in postal and telephonic communications was also of considerable significance for the movement, as well as for the advertising and ordering, of retail products. The extension of the postal services proved of particular value to retailers and shoppers in rural areas of the country. The first half of the century saw some improvement of roads, the establishment of regular stagecoach routes, and the use for the first time of steam-powered boats. In early nineteenth-century Manitoba, for instance, delivery of the mail was dependent on the Hudson's Bay Company's twice-yearly service. The establishment in 1853 of a monthly service between Fort Garry and Fort Ripley, Minnesota, was followed by further extensions and improvements so that by the 1870s a regular service had been introduced to many Manitoba communities – while in those areas without a service the mails were often carried by members of the North-West Mounted Police (Friesen and Potyondi, 1981, p.32; Osborne and Pike, 1984, p.202).

The extension of the railway network during the second half of the century proved the crucial development. 'For example, mail delivery between Quebec and Windsor which in 1853 had taken ten and a half days was reduced four years later, after the advent of the railway, to forty-nine hours. Between Quebec and Toronto, the reduction in mail passage was from a week to forty hours' (Osborne and Pike, 1984, p.202). The second half of the century saw too a massive increase in the number of post offices: from 601 (one for every 4,059 people) in 1851, to 3,943 (one for 936 people) in 1871, 8,061 (one for 600 people) in 1891, and 13,324 (one for 541 people) in 1911 (Urquhart and Buckley, 1965, pp.555–6; Osborne and Pike, 1988, p.3). Indeed by the end of the period post offices were generally most common in the rural provinces where they were most needed. In the Maritimes there was one post office for every 243 people, on the Prairies one post office for every 502 people, in British Columbia one for every 640 people, in Ontario one for every 667 people, and in Quebec one post office for every 837 people (Urquhart and Buckley, 1965, p.555; Guest, 1986). It will be seen in subsequent chapters that the improvements to the postal system exercised a profound impact upon retailing in the rural areas of the country. For these improvements both encouraged the growth of mail-order selling, and 'accelerated and insured the demise of certain functions of the post office's early host, the general store' (Osborne and Pike, 1984, p.221).

The invention of the telephone proved of value to shopkeepers and middle-class shoppers in urban and rural areas alike. The first telephone exchange in the British Empire was opened in Hamilton in 1878. Thereafter the number of telephones in use multiplied rapidly: from just 13,000 in 1886, to more than 52,000 at the end of the century, and 542,000 in 1914, a figure which, large though it seems, was equivalent to only one phone for every 13 members of the population – which meant that domestic phones were confined almost exclusively to members of the middle class (Urquhart and Buckley, 1965, p.559; Drummond, 1987, pp.259–60; Pike, 1989, p.42). Nonetheless, established retailers were able to use the phone for ordering stock from manufacturers and wholesalers, while customers with access to a telephone were able to use it for ordering the items that they required from departmental and other large established stores. By the end of the century, concludes one recent commentator, 'householders were already extensively shopping over the telephone' (Martin, 1987, p.375).

The expansion of the secondary and tertiary sectors of the economy during the second half of the nineteenth century proved of crucial importance, for it meant that retailers were able – indeed needed – to stock a growing, and increasingly sophisticated, supply of indigeneous and imported products. A glance through the pages of any major provincial newspaper will confirm that by the end of the century both manufacturers and retailers were advertising a vast array of nationally known, branded products. They advertised Canadian goods ranging from 'Black Cat' cigarettes, to the 'Vapo-Cresoline' inhaler, and the Canada Cycle and Motor Company's 'Cushion Frame Bicycle'; they advertised British products encompassing everything from 'Yale' locks, to 'Beecham's Pills', 'HP Sauce', and 'Salada' tea – the latter described during the Boer War as 'British To The Core', 'Grown by Britishers. Sold by Britishers. Drunk by Britishers'. Many of these manufacturing firms, it was claimed at the time, were 'great advertisers, their goods known in the smallest hamlet and the largest cities' (*Retailer*, July 1917).

This brief survey, it must be repeated, has not been intended to provide anything approaching a comprehensive economic and social history of nineteenth- and early twentieth-century Canada. It is hoped, however, that it has been successful in indicating some of the major changes that took place during this period in consumer demand and in consumer supply; thereby providing a useful background to explain the developments in Canadian retailing, that will be discussed in subsequent chapters of this volume.

References

Acheson, T.W., 1971, The social origins of Canadian industrialism: a study in the structure of entrepreneurship, PhD thesis, University of Toronto

Archer, J.H., 1980, *Saskatchewan: A History*, Western Producer Prairie Books, Saskatoon

Artibise, A.F.J., 1975, *Winnipeg: A Social History of Urban Growth 1874–1914*, McGill-Queen's University Press, Montreal and London

Artibise, A.F.J., 1982, The urban west: the evolution of prairie towns and cities to 1930, in R.D. Francis and D.B. Smith (eds.), *Readings in Canadian history: Post-Confederation*, Holt Rinehart & Winston, Toronto

Babcock, R.H., 1979, Economic development in Portland (Me.) and Saint John (N.B.) during the age of iron and steam, 1850–1914, *American Review of Canadian Studies*, 9: 3–37

Benson, J., 1988, Penny capitalism and capitalism in Canada, 1867–1914, *British Journal of Canadian Studies* 3 (1): 67–82

Benson, J., 1990, *Entrepreneurism in Canada: A History of "Penny Capitalists"*, Edwin Mellen Press, Lewiston, Queenston and Lampeter

Bercuson, D.J., 1974, *Confrontation at Winnipeg: Labour, Industrial Relations, and the General Strike*, McGill-Queen's University Press, Montreal

Bercuson, D.J., 1987, The era of industrialization, in D.J. Bercuson (ed.), *Canadian Labour History: Selected Readings*, Copp Clark Pitman, Toronto

Bertram, G.W. and Percy, M.B., 1979, Real wage trends in Canada 1900–26: some provisional estimates, *Canadian Journal of Economics*, 12 (2): 299–312

Blake, H.W., 1971, *The Era of Interurbans in Winnipeg 1902–1939*, H.W. Blake, Winnipeg

Bliss, I.M., 1987, *Northern Enterprise: Five Centuries of Canadian Business*, McClelland & Stewart, Toronto

Bradbury, B., 1984, Pigs, cows, and boarders: non-wage forms of survival among Montreal families, 1861–91, *Labour/Le Travail*, 14: 9–46

Burns, R.J., 1985, *Packaging Food and Other Consumer Goods in Canada, 1867–1927: A Guide to Federal Specifications for Bulk of Unit Containers, their Labels and Contents*, Parks Canada, Ottawa

Calgary Daily Herald, 1913

Canada Farmer

Careless, J.M.S., 1989, *Frontier and Metropolis: Regions, Cities and Identities in Canada before 1914*, University of Toronto Press

Census of Canada, 1911

Copp, T., 1974, *The Anatomy of Poverty: The Condition of the Working Class in Montreal, 1897–1929*, McClelland and Stewart, Toronto

Cross, D.S., 1969, The Irish in Montreal, 1867–1896, MA thesis, McGill University

Daily World, Vancouver, 1900

Darroch, A.G., 1983, Early industrialization and inequality in Toronto, 1861–1899, *Labour/Le Travailleur*, 11: 31–61

Davies, C., 1987, *Bread Men: How the Westons Built an International Empire*, Porter Books, Toronto

Deane, P. and Cole, W.A., 1969, *British Economic Growth 1688–1959: Trends and Structure*, Cambridge University Press

Doucet, M., 1982, Politics, space and trolleys: mass transit in early twentieth-century Toronto, in G.A. Stelter and A.F.J. Artibise (eds.), *Shaping the Urban Landscape: Aspects of the Canadian City-building Process*, Carleton University Press, Ottawa

Drummond, I.M., 1987, *Progress Without Planning: The Economic History of Ontario from Confederation to the Second World War*, University of Toronto Press

Due, J.F., 1966, *The Intercity Electric Railway Industry in Canada*, University of Toronto Press

Easterbrook, W.T. and Aitken, H.G.J., 1961, *Canadian Economic History*, Macmillan, Toronto

Feustel, R.M., 1913, Report on the Winnipeg Street Railway Service, 1913, Legislative Assembly of Manitoba, Report of Public Utilities.

Fowke, V.C., 1962, The myth of the self-sufficient Canadian pioneer, *Transactions of the Royal Society of Canada*, 56 (3): 23–37

Friesen, G. and Potyondi, B., 1981, *A Guide to the Study of Manitoba Local History*, University of Manitoba Press, Winnipeg

Glazebrook, G.B. deT., 1938 (1964), *A History of Transportation in Canada*, Ryerson Press (McClelland and Stewart), Toronto

Greer, A., 1985, Wage labour and the transition to capitalism: a critique of Pentland, *Labour/Le Travail*, 15: 7–22

Guest, H., 1986, *A History of the Dawson Post Office with Some Comment on the Klondike Mail Service, 1897–1924*, Parks Canada, Ottawa

Innis, M.Q., 1935, *An Economic History of Canada*, Ryerson Press, Toronto

Kealey, G.S., 1980, *Toronto Workers Respond to Industrial Capitalism, 1867–1892*, University of Toronto Press

Koltun, L.A., 1979, *The Cabinetmaker's Art in Ontario c.1850–1900*, National Museums of Canada, Ottawa

Labour Gazette, Ottawa

Langdon, S.W., 1972, The political economy of capitalist transformation: central Canada from the 1840s to the 1870s, MA thesis, Carleton University

McKay, I., 1978, Capital and labour in the Halifax baking and confectionary industry during the last half of the nineteenth century, *Labour/Le Travailleur*, 3: 63–108

Makahonuk, G., 1982, The Regina painters' strike of 1912, *Saskatchewan History*, 35: 108–15

Martin, M., 1987, Communication and social forms: a study of the development of the telephone system, 1876–1920, PhD thesis, University of Toronto

Napanee Beaver, 1908

Nelles, H.V., 1970, The politics of development: forests, mines and hydro-electric power in Ontario, 1890–1939, PhD thesis, University of Toronto

Osborne, B. and Pike, R., 1984, Lowering 'the walls of oblivion': the revolution in postal communications in central Canada, 1851–1911, *Canadian Papers in Rural History*, 4: 200–25

Osborne, B. and Pike, R.M., 1988, From 'a cornerstone of Canada's social structure' to 'financial self-sufficiency': the transformation of the Canadian postal service, 1852–1987, *Canadian Journal of Communication*, 13 (1): 1–26

Ostry, S. and Zaidi, M.A., 1979, *Labour Economics in Canada*, Macmillan of Canada, Toronto

Palmer, B.D., 1983, *Working-class Experience: The Rise and Reconstitution of Canadian Labour*, Butterworth, Toronto

Pentland, H.C., The development of a capitalistic labour movement in Canada, *Canadian Journal of Economics and Political Science*, 25: 450–61

Pike, R.M., 1989, Kingston adopts the telephone: the social diffusion and use of the telephone in urban central Canada, 1876–1914, *Urban History Review*, 17 (1): 32–48

Piva, M.J., 1979, *The Condition of the Working Class in Toronto – 1900–1921*, University of Ottawa Press

Porter, J., 1965, *The Vertical Mosaic: An Analysis of Social Class and Power in Canada*, University of Toronto Press

Rasmussen, L., Savage, C. and Wheeler, A., 1976, *A Harvest Yet to Reap: A History of Prairie Women*, Canadian Women's Educational Press, Toronto

Reid, D.J., 1975, Company mergers in the Fraser river salmon canning industry, 1885–1903, *Canadian Historical Review*, 56: 282–302

Retailer, 1917

Russell, P.A., 1983, Wage labour rates in upper Canada, 1818–1840, *Histoire sociale/Social History*, 16: 61–80

Sacouman, R.J., 1977, Underdevelopment and the structural origins of the Antigonish movement co-operatives in eastern Nova Scotia, *Acadiensis*, 7 (1):66–85

Sanger, S.W., 1973, Technological and spatial adaption in the Newfoundland seal fishery during the nineteenth century, MA thesis, Memorial University of Newfoundland

Santink, J.L., 1990, *Timothy Eaton and the Rise of his Department Store*, University of Toronto Press

Spry, I.M., 1968, The transition from a nomadic to a settled economy in western Canada, 1856–96, *Transactions of the Royal Society of Canada*, 6: 187–201

Struthers, J., 1984, *Canadian Unemployment Policy in the 1930s*, Trent University, Peterborough

Urquhart, M.C. and Buckley, K.A.H., 1965, *Historical Statistics of Canada*, Cambridge University Press

Voice, Winnipeg

Weaver, J.C., 1982, *Hamilton: An Illustrated History*, James Lorimer, Toronto

Wells, D., 1982, The hardest lines of the sternest school: working class Ottawa in the depression of the 1870s, MA thesis, Carleton University

Part II: Fairs, markets, pedlars and small-scale shops

Part II
Fairs, markets, pedlars and small-scale shops

It is easy to overlook the importance of small-scale – and especially of non-fixed-shop – forms of retailing. In most countries of the world the study of fairs, markets, the itinerant trades and small fixed shops seems to have been marginalised by a combination of empirical difficulty and ideological assumption: the paucity and complexity of the surviving primary data; and the preoccupations of historians, geographers and economists who seem concerned primarily with size, growth and success. Indeed it is a fundamental paradox of retailing history that the more attention is directed towards large-scale organisation, the more misunderstandings seem to persist about small-scale forms of distribution.

Accordingly it is the aim of the following three chapters to bring together what (little) is known about the retailing functions of fairs, markets, the itinerant trades and small fixed shops in Britain, Germany and Canada during the nineteenth and early twentieth centuries. For not only is such a task important in its own right, but it is only when it is completed that it will be possible to understand properly the growth and impact of the large-scale forms of retailing that are examined in the final section of the book.

The following three chapters confirm the resilience, and importance, of small-scale forms of retailing. Indeed the evidence produced in this section of the book suggests that these easily overlooked forms of distribution adapted with surprising success to the economic and demographic changes brought about by industrialisation and urbanisation.

It is clear, for example, that the nineteenth century saw the survival, rather than the demise, of the periodic market. The scholars who contribute to this section of the book show that the city-centre market retained a dual role in the retail systems of each of the three countries under discussion. The market remained the geographical focus of a good deal of urban retailing activity; it was the place where stall-holders, itinerant traders and shopkeepers were to be found competing alongside one another. The market also retained a major functional role as an intermediary between rural producers and urban consumers; it was the place where farmers and smallholders came to sell, and working people in particular came to buy, the meat, vegetables and fresh fruit that had been produced in the surrounding countryside.

It seems clear that itinerant trading too maintained a significant – and in

Germany a growing – role in the retail systems of expanding urban areas. The authors of the following three chapters show that hawkers and pedlars, like market stall-holders, performed a dual role in the urban economies that were developing so rapidly during the nineteenth and early twentieth centuries. For the itinerant trades contributed not only to the maintenance of urban food supplies but also to the provision of work and income for members of some of the most disadvantaged groups to be found competing in urban labour markets. In fact, the survival of hawking and peddling has implications for the study not simply of retailing, but of many other aspects of urban and working-class life.

Nonetheless, the significance of periodic markets and itinerant trading should not be exaggerated. For as the contributors to this section of the book make clear, the outstanding development in small-scale retailing was the growth, and increasing importance, of the fixed shop. It is a development that can easily be overlooked. For the emphasis in so much of the literature upon the growth and success of large-scale fixed-shop retailing tends to suggest that small, independently owned shops were in absolute, as well as in relative, decline from the late nineteenth century onwards. This, as will be made clear, was simply not the case. In all three countries, small fixed shops retained a vitality, and an importance, that should not be overlooked or undervalued.

The survival, and success, of these small-scale forms of retailing throws into question some of the assumptions that are commonly made about the determinants of retail development. For while the contributors to this section of the book show, time and time again, that changes in consumer demand constituted the primary determinant of retail development, they suggest too that broader economic, social, political and legislative changes should not be ignored. It seems, for example, that in both Britain and Canada the survival of itinerant trading and general storekeeping owed a good deal to the needs of members of the working and lower middle classes to supplement and/or replace their other sources of income, while in Germany the late nineteenth- and early twentieth-century expansion of itinerant retailing and specialised shopkeeping owed a good deal to the legislative changes that were introduced from the late 1860s onwards.

It is easy then to stress the resilience of markets, itinerant trading and small fixed shops in Britain, Germany and Canada, and it is tempting perhaps to exaggerate the implications that their survival has for the understanding of retail development in advanced, industrialising countries. However, much remains to be done. What is needed now, all the contributors to this section would agree, is a series of serious, sustained and sophisticated investigations of the still neglected world of small-scale retailing.

Chapter 4

The evolution of markets and shops in Britain

Martin Phillips

4.1 Introduction

Historical retail studies in Britain, and arguably elsewhere, are at present caught between the concerns and dilemmas of two overlapping philosophies. First, there have been attempts to introduce positivist models of retail change (see Shaw, 1988 and Chapter 1 of this volume). Second, and more importantly, studies of retailing in nineteenth- and early twentieth-century Britain have been dominated by a series of monumental empirical studies which have provided a pivot around which much subsequent work has focussed. Jefferys' *Retail Trading in Britain, 1850–1950* and the work of Everitt (1967), Gras (1926) and Westerfield (1915) have been pre-eminent, each spawning a series of more or less critical studies: Alexander (1970), Blackman (1962–4), Burnett (1983), Davis (1966), Mathias (1967) and Yamey (1954). Whatever the value of the initial study, the empiricist nature of the subsequent discourse has both created a wealth of information on retailing in the period and encouraged the smuggling in of many assumptions as uncontestable 'fact'.

Naturally, not all these issues can be taken up here. Accordingly, this chapter seeks to address just three major questions. It will consider the nature of retailing in the 'long century' after 1800, and will seek to avoid the tendencies of many existing studies to view the transformation of retailing solely in terms of competition between markets and shops. It will also seek to extend our understanding of developments in the distributive trades by considering the geographies of change. For much of the existing work on retailing in this period pays little attention to the significance of spatial aspects of market exchange, and thus to the imaginative work of scholars such as Braudel (1985a, 1985b) and Polanyi (1957) and the more recent work of geographers such as Dodgshon (1987), Gregory (1987, 1988), Harvey (1973, 1982) and Langton (1984, 1988). The third issue to be addressed relates to the question of whether changes in the organisation of commerce should be seen as caused by changes in demand and supply. It will be argued here that production and consumption should not be seen as autonomous, independent causal factors but rather that they should be considered in the context of what Marx termed 'a separation in unity' (Marx, 1973).

4.2 Itinerant trading

One common view is that itinerant traders, along with market traders, were of declining significance during the nineteenth century. For instance, McCulloch argued as early as 1833 that the number of itinerants had declined, 'since shops for the sale of almost every sort of produce have been opened in every considerable village throughout Britain'. This argument, unlike that for markets, has been subjected to considerable examination. Alexander (1967), for example, has described such comments as 'misleading' in at least three respects. First, the growth of fixed-shop retailing did not necessarily lead to a decline, either in relative or absolute terms, in the number of itinerant traders. Second, such a view fails to distinguish between country peddling, which was in decline, and urban itinerancy, which was on the increase. Third, it is a view which relies, not on firm occupational statistics, but on what Alexander considers to have been the misleading views of middle-class political economists who favoured retailing in fixed shops. This last point leads to two related problems which have bedevilled empirical studies of the itinerant trades. For, as Benson (1984) has discussed, the definition of itinerant traders is complex and, as Alexander (1967) has explained, the two major official sources on itinerant traders, the licences for hawking and the census returns, are only partial indicators of the distribution of itinerant traders. The problem is seen clearly in the difference between the number of itinerants recorded in the two sources in 1840–1: the census lists 14,662 hawkers, pedlars and hucksters, while the number of licensed hawkers and pedlars is less than half that.

Alexander (1967) suggests that even the census figures do not indicate the full extent of itinerant trading. First, many itinerant traders were illiterate and could not (or would not) complete the census returns; second, the census failed to enumerate both country people selling in urban markets and dealers in manufactured goods who sold their products at the market place and/or in the streets; and, third, the census ignored people who, at times of hardship, took temporarily to hawking. Overall, Alexander concludes, the census returns give, at best, an indication of the size – and one can add the spatial distribution – of only 'the permanent core of full-time hawkers and pedlars' (Alexander, 1967, p.62). They suggest, as Benson (1984, p.103) has shown, an increase, rather than a decrease, in numbers between 1851 and 1911.

They show that absolute numbers rose two and a half times, from 25,747 in 1851 to 69,347 in 1911. They show, too, an increase in the number of street salesmen compared with the rest of the population: in 1851 there was one such trader to 696 other people; in 1911 one to 520, a relative increase of 25 per cent. For all their limitations, then, the census figures provide no indication at all of a decline in the permanent core of full-time street sellers. Moreover, the census returns provide a useful guide to the geographical differentiation of itinerant trading. For instance, both Alexander (1967, 1970) and Shaw (1986) have commented on the strongly urbanised pattern of the distribution of itinerant traders recorded in the census. This

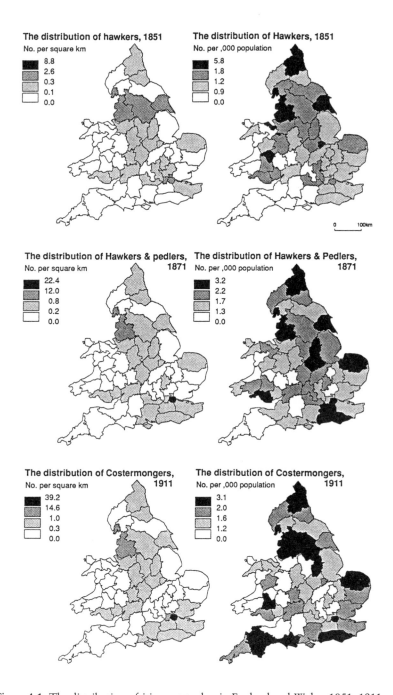

Figure 4.1 The distribution of itinerant traders in England and Wales, 1851–1911

feature is clearly shown in Figure 4.1 which plots the distribution of hawkers and pedlars in England and Wales 1851–1911. Shaw has described the mid-nineteenth-century situation as follows:

Heavily urbanised counties, such as Lancashire, the West Riding and the central lowlands of Scotland, had the highest proportion of traders. In contrast most of the agricultural counties, especially in Wales, northern Scotland, and south west England, possessed very low levels of itinerant traders. This situation was probably further intensified by an absolute decline in the more established country trade, possibly through a combination of rural depopulation and competition from shops (Shaw, 1986, p.182).

Rather less attention has been paid to the distribution of itinerant traders in the late nineteenth and early twentieth centuries. Yet, as Figure 4.1 shows, there were significant changes in the distribution of these traders, between 1851, 1871 and 1911. By 1911, although Lancashire and the West Riding continued to have relatively high numbers of traders relative to their populations, there are clear concentrations in the counties along the south and east coasts. This pattern suggests that any relationship with urbanisation which had existed in the northern counties, had been affected by other influences. Among these one can suggest the extensive penetration of wage labour into, and the shedding of labour from, capitalistic agriculture. Such changes would provide both the necessary conditions, and the compulsion, for small-scale itinerant trading, which in relative terms was equal to that in the northern urbanised/industrialised counties. Indeed, as in the case of marketplace improvements, one can suggest that there were distinct and changing regional geographies (Lee 1981, 1984).

In all events, small-scale agents of exchange continued to play an important role. When Matthew Boulton described the commercial system of the late eighteenth century, he acknowledged the significance of traditional practices and of small agents of exchange. In one of his letters, for instance, he comments:

We think it of far more consequence to supply the People than the Nobility only; and you speak contemptuously of Hawkers, Pedlars and those who supply *Petty Shops*, yet we must own that we think they will do more towards supporting a great Manufactory, than all the Lords in the Nation, and however lofty your notions may be, we assure you we have no objection to pulling of our Hats and thanking them 4 times a year (quoted in McKendrick, 1982, p.77).

When a working-class couple in Bristol described the distribution system that operated in the city during the 1920s, they explained that

of course you used to have all the tradesmen going round. The cockle woman, she used to go round with a big bath on her head and then eels, you've seen these, baby eels, well they'd go round with those . . . And then there would be the bloke with the flypapers, with a top hat . . . you had somebody continually knocking on your door from morning till night. (Benson, ND, p.5).

4.3 Markets

It is not easy to define a market. In fact, the term 'market' has been perceived in two basic ways: 'physically', in terms of a zone of exchange, and 'abstractly', as a process of exchange. These two meanings have interpenetrated each other in complex ways. Walker (1988), for instance, has remarked that the 'neoclassical' concept of the market beloved by some contemporary New Right philosophers is 'nothing more' than an idealisation of a village marketplace into which people come to buy and sell. Indeed, it can be argued (Phillips, 1991) that there is a need to consider both physical and abstract notions of marketplaces if one is to understand the nature of the activities that went on in them, and the range of forces and social relations that operated within them.

These alternative, and changing, notions of what constitutes a market raise awkward questions for those attempting a study of this form of selling. In this chapter, attention is paid to publicly defined markets, that is markets which were described within publicly available literature as weekly markets, great markets and fairs. These markets lie somewhere between the total set of markets and the set of markets defined formally/legally as such by charter or prescription. This publicly defined set of markets will no doubt omit many informal and private markets such as those held in inns and private houses (Everitt, 1967). However, Scola, in one of the few detailed studies of markets, has remarked that whatever the problems their study entails, they did have the particular virtue of generating records.

They occupied central sites; they spilled out into the highway and generally disrupted the life of surrounding areas; market authorities jealously guarded their rights and often clashed with their tenants; the building of covered market halls were matters of civic pride (Scola, 1982, p.157).

In the seventeenth and early eighteenth centuries market buildings were generally limited in extent. The most permanent element of the marketplace was generally the butchers' shambles, which were usually rows of covered-in stalls or shops. These shambles were frequently incorporated into town and market halls, and these halls formed the principal building in many marketplaces up until the eighteenth century. They were generally built within the bounds of existing open marketplaces and often had a row of shops at one end. In the eighteenth century a new form of marketplace began to be constructed: this was the cloth hall, which was typically a large rectangular building with a central courtyard and long rows of stalls at which clothiers exhibited their cloth for the merchants, who walked up and down comparing prices and quantities (Grady, 1980). From the mid-nineteenth century these buildings became larger and more impressive. This was a trend which, Grady argued, was present in 'almost all the marketing and commercial buildings, and corn exchanges' erected after 1750 (Grady, 1980, p.69). This argument is clearly supported when one considers the description of the new market of Liverpool which was built in 1822 at a cost of some £35,000:

Viewed from one end, the interior is divided into five avenues, there being four rows of handsome cast-iron pillars, 23 feet high, supporting the conjoined abutments of the roofs along the entire building . . . The walls are lined by 62 shops and offices . . . The great body of the market is occupied by four ranges of stalls, tables, &c. running in a line with the pillars from end to end, including 1600 stalls three yards each (*The Economist and General Adviser*, 1822, p.226).

Despite the increasing material presence of marketplaces during the nineteenth century, the work of Grady remains the most detailed study of their construction, although remarks on the rebuilding of marketplaces appear in local histories and in studies of the commercial structure of selected towns. However, there have also been general surveys of the spacio-temporal distribution of market improvements Acts, by which local administrations sought powers to improve and regulate markets. According to Alexander (1970), Acts incorporating market re-organisation date back to the sixteenth century, although they became much more significant as part of the comprehensive urban improvement measures which emerged from the late eighteenth century onwards. Almost 400 local and private town and market improvement Acts were passed by Parliament between 1785 and 1850. In the period 1800–1890 64 towns, excluding London, apparently obtained Acts to restructure their markets, while in London 14 new markets were opened during the course of the nineteenth century. Table 4.1 shows the temporal distribution of these Acts.

Table 4.1 The temporal distribution of market improvement Acts in England and Wales, 1800–1890

Period	Number of Acts passed
1800–10	42
1811–20	27
1821–30	34
1831–40	44
1841–50	56
1851–60	78
1861–70	60
1871–80	30
1881–90	3

Source: Table III of Shaw and Wild, 1979, pp.278–91

In interpreting these figures it is important to note that, up to about 1820, market improvements were largely included within general town improvement schemes. As a result, the figures for the first two decades of the nineteenth century represent an underestimate of the amount of legislation which impinged upon marketplaces. Nonetheless, it can be suggested that the initial decade of the century saw a high degree of activity in relation to Acts of market improvement, and that this activity declined somewhat in the following two decades. From 1831 to 1860 there was a generally increasing rate in the number of Acts passed per decade, which reached a peak of 78 between 1851 and 1860. The number of Acts declined slightly in the period 1861 to 1871, and then declined rapidly (to three) in the years 1881–90.

Shaw (1985) has shown that these market improvement Acts became distributed throughout the settlement hierarchy, and across the length and breadth of the country. However, more significant patterns are revealed when the space/time distribution and form of market improvements are examined. Figure 4.2 shows the spatial distribution of local, local and private, and provisional Acts relating to

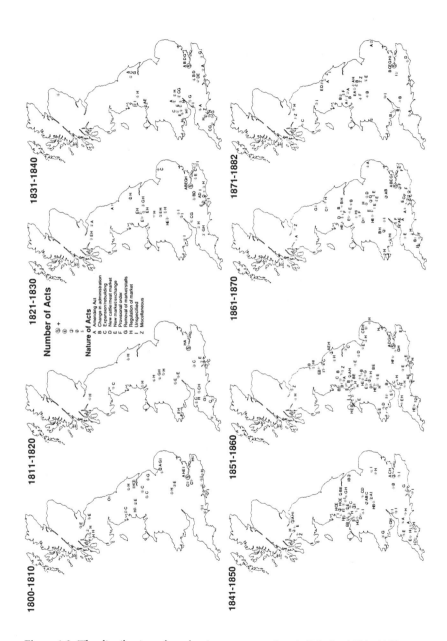

Figure 4.2 The distribution of market improvement Acts in Britain, 1800–1882

markets passed for similar time spans to those in Table 4.1. The market improvement Acts appear to be distributed throughout the country, although London was the dominant site of such improvements in all periods except 1841–50. Despite this degree of spatial continuity, there are distinct differences in the pattern of improvement between the periods recorded here. There appear to be distinct regional clusters in the patterns of improvement, and it is worthwhile considering how one might seek to explain this 'regional geography'.

Those researchers who have examined the issue have argued that improvements in marketplaces were generally a direct result of the pressures of a growing population. Alexander argues that

Urbanisation and the rapid population growth in this period [the eighteenth and nineteenth centuries] placed heavy demands upon existing market facilities . . . while quantitative evidence is lacking it is clear that considerable quantities of capital was invested in market improvements . . . [which] were an investment in that part of the distribution system which gave the greatest benefit to the mass of the population (Alexander, 1967).

However, an examination of the distribution of market improvement (at least as evidenced by the lists of local, market, and local and personal Acts relating to market improvements listed in the Report of the Royal Commission of Market Rights and Tolls) suggests that the situation may not be quite as straightforward as Alexander, among others, has suggested.

Two areas are worthy of particular examination. First, it is interesting to note that Lancashire, an area where there have been a number of studies on market improvement, appears to have experienced relatively few market improvements during the 1820s and 1830s, although there was considerable population increase in both relative and absolute terms. Lancashire's apparent lack of market improvements had changed by the period 1841–61, when there was also considerable further population growth. The studies by Redford (1939) and Scola (1975, 1982) have stressed how in Manchester, at least, it was felt necessary to expand the markets to cope with an expanding population. Manchester, and perhaps other Lancashire towns, may therefore be cases where population growth contributed greatly to attempts to improve markets, but only in the period after 1841. Second, it is interesting to see that in the south-west of England, the distribution of Acts (see Table 4.2) is rather different from that nationally. Moreover, the distribution reinforces the argument against viewing marketplace improvements purely as a response to population increase because fluctuations in the number of market improvement Acts in Cornwall and Devon do not correspond directly to changes in population levels in the two counties.

This is not to say that broad-scale changes exercised no influence. In fact, the distribution of the Acts is suggestive of at least two such influences. First, the decline in the 1820s seems to correspond with the agricultural depression of the decade; for a decline in agricultural production, one might expect, would lead to falling investment in marketplaces. Second, the peak of market improvement Acts between 1831 and 1850 might reflect the emergence of the railways and their penetration into the counties. In fact, two rather different accounts of the relationship between railways and market improvements can be suggested, dependent upon how one views the impact of railways upon the general circulation of commodities. One

Table 4.2 The physical restructuring and regulation of markets in Cornwall and Devon, 1801–1880

Period	Number of market improvement Acts	Number of market 'improvements'
1801–10	0	4
1811–20	4	4
1821–30	2	12
1831–40	5	15
1841–50	6	9
1851–60	3	5
1861–70	4	3
1871–80	1	1

Sources: Billing's Directory and Gazetteer of the County of Devon (Birmingham: Billing, 1857); *Pigot and Co.'s Royal, National and Commercial Directory* (Slater, 1844); *Slater's (late Pigot and Co.) Royal, National and Commercial Directory and Topography* (London and Manchester: Isaac Slater, 1852–3); *White's History, Gazetteer and Directory of the County of Devon* (Sheffield: White, 1850); *Post Office Directory of Devonshire and Cornwall* (London: Kelly & Co. 1856, 1866, 1873); Royal Commission on Market Rights and Tolls (BPP, 1889)

might argue that railways created a general increase in the circulation of commodities which led to more demands being placed upon market facilities. Alternatively, one can argue that railways led to a concentration of circulation at certain localities, creating a situation where the existence of some markets became endangered; in such instances one might expect the responsible authorities to endeavour to attract more business by improving the facilities at their marketplace.

However it is important not to jump to too hasty a focus upon the railways as an explanation. For example, Perren (1989) has remarked that many changes associated with the arrival of the railways, including the re-organisation of marketing, may in practice either pre-date it or be influenced more by other changes in the economy, principally, he argues, by a growth in demand after 1830. (His arguments find some support in the figures for market improvement Acts in Devon and Cornwall; for whereas the first major railway line only reached Devon in 1844, the increase in market improvements probably began in the 1830s.)

Nonetheless, before too many implications are drawn from these distributions, it must be noted that the distribution of market improvement Acts does not necessarily correspond to the distribution of marketplace improvements. An analysis of the marketplace improvements listed in directories suggests that market improvements may have been more widespread than is indicated by the list of legislation provided in 1888 (see Table 4.2). All that can be suggested therefore is that before any interpretation of the distribution of market improvements can reasonably be put forward, rather more detailed work must be undertaken on the motives for, and the nature of, marketplace improvement. Overall, it would seem that no general evolutionary explanation appears to account completely for the geography of market improvement. Instead a more contextual approach is required, one which recognises the social relations within a marketplace, social relations which relate both to the material existence of the place and to the more abstract processes of market exchange.

One of the major reasons why marketplaces and marketplace-based trading have been relatively ignored is that there is a contention, albeit frequently implicit, that the marketplace as an institution for commercial exchange had become unimportant by the nineteenth century. This is clearly seen within one of the most recent studies of commercial organisation, that of Mui and Mui, who pay no attention at all to the role of markets and fairs, arguing that by the end of the eighteenth century,

the wholesale functions once performed by the fair had long since fallen into desuetude. All that remained of the great fairs was the trade in livestock and some foodstuffs . . . The retail trade had also shifted. In the seventeenth century, the fair was still an important source of supply for the great houses, but the eighteenth century witnessed the demise of all its retail trade except for trifles . . . Nor is there any evidence that the weekly market was a buoyant, flourishing institution. Rather, the picture is one of decline (Mui and Mui, 1989)

Mui and Mui do not provide any direct supporting evidence for this forceful claim. Instead they appeal to the indirect evidence of consumption studies, suggesting that markets were only significant routes of exchange for foodstuffs. The interpretation of such evidence is notoriously difficult, as witnessed by the seemingly interminable 'standard of living debate'. With reference to the links between consumption habits and retail outlets, Shaw (1985, p.286) has argued, using some of the same studies as Mui and Mui, that 'many of the urban poor purchased . . . supplies of meat and vegetables late on Saturday evening, usually because prices were reduced at this time in the marketplace'. Whatever the relationship between consumption and purchasing behaviour, it can be suggested that there is considerable direct evidence that contradicts Mui and Mui's assertion that market exchange had largely moved, as early as the mid-eighteenth century, beyond the bounds of the marketplace. Indeed, one can detect some signs of a revision in the historiography of markets and fairs. Chartres (1990), for example, has argued that, while the general model of 'rationalisation' (by which he means decline) over time still holds, there is a need for caution in applying it too readily. This caution is necessary, he argues, for at least three reasons: that work on the sixteenth and seventeenth centuries tends to overstate the number of such markets; that work on the seventeenth and eighteenth centuries has underestimated the significance of fairs; and that work on the eighteenth and nineteenth centuries has focussed too readily on the rise of private markets, assuming that this was necessarily associated with the demise of public markets. Given such problems with existing interpretations, it seems time for a detailed re-examination of the role of markets and fairs.

A regional perspective may prove valuable, so we consider very briefly the distribution of markets in the two counties of Devon and Cornwall. An examination of the directories of these counties suggests that the total number of market days appears to have increased from a low level in 1782–3 to a much higher, and fairly constant, level in the 1790s, 1810s, and 1840. Comparing this last cross-section with that of 1888 produces, once again, a picture of enormous decline. However, the addition of more frequent cross-sections produces a markedly different picture for the period after 1840. For, rather than a decline, there appears to be a continued upward movement in the number of markets, right through to

1870. Indeed it is only at this cross-section that there appears to be a dramatic decline in the number of markets. This then would date any decline in the distribution of weekly markets to the 1870s and 1880s.

Naturally, it is difficult to generalise upon the basis of a particular regional investigation. Nevertheless, one can suggest that, at least up until the 1870s and possibly beyond, markets remained a much more significant feature than has generally been supposed. However, since this interpretation, like many previous suggestions of decline, is based upon the distribution of market days, further detailed work is clearly required in order to investigate how the institutional arrangements of market days actually related to commercial activity in the marketplace (see Phillips, 1991).

4.4 Shopkeeping

Any empirical study of small-scale, fixed shopkeeping runs into immediate problems. For even the term 'shopkeeper' is problematic in that it appears to have been used in the eighteenth and early nineteenth centuries to refer to wealthy traders who sold goods to the public from fixed premises, whatever the size of the establishment, and whether or not the seller had produced the goods. However, in the course of the nineteenth century the word shopkeeper was increasingly, although by no means exclusively, reserved in trade circles, in the pages of commercial directories and in imaginative literature, to refer to small, non-specialised retailers who lacked capital or social standing.

The changing definition of the term shopkeeper means that its application shifted in regard to traders who experienced no change in their position in the division of labour. Thus while in the eighteenth century a substantial trader dealing in foreign goods might be described as a grocer or a shopkeeper, by the mid-nineteenth century only the former term would probably be applicable. Likewise, while a small-scale trader in household goods might be called a provisions dealer in the eighteenth century, by the nineteenth century he might be described as a shopkeeper. Moreover, there is the question of social status and its influence upon the producers of information used by the historian. Winstanley, for example, has commented that the 'substantial dealers' obvious desire to be included in trade directories as recognised specialist tradesmen on a par with the merchants and manufacturers listed there clearly caused considerable headaches for the compilers, who had to resort to an elaborate system of cross-referencing to avoid labelling them simply as "shopkeepers"' (Winstanley, 1983, p.12). The commercial reason for avoiding such a description is clear. However, the concern over status had wider connections with respect and authority, and can be seen to affect sources other than directories. In the census, for instance, there was, according to Mills and Pearce (1989, p.4), a 'reluctance of respondents and enumerators to enter "master" or "journeyman" against many tradesmen and craftsmen, including shopkeepers'. Such influences on the production of information must caution one against any over-hasty interpretation of the seemingly authoritative distributions derivable from the census returns.

The approach adopted here is to consider a variety of 'retail' trades, even though such a designation has arguably obscured any recognition of their wholesaling and producing activities. Bakers, butchers, grocers and 'shopkeepers' will be the 'retailers' examined, for they were the major constituents of the 'food trades' as identified by Perren (1978).

By the beginning of the nineteenth century, grocers dealt principally in foreign produce, dried fruits, condiments, spices, tea, coffee and sugar, and drew their customers from the middle- and higher-income groups. 'Provision merchants' dealt in more basic, domestically produced foods: butter, eggs, hams and salted beef. (Blackman, 1976, p.149; Mui and Mui, 1989, p.23). During the nineteenth century the distinction between the grocery trade and provisions was transformed, although both the nature and the timing of the change is a matter of considerable debate. Jefferys (1954), for example, suggested that the grocery trade changed in the latter half of the nineteenth century. Certainly, census returns indicate a substantial expansion in the grocery trade, and to a lesser extent the provisions trade, during the second half of the century.

Moreover, some scholars, such as Mathias (1967), have argued that the grocery trade experienced a 'revolution in retailing' moving towards the specialised practices of mass retailing where agents stocked one, or perhaps two, specialised lines of commodities in bulk. On the other hand, Blackman (1976) has suggested that by the mid-nineteenth century grocers had become increasingly involved in selling a wider range of commodities to the working class. In performing this task they were competitive with (Winstanley, 1983), or complementary to (Mui and Mui, 1989, pp.219–20), a growing number of provision dealers, shopkeepers and co-operative stores. Either way, there is seen to be a decreasing degree of specialisation, with traditional grocery products being handled by a greater range of agents, and formerly specialised trades, such as groceries and provisioning, becoming much more widely based.

Mui and Mui have provided perhaps the most extreme version of this argument, suggesting that the activity of tea dealing became widespread across a range of agents to such an extent that by the late eighteenth century one could reasonably say that there had been 'a quiet revolution well before the explosive events of the industrial sector' (Mui and Mui, 1989, p.200). In support of their argument they point to an apparent change in the geography of retailing between 1759 and 1795–6. Figure 4.3 illustrates the results of an excise enumeration of retail shops in 1759 and an excise account of tea licences in 1795–6. Mui and Mui argue that these reveal a number of highly significant features. First, it appears that a substantial number of shops were licensed for selling tea – hence the argument that tea dealing was not purely a prerogative of high-class grocers. Second, they argue that there was a dramatic change in the geography of retailing with counties north of a line stretching from Lincolnshire through Leicestershire, Warwickshire and Gloucestershire to Somerset on the south-west coast experiencing a dramatic increase, although still lagging in absolute terms behind the counties south of that line. The rise in the northern counties, which were undergoing industrialisation at this time, is perhaps not unexpected, although the scale of the increase probably is. Perhaps of more immediate interest is the reason for the dominance of the southern counties. As Mui and Mui remark,

Convention at least links a great increase in retail shops with industrialisation, either concomitant or trailing after, and with urbanization. In England, at least, that increase

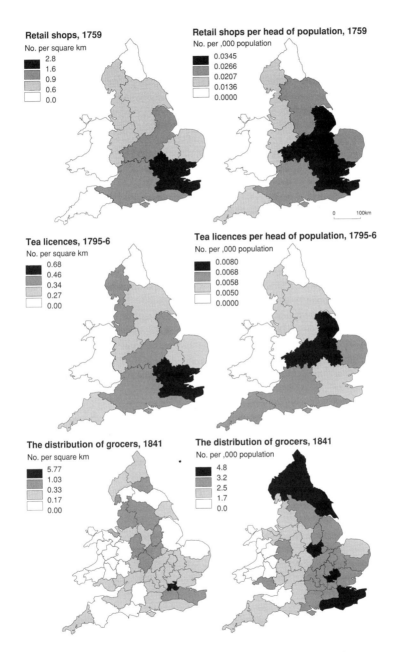

Figure 4.3 The distribution of retail shops (1759), tea licences (1795–6) and grocers (1841) in England and Wales

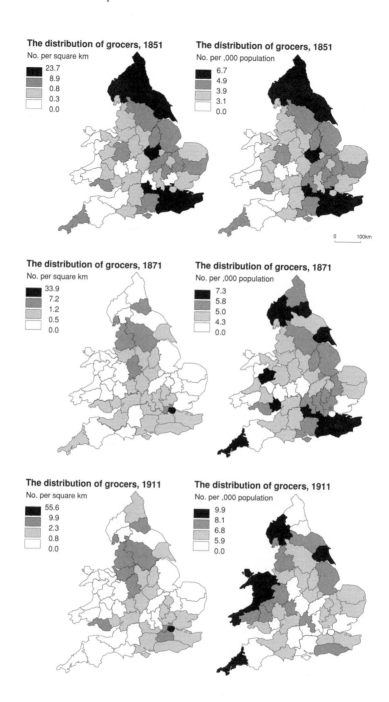

Figure 4.4 The distribution of grocers in England and Wales, 1851–1911

appears to have taken place before the industrial sector had achieved revolutionary changes and when the proportion of the population living in urban centres of 5,000 or more may have been no more than 20 per cent (Mui and Mui, 1989, pp.44–5).

Differences in the density of grocers in England and Wales in 1841 (Figure 4.3) would tend to support their argument, with London, Lancashire and the counties of the Midlands all having higher than average densities. However, the distributions of grocers in relation to population are less supportive of their argument, with London and its neighbouring counties having above average numbers of grocers in comparison with their population. The west of England appears to have the lowest relative number of grocers. The distribution is maintained in 1851 (Figure 4.4), although there are a number of areas (including London) with a lower than average number of grocers per thousand population. This would seem to support the arguments of Mui and Mui although there does not appear to be, as their arguments seem to imply, an increase in traders in the counties with growing industrial centres of such a magnitude as to overshadow growth elsewhere. Instead it appears that grocers were, in the 1840s and 1850s at least, of most prominence in counties with relatively few centres of large population. Although the distributions of grocers relative to population in 1871 show this trend to only a limited degree, it appears extremely marked in the distribution of 1911 (Figure 4.4). This pattern of grocers may not be as surprising as initially thought. For, as it is argued above, the term 'grocers' was increasingly taken to refer to traders with a relatively wealthy clientele, so it might be expected that their relative significance in terms of population size would decline in areas where there was a large increase in the size of the working-class population.

The possibility of the different dynamic of exchange can be usefully highlighted by comparing two other food 'retailers': bakers and butchers. The maps of the distribution of bakers for 1851 and 1871 (Figure 4.5) suggest a clear regional divide in the distribution relative to population. The areas south of a line running from the Wash to the Severn, excluding Cornwall, all appear to have a relatively high distribution of bakers. The distribution echoes the statement by Mui and Mui on retail trading in the mid-eighteenth century.

An agricultural map shows that these counties (with a high number of retail shops) lie within the lowland zone, an area characterised by mixed husbandry. In the lowland zone the nucleated village was the predominant type of settlement, in contrast to the isolated farmhouse and small hamlet of the pastoral zone. The lowland area was also well served by market towns . . . Both these conditions, ancient in origin, would help facilitate the spread of shopkeeping as a means of inland communication improved, as commercial activities quickened and as an ever-larger proportion of the working and consuming population became increasingly dependent upon local markets *and* shops for their daily 'necessities' and 'luxuries'. Counties outside the lowland, with their isolated farmhouses and hamlets, lacked an economically viable settlement pattern and in these areas shopkeeping lagged behind the rest of the country (Mui and Mui, 1989, p.41).

It is interesting to speculate about the extent to which this interpretation of retailing in the mid-eighteenth century may account for the distribution of bakers in the mid-nineteenth century. Certainly corn was largely produced and circulated in southern England and hence the distribution of bakers can be seen as an expression

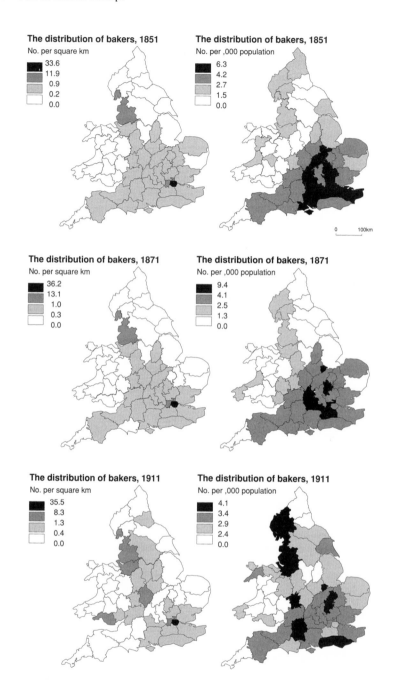

Figure 4.5 The distribution of bakers in England and Wales, 1851–1911

of the influence of production on circulation. In a period of expanding grain production there would be a considerable need for the value embodied in it to be realised: dense settlement and good communications would help this process by minimising any loss of value within exchange, while the increasing penetration of capitalist social relations within agriculture would ensure the necessary separation of production and consumption for market exchange to function. The pattern of bakers relative to population in 1911 is rather different from those of the nineteenth century discussed above. In particular the counties of north-west England join those of southern Britain in having a higher than average number of bakers relative to their population. In part the differences may reflect a change in the classifications of the census, which in 1911 distinguished between bakers as retailers of bread and as makers of bread and biscuits. The image presented may therefore indicate how the influence of production diminished in comparison with that of a more distinctly 'retail' sector.

Fortunately, the occupational category 'butchers' is reasonably well defined, although the maps of their distribution as recorded in the censuses of 1841, 1851, 1861 and 1911 reveal a considerable amount of variation, particularly in relation to population numbers (Figure 4.6). The 1841 and 1861 cross-sections have been used to accentuate the seemingly complex nature of changes in the distribution of butchers which appear to have occurred in the nineteenth century. Considering relative densities first, there is considerable apparent change between the distributions of 1841 and 1861. The map of 1841 shows a relatively high concentration of butchers in London and the neighbouring counties of Surrey and Kent, and in a broad belt extending northwards from Gloucestershire through the midland counties (with the exception of Derbyshire) into Lancashire, Cheshire and the West Riding of Yorkshire. The distribution of butchers in these years can be seen to be a clear reflection of two broad factors: the significance of the London market, and the distribution of pastoral agriculture. By 1911 the pattern had changed once more, with the counties of the south-west joining the areas with higher than average numbers of butchers relative to their population.

Such major, and fluctuating, variations pose many problems of interpretation. Not least is the issue of whether they reflect changes in the classifications in the census as opposed to changes in the geography of the trade. In this respect it is interesting to note that the changes in the 1860s and 1870s correspond, at least temporally, with the rise in imports of livestock and with the movement of agrarian capital from cereal to livestock production. Thus there was the clear possibility of a rising circulation of livestock; fortunately for the growth of the butchery trades, rising population, increased monetary returns to labour, and a continued preference for meat within the diet permitted the expanded circulation of livestock.

Some scholars have also argued that during the period covered by this book there was not simply an increase in the number of butchers and meat salesmen, but also a change in the nature of these agents and in the organisation of the meat trade. Shaw, for example, has claimed that 'the meat trade in the first half of the nineteenth century was dominated by producer–retailers, large-scale butchers who also did their own slaughtering . . . [and] in turn supplied the small-scale meat retailer' (Shaw, 1985, pp.287–8). Throughout the first half of the century there occurred an increasing separation both in operations of business and in physical location. In Sheffield, for example, the slaughter houses and the live cattle market

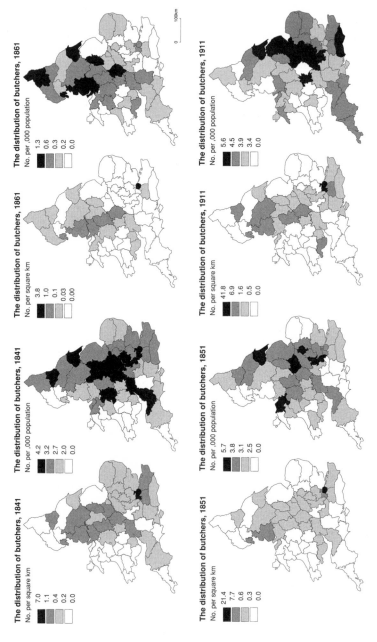

Figure 4.6 The distribution of butchers in England and Wales, 1841–1911

were both removed from the centre of the town, with the result that the carcass and retail meat markets were located in different parts of the town and held on different days of the week. However, there are obvious problems about generalising from the as yet restricted number of studies of the meat trade, which have been based predominantly on London or on northern industrial towns.

The case of shopkeepers is also instructive. For during the nineteenth century (Figure 4.7), the counties of Lancashire and the West Riding of Yorkshire, for example, appear in all the decennials with an above average figure for the number of shopkeepers per thousand population. However, the manufacturing districts of the north were not the only counties with high numbers of shopkeepers relative to population. The counties of Norfolk, Essex, Gloucestershire, Somerset, and North and West Wales all had consistently high figures while the counties south of London were below average, at least until 1911. These variegated patterns of shopkeepers per thousand population stand in great contrast to the maps of absolute distributions which are all very similar (London and Lancashire being the only areas with above average distributions). Over the period 1851–1911 there appears to be a general increase in the average number of shopkeepers, with a rather faster climb in the higher-density counties. Hence, the variation in the number of shopkeepers per thousand population would seem to reflect rather more the variability of population change than any differential growth of the trade. By implication therefore, it could be argued that population pressure was not the crucial influence on retail growth at least as far as shopkeepers were concerned. Indeed one can suggest that rather than looking for a simple cause and effect relationship between retail growth and macro-scale features of the economy, one needs to develop an approach that is much more sensitive to the dynamics of market exchange. As Ducatel and Blomley (1990) have argued, retailing is caught within a complex set of relations and contradictions. Yet they indicate only two positions: first, between production and realisation of capital; and second, between exchange of values and consumption. The working out of these contradictions lead, so they argue, to processes of centralisation and concentration, and hence to increased division and integration of labour.

The arguments of Ducatel and Blomley are couched in a 'capital logic' framework, which arguably runs the risk of reducing everything to an abstract, reified logic. That said, their analysis seems to illuminate important facets of the dynamics of market exchange. For, as revealed in this analysis of shopkeeping, not all retailing appears to be locked into reactive changes to the 'demands' of consumption. Rather than responding to the distribution of population, shopkeeping appears to have followed its own dynamics, related perhaps to its association with other economic activities and with the general divisions of capital. (This is not to say of course that in other times/spaces, or in other trades, the relation of retailing to consumption was not crucial).

This examination of changes in the grocery, bakery, butchery and 'shopkeeping' trades raises a number of interesting, important and complex issues. Indeed the range of factors affecting retailing has led some commentators (see Ducatel and Blomley, 1990) to reject any movement towards a theoretical input in the study of retail change. Yet, as they argue, retailing needs to be considered in relation to particular social relations, specifically those contradictory capitalist relations which lie within, and between, production and consumption. Such issues, unfortunately, lie beyond the scope of this chapter (but see Phillips, 1991).

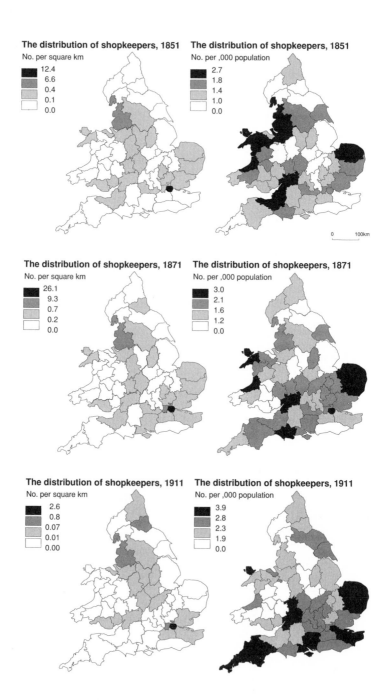

Figure 4.7 The distribution of shopkeepers in England and Wales, 1851–1911

4.5 Conclusions

The purpose of this chapter has been to widen discussion on the processes of 'retail evolution' in three directions. First, it has been argued that there is a need to avoid the assumption of a single chronology of change that is based upon retail shops. Attention has been directed, therefore, to another, frequently ignored, aspect of retailing, that of marketplace-based trading. It has been shown that it is impossible to use one piece of evidence, the number of market days, to support the argument that marketplace trading was of declining significance during the nineteenth century. Second, it has been argued that the spatial distributions of marketplace improvements, of itinerant traders and of various 'retail' food trades all had distinct geographies. It is suggested that there is clearly a need to consider such geographies further, particularly as they do not seem to correspond to many of the existing macro-scale, 'evolutionary' explanations of retail development. Third, it has been argued that such explanations are in any case deficient in that they ignore the social context of, and the interrelations between, the 'factors' that they take as causal. In particular, it has been suggested that the notion of autonomous forces of demand and supply is untenable, particularly within the context of capitalistic relations of accumulation. It has been argued therefore that a deeper understanding of retailing can be gleaned through a consideration of the various social contexts in which, and through which, it operated. The social relations involved in retailing are not restricted to those associated with a geographically variegated division of labour, but include a variety of cultural, administrative and political relationships. What is needed, of course, is much further work of both an 'empirical' and a 'theoretical' nature in order to examine the nature of such social relations and how they were constituted.

References

Alexander, D., 1967, Retail trade in Great Britain 1800–1850, unpublished PhD thesis, University of London

Alexander, D., 1970, *Retailing in England During the Industrial Revolution*, Athlone Press, London

Benson, J., 1984, *The Penny Capitalists: A Study of Nineteenth-Century Working Class Entrepreneurs*, Gill and Macmillan, Dublin

Benson, J., N.D. Hawking and peddling in England and Wales, 1850–1939, unpublished paper

Blackman, J., 1962–4, The food supply of an industrial town, *Business History*, 5–6: 83–97

Blackman, J., 1976, The corner shop: the development of the grocery and general provisions trade, in D.J. Oddy and D.S. Miller (eds.), *The Making of the Modern British Diet*, Croom Helm, London, pp.148–60

Braudel, F., 1985a, *Civilisation and Capitalism, 15th–18th Century: Volume 2 The Wheels of Commerce*, Fontana, London

Braudel, F., 1985b, *Civilisation and Capitalism, 15th–18th Century: Volume 3 The Perspective of the World*, Fontana, London

Burnett, J., 1983, *Plenty and Want*, Methuen

Chartres, J.A., 1973, The marketing of agricultural produce in metropolitan western England in the late seventeenth and eighteenth centuries, in M. Havinden (ed.), *Husbandry and marketing in the South West, 1500-1800: Exeter papers in economic history, no. 8*, University of Exeter, Exeter

Chartres, J.A., 1986, The marketing of agricultural produce, Chaper 17 of *The Cambridge Agricultural History of England and Wales*, Vol. 5, Cambridge University Press; reprinted in Chartres, J. (ed.) *Chapters from the Agrarian History of England and Wales: Volume 4 Agricultural Markets and Trade 1500-1750*, Cambridge University Press

Chartres, J.A., 1990, Introduction in J. Chartres (ed.), *Chapters from the Agrarian History of England and Wales: Volume 4 Agricultural Markets and Trade 1500-1750*, Cambridge University Press

Census of Great Britain, 1854

Census of Great Britain: Report of occupations, 1911

Davidoff, L. and Hall, C., 1987, *Family Fortunes: Men and Women of the English Middle Classes, 1780-1850*, Hutchinson, London

Davis, D., 1966, *A History of Shopping*, Routledge Kegan Paul, London

Dodgshon, R.A., 1987, *The European Past: Social Evolution and Spatial Order*, Macmillan, London

Ducatel, K. and Blomley, N., 1990, Rethinking retail capital, *International Journal of Urban and Regional Research* 14 (2): 207-27

Everitt, A., 1967, The marketing of agricultural produce, 1500-1640, in J. Thirsk (ed.), *The Agrarian History of England and Wales, Volume 4: 1500-1640*, Cambridge University Press, pp.466-592; reprinted in Chartres, J. (ed.), 1990, *Chapters from the Agrarian History of England and Wales, Volume 4: Agricultural Markets and Trade 1500-1750*, Cambridge University Press, pp. 15-138

Finch, G., 1984, The experience of peripheral regions in an age of industrialisation: the case of Devon, 1840-1914, unpublished PhD thesis, Oxford University

Grady, K., 1980, The provision of public buildings in the West Riding of Yorkshire, c.1600-1840, unpublished PhD thesis, Leeds University

Gras, N.S.B., 1926, *The Evolution of the English Corn Market from the Twelfth to the Eighteenth Century*, Oxford University Press

Gregory, D., 1987, The friction of distance? Information circulation and the mails in early nineteenth century England, *Journal of Historical Geography*, 13 (2): 130-54

Gregory, D., 1988, The production of regions in England's industrial revolution, *Journal of Historical Geography*, 14 (1): 170-6

Harvey, D., 1973, *Social Justice and the City*, Edward Arnold, London

Harvey, D., 1982, *Limits to Capital*, Basil Blackwell, Oxford

Jefferys, J.B., 1954, *Retail Trading in Britain, 1850-1950*, Cambridge University Press

Langton, J., 1984, The industrial revolution and the regional geography of England, *Transactions Institute of British Geographers*, new series, 9: 145-67

Langton, J., 1988, The production of regions in England's Industrial Revolution: a response, *Journal of Historical Geography*, 14 (2): 170-4

Lee, C.H., 1981, Regional growth and structural change in Victorian Britain, *Economic History Review*, 2nd series, 34: 438-52

Lee, C.H., 1984, The service sector, regional specialisation and economic growth in the Victorian economy, *Journal of Historical Geography*, 10: 139-55

Mathias, P., 1967, *Retailing Revolution*, Longman, London

Mathias, P., 1976, The British tea trade in the nineteenth century, in D.J. Oddy and D.S. Miller, *The Making of the Modern British Diet*, Croom Helm, London, pp.91-116

Marx, K., 1973, *Grundrisse*, Penguin, Harmondsworth

McCulloch, J.R., 1833, *On Commerce*, Library of Useful Knowledge, London

McKendrick, N., 1982, The commercialisation of fashion, in N. McKendrick, J. Brewer and J.H. Plumb, *The Birth of Consumer Society: The Commercialisation of Eighteenth*

Century England, Hutchinson, London

Mills, D. and Pearce, C., 1989, *People and Places in the Victorian Census: A Review and Bibliography of Publications Based Substantially on the Manuscript Census Enumerators Book 1841–1911, Historical Geography Research Series, no. 23*, Historical Geography Research Group

Mui, H.-C. and Mui, L.H., 1989, *Shops and Shopkeeping in Eighteenth-century England*, Routledge, London

Perren, R., 1978, *The Meat Trade in Britain, 1840–1914*, Routledge Kegan Paul, London

Perren, R., 1989, Market and marketing, in G.E. Mingay, *The Agrarian History of England and Wales, Volume 6: 1750–1850*, Cambridge University Press

Phillips, M., 1991, Market exchange and social relations: the practices of food circulation in and to the 'Three Towns' of Plymouth, Devonport and Stonehouse, 1800–1875, unpublished PhD thesis, University of Exeter

Polanyi, K., 1957, *The Great Transformation*, Beacon Press, Boston

Redford, A., 1939, *The History of Local Government in Manchester*, 2 vols, Longman, London

Royal Commission on market rights and tolls, Volume 1, 1889, British Parliamentary Paper, cd 5550

Scola, R., 1975 Food markets and shops in Manchester, 1770–1870, *Journal of Historical Geography*, 1 (2): 153–69

Scola, R., 1982, Retailing in the nineteenth century town: some problems and possibilities, in J. Johnson and C. Pooley (eds.), *The Structure of Nineteenth Century Cities*, Croom Helm, London, pp.153–69

Shaw, G., 1985, Changes in consumer demand and food supply in nineteenth century British cities, *Journal of Historical Geography*, 11 (3): 280–96

Shaw, G., 1986, Retail patterns, Chapter 23 of J. Langton and R.J. Morris (eds.), *Atlas of Industrialising Britain 1780–1914*, Methuen, London, pp.180–3

Shaw, G. 1988, Recent research on the commercial structure of nineteenth-century British cities, in D. Denecke and G. Shaw (eds.), *Urban Historical Geography: Recent Progress in Britain and Germany*, Cambridge University Press, pp.236–49

Walker, R., 1988, The geographical organization of production-systems, *Environment and Planning D: Society and Space*, 6 (4): 377–408

Westerfield, R.B., 1915, *Middlemen in English Business: Particularly Between 1660–1760*, Yale University Press, New Haven

Winstanley, M.J., 1983, *The Shopkeeper's World, 1830–1914*, Manchester University Press

Yamey, B., 1954, The evolution of shopping, *Lloyds Bank Review*, NS 31: 31–44

Chapter 5
Traditional retail systems in Germany
Dietrich Denecke and Gareth Shaw

5.1 Introduction

Unfortunately, there has been little research on the evolution of retailing in Germany, and those studies that do exist date in the main from the early twentieth century. Many of these early studies focussed specifically on the threat that large-scale retail firms posed to the small, independent shopkeeper (Mataja, 1891; Göhre, 1907; Lux 1910). Other studies have placed the development of retailing within the context of urban social topography and have been concerned merely with the location of shops. This work has been undertaken mainly by geographers and was stimulated by Dorries' early studies during the 1920s (Denecke, 1988). There are also studies by economic and business historians which have focussed on a few large firms, but have added little to our understanding of the general evolution of German retailing (Tietz, 1965). Indeed, most of these publications, because of their subject matter, have stressed developments only in the very large cities, especially Berlin, and failed to recognise that the pace of change varied considerably between these areas and the many small market towns. Finally, the difficulties of investigating early trends in nineteenth-century German retailing are enhanced by the political and commercial fragmentation of the country before the 1870s. As a result data are often available only at regional or local levels making it difficult to gain an overall picture.

Against this limited background of past work this chapter will attempt to consider a number of key issues relating to retail change in Germany. Such issues range from the importance and changing role of fairs and markets, the phase of transition from producer-retailing towards shopkeeping, and the pace of change within different parts of the settlement hierarchy. In some cases explanations may of necessity be restricted to regional or even local examples – a reflection once again of the early stages within which research in Germany is still anchored.

5.2 Fairs

Medieval fairs had, even by the late eighteenth century, witnessed a significant decline in importance, a trend brought about by the changing nature of trade and the consequent expansion of other parts of the distribution system. In Germany during the nineteenth century large-scale fairs such as those at Frankfurt and Leipzig were still important events that attracted considerable trading activity. In the main this was of a wholesale nature, with dealer meeting dealer, although the fairs also had their retail elements. The so-called 'golden age' of German fairs had been during the sixteenth century, with the fair at Frankfurt am Main being pre-eminent, to be followed after the Thirty Years War by Leipzig (Allix, 1922, pp.537–8). According to contemporary eighteenth-century commentators quoted by Braudel (1982, p.93), the fair was seen as an archaic form of exchange and 'wherever it reigned without competition, the economy did not do well'. In more economically backward rural areas, fairs tended to persist but 'when economic life moved ahead fairs were like old clocks which would never catch up' (Braudel, 1982, p.94).

In nineteenth-century Germany, fairs did survive but with considerably changed functions which involved different evolutionary pathways. One of these was the specialisation in cattle fairs, while another group within the growing industrial cities became pleasure fairs with hardly any retail functions. Finally, some changed and became trade fairs for businesses and middlemen. One of the best examples of trade fairs is Leipzig, whose fair was founded in 1268. During the nineteenth century the Leipzig fair was in serious decline and by the 1890s specialised almost entirely in books and furs; moreover, even the retailers of these products were beginning to desert the fair and establish themselves in permanent quarters within the city (Allix, 1922, p.557). By around 1897 major attempts were being made to save the fair by preserving its wholesale trade and preventing it from becoming a mere local retail fair. The new business methods involved the idea of wholesale dealing at the fair but without immediate delivery, with merchants only being shown samples. In this way major fairs like Leipzig could survive, but on the whole many others changed their functions and succumbed to competition.

5.3 Markets

In a sense the fair was never a major retail institution in Germany, although by its very nature it attracted both retailers and consumers. However, in Germany, as in other European economies, the market played an early and dominant role in the country's retail system. The first wave of market development was related to the growth of towns and the increase of trade from the sixteenth century onwards. General statistics on the development of markets in Germany are sadly lacking, although a few regional studies, such as that by Schremmer (see Braudel, 1982, p.42) on Bavarian markets in the eighteenth century, do provide a basis for further research. During the later middle ages and the early modern period the number of market days tended to increase, an extension that applied to both weekly and annual markets. In smaller towns, where economic development had stagnated, the right to hold a market had sometimes been abandoned or was no longer exercised, but in general traditional markets were still held in most towns during the nineteenth century. Indeed, there was an increase in the number of new markets towards the end of the century as populations grew and consumption levels started to increase.

Three main types of markets were in operation by 1800: the market mainly for the sale of food; the annual market (termed *Dult* in southern Germany) for the sale of haberdashery, small wares and livestock; and the 'special' market for the sale of grain, hops, wool and animals. The special markets in particular were held in major centres of agricultural areas and market towns of some importance were to develop from these. In northern Germany special markets for the sale of pigs were held in Bassum, Bleckede, Cloppenburg and Buxtehude. Annual and special markets experienced fluctuations in their relative importance, while the coming of the railways tended to increase functional concentrations. Cloppenburg, in northern Germany for example, had become South Oldenburg's largest animal market by 1900 (Heumann, 1987).

Within the growing nineteenth-century towns and cities food markets maintained their role, especially among the working classes. These markets were closely regulated by the local authorities and dealt almost exclusively in food. Indeed, within the largest cities market development was seen as an important means by which food supplies could be improved. As in Britain, though often at a later date, the major influences that led to market developments in the nineteenth century were food and health regulations and improvements in the organisation of supply. Very often these ideological and economic developments culminated in the construction of indoor markets from the late 1870s. Within Berlin, for example, eight such market halls were opened between 1886 and 1888, and by 1900 the city had some fifteen halls with the two central buildings being the largest (Krüer, 1914). Berlin's markets represented a substantial investment estimated at some £1.4 million, of which one half was accounted for by the costs of the sites. They carried out considered trade in meat, fish and vegetables, and in 1905 the two main central markets received almost 100,000 tons of goods by rail alone (Board of Trade, 1908, p.32). Many of the other cities' markets were built in the centres of rapidly growing working-class residential areas, such as Berlin–Kreuzberg. By 1897 there were twelve German cities, excluding Berlin, that had invested in new market halls: Braunschweig, Chemnitz, Dresden, Frankfurt am Main, Hannover, Köln, Leipzig, Lubeck, Metz, Nürnberg, Strassburg and Stuttgart (Krüer, 1914).

These halls were extremely important to the working classes, and in the cities there also operated a formal system of offering poor-quality meat to the lowest-income groups. In Berlin, for example, as in other large centres, inferior meat was passed to the so-called 'Freibank' shops for sale to the most disadvantaged consumers. Within Berlin there were four such shops located in working-class areas and demand for products always exceeded supply, with crowds of women gathering long before the opening hour to take advantage of the very low prices (Board of Trade, 1908, p.33).

Even by the turn of the century, market halls had still not been constructed in many towns and cities. Indeed, some places, like Stuttgart, could only aspire to constructing covered markets to replace the small outmoded buildings. Other centres, like Dusseldorf and Bochum, relied even in 1905 on large open-air street markets. Many of these were supplied on a daily basis by farmers from the surrounding countryside. In Bochum, there were several open-air markets for fruit and vegetables held in different parts of the town, with the local authorities allowing 'much latitude as to the small stall-holders who frequent odd corners and vacant spaces in the town' (Board of Trade, 1908, p.36). Many of these stallholder/costermongers (*Hökerhandel*) sold small quantities of foodstuffs to lower-income consumers, and by the late nineteenth century they also frequently sold their products along main routes to work and, particularly, outside major railway stations. Thus, given the existing state of knowledge it is extremely difficult to comment in any precise way upon the scale, regional diversity and importance of market selling. However, this is not to suggest that markets did not play a significant part in urban food retailing. Indeed, they continued to perform a crucial role in supplying the basic needs of some of the most disadvantaged of late nineteenth- and early twentieth-century German consumers.

Unfortunately, it is difficult to arrive at any general conclusions as statistically these stall-holders are not identified as a distinctive group. There are, however, numerous local monographs about the *Hökerhandel*, though as yet there is not a single region of Germany for which any detailed, systematic research has been undertaken.

5.3 Itinerant retailing

The development of itinerant retailing, at least in terms of the number of people engaged in it and its economic importance, depended to some extent on restrictive rules and changes in legislation. Until well into the nineteenth century itinerant retailing (or peddling) was quite severely restricted by the statutes of various guilds. These organisations not only restricted the number of pedlars permitted to trade but in many areas prohibited the practice altogether. (However, an important exception seems often to have been made for those buying-up agricultural raw materials, clothing and second-hand goods.)

The relaxation of restrictions on itinerant trading came with the passing of a new Trade Regulations Act in 1869, which permitted the peddling of virtually any goods. In effect this form of distribution was placed in a position of virtual legal equality with the more regular forms of retail trade. This liberalisation resulted in a sudden surge in itinerant retailing, an expansion which does not seem to have been adversely affected by increases in the cost of the trade permits which were introduced in 1883.

As in most other countries it is difficult to gain any precise measure of the numbers involved in itinerant retailing from the German census of occupation of 1895 which lists only those 113,329 self-employed pedlars who had obtained a permit. However there were also 13,556 assistants, and an unknown number of commercial travellers/travelling salesmen, shop delivery workers and pedlars operating in the area in which they lived.

From the limited evidence it seems certain that there was a substantial increase in itinerant trading in the larger cities towards the end of the nineteenth century. In Berlin, for example, there were around 20,000 pedlars in 1900 (Steida, 1900). The incidence of itinerant retailing showed wide variations throughout Germany, with Saxony having the highest relative concentrations of 9 pedlars per 1,000 employed. To be added to these figures for Saxony were a larger number of pedlars from Bavaria, Silesia and Bohemia who often visited Saxony. The regions of Alsace–Lorraine, Wüttemberg, and Baden had the next highest incidence of itinerants, with many pedlars coming from Hesse and the Rhineland – areas which themselves had a relatively low rate of itinerants. Bavaria had the lowest recordings of pedlars due in the main to its particularly restrictive legislation, which caused many Bavarian pedlars to ply their trade in neighbouring regions.

When considered in detail it becomes clear that itinerant retailing covered a range of activities, and in Germany four distinctive groups may be identified.

1. Pedlars selling goods that either were produced by themselves or were agricultural/trade products bought at their place of residence. These pedlars would often undertake more extensive seasonal travel or work regular rounds in the area from which the products came.
2. Pedlars from areas with weak economies who would buy goods, mostly industrial products made elsewhere, and sell them independently as they travelled.
3. Pedlars employed in significant numbers by firms or even shop owners whose goods they sold; strictly speaking they were door-to-door salesmen.
4. Pedlars to whom hawking was in part a pretext to enable them to beg, move around the country and avoid settling down to work. These were mostly operating without permission, with peddling as casual employment mixed with vagrancy.

In general, the pedlars dealing in their own products often did so because of insufficient demand within their home area. As a consequence they were forced to retail their goods to more distant markets. Within Germany a whole range of small specialised production areas emerged, either over a long period of time or specifically during the nineteenth century, from which the selling of local products was organised in the form of peddling. This was usually undertaken by members of the family, especially women, with farmers' wives attending many of the town markets.

Within the agricultural sector, for example, Effeltrich in Upper Franconia specialised in the cultivation and selling of fruit, while Baiersdorf and neighbouring villages focussed on the growing of horse radish. In Bardowick, Lower Saxony, the specialism was the growing and selling of vegetables and flower seeds. Among the trade products sold by pedlars were, for example, potters' wares from Coppengrave in Lower Saxony or Urberach in Hesse. Other products included brushes from Nernbach in the Palatinate, or from Todtnau in the Black Forest region, lace from the mountainous area between Saxony and Bohemia, wooden utensils from the Sauerland, and carved cuckoo clocks from the Black Forest.

In investigating peddling of this kind, however, it is essential to establish to what extent the pedlars (or their families) were the producers of the goods, or had bought their goods from other producers. A thoroughly researched example of the development of a particular kind of peddling within the social framework and conditions of the nineteenth century is the trade in horse radish in Baiersdorf in Franconia and villages in the vicinity (Heinritz, 1971). In that particular area, the growing of horse radish had become very important since the beginning of the nineteenth century. Medium-sized farms (5–10 hectares) were the producers; the sale was largely in the hands of the wholesalers. Before 1850, peddling of any kind was not much practised in the area, apart from some hawking by Jews. It was the growth of the rural proletariat (already in existence) in the nineteenth century that led to the development of peddling. The pedlars of this type did not farm themselves but usually had a craft or worked as day labourers. Peddling was usually a seasonal activity in which they often sold inferior, mostly industrial, products. In those villages in which conditions such as the ownership of land was concentrated in few hands or a general population policy led to a disproportionate increase in the rural proletariat, the result tended to be a surge in peddling.

In Baiersdorf and the surrounding area the sale of horse radish produced by local farmers was taken up by pedlars from about 1870 onwards. This specialisation developed rapidly, with sales as far afield as Bavaria, Austria and northern Germany. Middlemen could thus be cut out, which suited both farmers and pedlars. By claiming to be selling their own products the pedlars could also avoid taxes on trading. This kind of trade reached its peak at the end of the nineteenth century. Its structure and development are typical of several different kinds of retail trade in the late nineteenth century, arising from rural pauperisation and the demand for daily supplies in cities and towns. Whilst the trade in horse radish was mainly practised in autumn and winter, other types of peddling followed the farming calendar (various farming tasks at certain times of the year, important religious festivals). Thus, the women from the border region between Saxony and Bohemia toured their areas three times a year: after Whitsun when they visited spas and health resorts, after the potato harvest until Christmas, and from the end of January until Easter. In essence, the organisation of this trade remained intact until the First World War; afterwards it went into a fairly rapid decline.

The goods were mostly carried in chests or wicker baskets holding from 50 to 150 pounds. The use of carts or barrows was rather rare. Thus, even as late as 1900, the potters of Coppengrave still travelled overland in large wagons. Travel was, as a rule, seasonal; the routes and destinations had long been established; they were visited annually, partly to build up a stock of regular customers. Rural areas and small towns were the main selling areas. Peddling of this kind went into a decline as the regular retail shops offered a widening range of products, as labour became more valuable, and as employment opportunities became more varied.

The group of pedlars who sold goods that they themselves had first bought, usually goods not locally produced, had a different structure. They engaged in this form of retail trade because they could not manage to make a living in their own locality. This may have been because of small-scale farming on poor soil, lack of employment, a decline in their craft, or often through overpopulation. Poor farming areas were generally ones with a high incidence of emigration, itinerant musicians, or domestic weaving. In nineteenth-century Germany, the Eichsfeld, the Westerwald, the Fichtelgebirge, the Vorderpfalz, the Saar, Alsace–Lorraine, the Mainhardter Forest, or places like Gönningen in the Swabian Alb and Wolfach and Ebergach in Baden were such areas.

Important centres of itinerant retailing were villages where domestic crafts were highly developed and the retail sale of locally produced goods was in the hands of pedlars, or villages in which the carriage of goods had provided the main livelihood. As modern developments brought about a decline in road haulage, a switch to peddling occurred, in which previous experience of routes and conditions proved to be helpful. Peddling of this kind, however, was often not associated with any particular locality but arose wherever pauperisation was widespread. The main selling areas were larger towns and industrial areas where housewives, shop assistants and domestic servants willingly bought the pedlars' goods. Inns were also visited by pedlars, often at regular intervals and by arrangement. The number of pedlars of this kind actually increased markedly during the second half of the nineteenth century.

The pedlars' routes were less traditional; they were forever looking for new areas to sell in, particularly in towns, travelling at those times in the year when they were not needed as day labourers for farm work. They formed the largest group of itinerants and were often also accused of molestation or sharp practices. The range of goods for sale was very wide, although individual pedlars tended to specialise in a particular field. From the point of view of labour efficiency, peddling was strongly criticised; at the same time, there was an element of social concern associated with its toleration – sometimes even support – for peddling alleviated the effects on backward areas of rapid industrial growth elsewhere.

In the period 1870–90, the number of pedlars greatly increased; in some places they even came to be dominant, particularly in parts of large towns and cities. The causes may be found in the decline of agriculture, fewer employment opportunities for day labourers, but also in the increased mobility of the rural population arising from improvements in transport. At the end of the nineteenth century (1895–1900) the statistics show a decline of about 25 per cent. During this period, however, there occurred a restructuring and intensification of peddling, particularly in the sale of cheap textiles, which was perceived as a serious threat by the regular textile trade. A new development was the emergence of 'large-scale' peddling, in which a number of employees were engaged and shops themselves sent out pedlars to sell their goods.

Thus, around 1900, peddling did have its specific significance, particularly in its restructuring and intensification alongside Germany's industrialisation and urbanisation. The struggle that occurred between the established retail trade in the hands of the middle classes and the migrant pedlars of the lower orders and from other areas was not merely an economic struggle but also had its socio-political dimension, as did the battle between independent and large-scale retailers.

5.4 The structure of shop growth

In German towns shops were already in existence during the medieval period, but it was in the nineteenth century that they increased in number and changed their characteristics. In the early nineteenth century many German shops still operated as craftsmen–retailers, producing or transforming a product and then selling it to the consumer. The associated retail craft guilds occupied important positions within the local economies of most towns, and exerted control over the types of trade undertaken. Most of the guilds were specifically to represent artisans and craftsmen, who viewed shopkeeping as outside their scope of activity. Even by 1800 most sales were retailed from craft or workshops with the artisan having made the products he sold. During the first part of the nineteenth century the number of shopkeepers, as opposed to craftsmen–retailers, started to increase and the term shopkeeper becomes more common in local directories. From admittedly somewhat limited evidence it appears however that the major growth of shopkeeping and indeed the retail system in general occurred after 1870. This reflected a number of factors, including;

industrialisation processes, increases in living standards and changes in the laws affecting local trading. The major legislation was the 1869 law on the freedom of trade (*Gewerbefreiheit*), passed by the North German Federation, which relaxed the controls over retailing of all types. This was incorporated into the full German Empire in 1871, although its origins lay in the late 1840s when attempts were being made to open-up trade (Gellately, 1974, p.24).

The transition from a retail system based on producer–retailers to one increasingly dominated by shopkeepers happened in a series of stages. After around 1850 and certainly by about 1870, producer–retailers had started to buy manufactured goods to add to their own products. With this trend they started to change their workshop into a retail shop proper. During this first phase of transition they transformed their economic base but not their locations. Between about 1850 and 1880 in most small towns shops tended to be scattered around the inner city area, reflecting in the main the earlier pattern of workshop locations. Specialised shopping streets did exist, especially around the market squares, but equally many shops were found in side streets or isolated clusters. It was really only after 1880, during the second phase of shop growth that the process of concentration into specialised shopping streets took place on a large scale. In some small German towns, as Heinritz (1986) has shown for Weissenburgs in Bavaria, the pattern of shop locations away from main streets persisted until well into the twentieth century. Such trends reflect the fact that in the smaller towns the pace of population change was often relatively slow and the shops established a stable and loyal set of customers. In some respects it reflects a continuation of the trade areas of the traditional producer–retailers, certainly in the period before 1850. Obviously, in the large towns and cities these changes in shop development occurred earlier as locational benefits became an important element of shop competition. Indeed, the coming of the railways and tramways provided new locational opportunities for shops; with retail concentrations developing in those main streets linking railway stations with the city centres.

As in other countries it is extremely difficult to estimate how quickly shops and shopkeeping expanded during the nineteenth century, especially in the period before 1860. Local evidence however shows an improvement in shop provision starting at least by the 1830s, if not earlier in some areas. For example, the number of food retailers in the Prussian provinces increased from 33 per 10,000 people in 1837 to 77 per 10,000 by 1895 (Schmoller, 1919). This region was economically one of the most backward and in other, more developed areas the progress was much more rapid, with Saxony, for example, having 256 retailers per 10,000 population in 1860 and 637 per 10,000 by 1895 (Sombart, 1903). These latter figures cover all types of traders, though Sombart thought that most of the increase was due to retailers. More localised statistics on shop growth would seem to confirm Sombart's view, as Table 5.1 shows. From this it can be seen that shops were growing at a much faster rate than population in a number of areas. In a developing city such as Brunswick, while population increased by 60 per cent between 1887 and 1901, over the same period the number of grocery shops grew by 90 per cent (Gellately, 1974, p.33).

Table 5.1 also shows that, even within this small sample of settlements, shop provision and rates of growth varied greatly. Such variations reflected rates of economic growth, especially the movement away from self-sufficient agrarian

Table 5.1   Variations in shop provision in selected German settlements

Period	Settlement	Population/shop	
1866	Baden (Black Forest)[1]	180.6	
1897	Baden (Black Forest)	91.7	
1866	Celle	577	(factory goods only)
1896	Celle	486	(factory goods only)
1872	Posen (area)	1,105	
1895	Posen (area)	1,061	

Note:
[1] 14 small settlements

Source: Gellately, 1974

communities, competition from other retail centres, the market areas covered by the surveys, and settlement size. Keeping in mind these variations, general figures on the growth of traders (the term covers more than just retailers) suggest that provision nationally increased at a much faster rate than population. Thus, in 1861 there was one trader per 83 people, by 1882 this had changed to one per 54 people and by 1907 to one per 30 people (Sombart, 1903; Rathgen, 1906–07).

Examining the changing structure of shop trades is also extremely difficult given the lack of any official information, certainly before the 1880s, and only a handful of published studies. Most material is contained in local town directories, although even these are problematical given the changing terminology used to describe different retail trades. For example, in the 1836 directory for Göttingen, a town in Lower Saxony, the term *Kaufmann* was frequently used to describe food retailers, and no mention was made of *Kolonialwarenhändler*, which became the term used to describe grocers in the 1864 and 1900 directories. Similarly, in 1826 the directory listed just two *Kleinhändler*, which we can take to be small shopkeepers. The 1826 directory abounds with listings of craftsmen, many of whom no doubt sold their own products direct to consumers. Thus, in the small but prosperous university town of Göttingen, with a population of 9,518 in 1821, the directory for 1826 listed some 114 shoemakers, or one for every 80 of the town's inhabitants. In contrast, the same directory listed only 18 butchers (one per 509 inhabitants) and 31 bakers (one per 295 inhabitants). Clearly at this time shopkeeping was not a predominant force in Göttingen's retail system compared with producer–retailers or the market, for which market tolls indicate a high degree of activity. In the 1864 directory the evidence is of a greater numerical importance of shopkeeping, with some 65 grocers and shopkeepers being listed, representing one shop per 217 inhabitants.

In many of the expanding towns and cities the suburbanisation of shops failed to keep pace with that of population, and there were often few stores in the newer suburbs. Even in a small town such as Göttingen population was expanding out from the central area, although by 1864 less than 24 per cent of grocers' shops had moved outside of the town walls. Within the larger cities the situation was even more acute and in those suburbs not served by shops consumers were either forced to make long journeys into the central shopping area or became dependent on pedlars and hawkers. Towards the end of the nineteenth century, retail provision in many of these suburban areas was supplemented by stores establishing door-to-door delivery services.

The changeover from producer–retailing to shopkeeping was in Germany, especially outside major cities, a fairly protracted process that in some places was only completed by the early twentieth century. Thus, in the small town of Gifhorn for example, of the 28 grocers operating in 1900, 11 had been artisans of some kind in their previous occupations.

The development of shopkeeping also brought with it not only changes in selling techniques, but also transformations of the range of products sold. In many cases it was the grocers who started to expand their product range in the second part of the nineteenth century. For example, in Münster by 1870 the local directory listed grocers who were also selling household goods (*materialwaarenhandlungen*); similarly a good number of bakers were also selling cakes and operating *Conditoren*. This was a trend which intensified after 1870 as the more successful stores attempted to increase their competitive edge and at the same time benefit from economies of scale within the shop. Thus, in Göttingen by 1900 at least seven of the larger grocers had diversified into other products ranging from medicines to household goods, and men's clothing. These trends led to increased competition at a time when the total retail system was expanding and large-scale, capital-intensive firms were starting to have an impact. There was increasing friction between different independent retailers as bakers complained that milk sellers, greengrocers and even schnapps sellers were encroaching on their preserves' (Blackbourn, 1984, p.41).

At the root of these difficulties was the growth and diversification of the retail system, especially a massive increase in the number of shops, both after 1860, when the number of customers per shop was halved, and more particularly after 1895. These two periods of shop development in a sense characterised different processes of growth. The first was largely dominated by the further transition of producer–retailers becoming shopkeepers and a general diversification of the types of products sold from shops. While the selling of new consumer products and the growth of new forms of shop retailing (see Chapter 9) formed a significant theme in the 1890s, another important pathway of shop expansion was through the growth of small shops. In many ways these were the underclass of shopkeeping, under-capitalised businesses that had made an appearance in cities like Köln even in the first half of the nineteenth century (Aycoberry, 1975). It was however during the 1890s that these very small retailers increased at their fastest rate, moving into the more marginal parts of the distribution system such as secondhand clothing, mixed food products, greengroceries and tobacco. In this period between 1890 and 1914, one study in Bremen has shown that 33 per cent of all shops listed in the town directories failed within six years (Haupt, 1982), and most of these were drawn from the smaller shops.

Those shopkeepers whose businesses had evolved from producer–retailer backgrounds in many instances attempted to hold on to their former organisations and guild structure. Thus, in many town directories those retailers who belonged to a guild would be indicated. This would obviously exclude grocers and small shopkeepers, but in Göttingen, for example, even in 1900 the directory indicated which of the bakers were members of the guild. The increased competition in the late nineteenth century brought a fresh demand for the re-introduction of guilds by craftsmen in an attempt to control entry by raising qualifications. For shopkeepers such a move was not practical, especially for the ranks of independent grocers, but as Gellately (1974, p.25) points out, shopkeepers did raise their political consciousness after 1890. They also attempted to control entry by introducing, somewhat unsuccessfully, qualifications and technical schools. In the end, for many shopkeepers ultimate survival depended on the use of self-help and the formation of trade associations, a process discussed more fully in Chapter 9.

References

Allix, A., 1922, The geography of fairs: illustrated by Old-World examples, *Geographical Review*, 12: 532–69. For a history of markets in Germany see K. Rathgen, 1881 *Die Entstehung der Märkte in Deutschland*, G. Otto, Darmstadt

Aycoberry, P., 1975, 'Der Strukturwandel in Kölner Mittelstand 1820–1850', *Geschichte und Gesellschaft*, 1: 85–92

Blackbourn, D., 1984, Between resignation and volatility: the German petite bourgeoisie in the nineteenth century, in G. Crossick and M-G. Haupt (eds.), *Shopkeepers and Master Artisans in Nineteenth-Century Europe*, Methuen, London

Board of Trade, 1908, *Cost of Living in German Towns*, Col. 4032, London

Braudel, F., 1985, *Civilization and Capitalism, 15th–18th century: The Wheels of Commerce*, Fontana, London

Denecke, D., 1988, Research in German urban historical geography, in D. Denecke and G. Shaw (eds.), *Urban Historical Geography: Recent Progress in Britain and Germany*, Cambridge University Press, Ch. 3

Gellately, R., 1974, *The Politics of Economic Despair: Shopkeepers and German Politics 1890–1914*, Sage, London

Göhre, P., 1907, *Das Warenhaus*, Die Gesellschaft, Rütten & Loening, Frankfurt, a.M.

Haupt, M.G., 1982, 'Kleinhändler und Arbeiter in Bremen zwischen 1890 und 1914', *Archiv für Sozialgeschichte*, 22: 105–116

Heinritz, G., 1971, Die Baiersdorfer Krenhausierer – Eine sozialgeographische Untersuchung, *Mitteilungen der Fränkischen Geographischen Gesellschaft*, 17: 69–148

Heinritz, G., 1986, Beobachtungen zum Wandel von Struktur und Standorten des Einzelhandels in Kleinstädten seit dem ende des 19. Jahrhunderts am Beispiel Weissenburgs in Bayern, in H. Heineberg (ed.) *Innerstädische Differenzierung und Prozesse Im 19. und 20. Jahrhundert*, Böhlau Verlag, Köln

Heumann, G.D., 1987, *Der Göttingische Ausruff von 1744*, E. Goltze, Göttingen

Krüer, H.E., 1914, *Die Markthallen und ihre Hilfskräfte als Faktoren der Lebensmittelversorgung in unseren Grosstädten*, Marcus & Weber, Berlin

Lux, K., 1910, *Studien über die Entwicklung der Warenhäuser in Deutschland*, Fisher, Jena

Mataja, V., 1891, *Grossmagazine und Kleinhandel*, Duncker & Humbold, Leipzig

Rathgen, K., 1906–07, Handelspolitik, *Wörterbuch der Volkswirtschaft* 2: 160–80

Schmoller, Gustav, 1919, *Grundriss der Allgemeinen Volkswirtschaftslehre* 2 vols Duncker & Humbold, München

Sombart, W., 1903, *Die deutsche Volkswirtschaft im 19. Jahrhundert*, G. Bondi Berlin

Strida, W., 1900, Die Lage des Hausiergewerbes in Deutschland, *Verhandlungen des Vereins für Socialpolitik*, 88: 102–36

Tietz, G., 1965, *Hermann Tietz: Geschichte einer Familie und ihrer Warenhäuser*, Tietz, Stuttgart

Chapter 6
Small-scale retailing in Canada
John Benson

6.1 Introduction

It has long been accepted that in Canada (as elsewhere) seasonal fairs, semi-permanent markets and itinerant trading were 'particularly associated with the initial stages of settlement' (Osborne, 1980, p.60; also Bank of Montreal, 1956, p.6; 1971, p.106; Kelly, 1978, p.71). As Brian Osborne has pointed out, 'The commercial activity of any society characterised by low population densities, low surplus and pronounced seasonal activity, may be dependent upon the interim adjustments provided by itinerancy and its concomitant periodicity of functions.' Indeed he has claimed 'that the demise of these periodic and mobile activities', and their replacement by more permanent, fixed-shop forms of selling, constitutes one important 'indicator of the maturing of a frontier society' (Osborne, 1980, p.60; also Kelly, 1971, p.106; Kelly, 1978, pp.71–2; Johnson, 1959, p.32).

It will be suggested in this chapter that such views are somewhat misleading. For while it is true that seasonal fairs, semi-permanent markets and itinerant trading were well suited to the early stages of Canadian settlement, this does not mean that they were therefore unsuited to subsequent stages of the country's development. There is no question that seasonal fairs succumbed to the changes brought about by industrialisation and urbanisation. But semi-permanent markets and itinerant trading most certainly did not. Semi-permanent markets survived by adapting to changes in consumer demand; while itinerant trading survived by responding to changes, both in consumer demand, and in the broader economic and social structure of Canadian society.

6.2 Seasonal fairs

Seasonal fairs at which goods could be displayed and sold were well suited to the needs of frontier society. Their establishment tended to follow the spread of permanent settlement, and they were usually held in Spring and Autumn, so avoiding the worst of the weather and conforming to the annual rhythms of the agricultural cycle. As farmers and merchants from the Bytown district of Ottawa explained, a twice-yearly fair 'would be of incalculable service to those engaged in the Lumber Trade by affording them an opportunity of disposing of their lean cattle to the Farmers in the spring after the conclusion of their winter work and of repurchasing supplies of cattle and Horses in the Fall' (Osborne, 1980, p.75).

Such fairs met the needs of rural producers, of urban wholesalers, and of urban consumers alike. It was claimed in 1836, for instance, that farmers throughout Ontario were learning 'that a Mart for horses, cattle, grain, etc. twice every year, where Cash is generally paid, and purchasers are waiting, is preferable to the farmers' ruinous practice of Trade, as it is technically termed, and the merchants, auctioneers, etc. anticipate the Fair with elated expectations, arising from an almost sure market for their various commodities' (Osborne, 1980, p.73; *Canada Farmer*, 15 February 1864). Indeed there seems little doubt that of the more than 150 fairs established in southern Ontario between 1800 and 1866, many assumed a considerable local significance. In 1836, for example, the Napanee fair handled 1,200 bushels of grain and 300 head of cattle, while the fair held at Guelph in October 1850 disposed of 1,500 head of livestock (Osborne, 1980, p.75).

Nonetheless, seasonal fairs proved unable to withstand the economic and social changes brought about by industrialisation and urbanisation. Their commercial functions were undermined, on the one hand by demand-side changes such as the growth of population and the improvement of transport, and, on the other hand, by increasing competition from markets, shops and other more flexible retail agencies. Fairs survived, it is true, but only as livestock shows or later as social events and/or agricultural exhibitions. Township fairs should be abolished, the *Canada Farmer* argued tellingly in 1864, because there were already far too many agricultural exhibitions in existence (*Canada Farmer*, 1 November 1864; also *Regina Leader*, 4, 11 October 1887; *Globe*, 6 February 1914; Osborne, 1980, pp.73, 77, 79).

6.3 Semi-permanent markets

Semi-permanent markets, opening one or several times a week, responded far more effectively than seasonal fairs to the changes brought about by industrialisation and urbanisation. For, while farmers' markets, like fairs, provided a forum at which rural producers were able to sell, and urban consumers to purchase, their food, fodder and fuel, there was a crucial difference between them: markets, unlike fairs, served the day-to-day, as opposed to the seasonal, needs of producers and consumers (Osborne, 1980, pp.69, 71; Pyle, 1971).

Markets were established in the urban centres of developing areas. In Ontario, and no doubt elsewhere, they appeared first in garrison and market towns like Kingston (1801), York (1814) and Niagara (1817) and later in centres such as Hamilton (1833), Prescott (1834), and Bytown, Dundas, London and Brantford (all in 1847) (Matthews, 1987, p.299; Osborne, 1980, p.69). By the middle of the century many towns with a population of a thousand or so had a market of their own, while many larger centres housed a number of specialised sites. Hamilton had four: a wood market, a hog market, a grain market and a central market. Quebec City had six: the Champlain, St Paul and Jacques Cartier markets in Lower Town, and the Finlay, Bertholet and St Andrews (fish and hog) markets in Upper Town (Van Hoorn, 1973; Campbell and Doyle, 1940, p.45).

Such markets assumed a major role in the retailing of agricultural products, their importance enhanced as local municipalities assumed control and attempted to improve facilities, to set minimum standards of cleanliness, and to control regrating and forestalling (*Maritime Grocer*, 9 February 1893; Matthews, 1987, pp.299–303; Van Hoorn, 1973, pp.131–3). Thus it has been claimed that in mid-nineteenth-century Ontario 'public marketplaces continued to function as the main forum for the buying and selling of agricultural produce' (Matthews, 1987, p.305; Wiesinger, 1985, pp.21, 26–7). Indeed it has been pointed out that public markets met the broader economic interests of those active in urban development; for by drawing farmers into the towns, and by concentrating commercial activity within them, they solidified the economic control that towns and cities were able to exercise over their hinterlands: 'The regulation of the public market functioned as an important development strategy by which nascent cities sought to establish themselves as dynamic metropolitan centres' (Matthews, 1987, p.314).

However it is generally agreed that during the final quarter of the nineteenth century markets throughout North America became less important as retailing centres, their role undermined by demand-side changes such as the growth of the urban population; by supply-side changes such as the specialisation of agriculture and the improvement of inter-urban transport; and by changes in the competitive environment, most notably the rise, as will be seen below, of the fixed-shop form of selling (Pyle, 1971, p.176; Wiesinger, 1985, pp.17–18; *Globe*, 13 January 1914). For example, improvements in inter-urban transport meant that consumers were no longer forced to rely upon their local market for the purchase of agricultural produce. So even in isolated prairie cities such as Calgary, fruit and vegetables could be brought into town by rail and displayed in the shops before it was possible to have locally grown produce on sale in the public market (*Calgary Daily Herald*, 19 April 1913; also *Globe*, 9 January 1914; Osborne, 1980, p.72).

Such arguments appear persuasive indeed. Yet they need to be approached with considerable caution, for the evidence of decline is less clear-cut than it sometimes appears. Indeed there is reason to believe that in many towns and cities the market continued to play a considerable role in the distribution of agricultural produce. There is the fact that new markets continued to be opened in small prairie centres such as Beausejour (just east of Winnipeg) and in large west coast cities such as Victoria and Vancouver (*Canadian Grocer*, 22 August 1980; Czuboka, ND, p.431; Roy, 1980, pp.29–30). There is the evidence – misleading though it can be – of the complaints that continued to emanate from the markets' competitors. From Halifax to Hamilton, from Montreal to Vancouver, shopkeepers fulminated against the unfair advantages said to be enjoyed by those selling in semi-permanent markets (*Canadian Grocer*, 1 March 1889, 14 March 1890, 21 June 1895; *Maritime Grocer*, 9 February 1893; *Hamilton Spectator*, 2 February 1926). There is also the testimony provided by the reports on local markets that appeared in the pages of the trade and provincial press. A few examples must suffice. The market wharf at New Westminster was an important local institution, claimed Vancouver's *Daily World* (15 December 1899). The Bonsecours market in Montreal was open every day of the week and did a large business in dairy products and home-made sausages, explained the *Canadian Grocer* a few years later (*Canadian Grocer*,

27 October 1905). The farmers' market in Hamilton, it was said, continued to attract sellers and buyers in large numbers. It was, claimed a city alderman in 1900, 'the natural market place of the district' (*Hamilton Spectator*, 15 September 1900; also *Globe*, 27 June 1910).

The resilience of the semi-permanent market owed much of course to its ability to cater to – or to circumvent – the changes that were taking place in the supply of, and in the demand for, agricultural produce. The market continued to meet the need of small rural producers for a convenient and flexible retail outlet, and the need of urban – and suburban – consumers for an inexpensive and unpretentious source of fresh food. However the resilience of the semi-permanent market also owed a good deal to broader political-cum-economic considerations. It seems that, as in the early and middle years of the century, members of the business community accepted that the existence of a centrally located market tended to encourage urban growth in general, and commercial development in particular (Matthews, 1985, pp.170–1; Pyle, 1971, p.167). Shopkeepers themselves recognised that farmers selling their produce in a market spent some of their profits in nearby shops, and that customers attracted to a market tended to patronise the surrounding retailers. In Hamilton, for example, a number of city-centre traders continued to believe in the benefits to be derived from the farmers' market: 'Merchants in the vicinity of the market swear by it and retailers in the outlying districts swear at it' (*Hamilton Spectator*, 27 January 1927; also 14 August 1919, 16 December 1922; Czuboka, ND, p.431).

6.4 Itinerant trading

Itinerant trading too responded surprisingly successfully to the changes brought about by industrialisation and urbanisation (Benson, 1985; Benson, 1990, pp.49–53, 69). For while it is true, and has long been recognised, that hawking and peddling constituted an important form of retailing in pre-Confederation Canada, it is no longer possible to accept the view that this form of selling declined so precipitously that 'by the end of the century' it was only in rural areas that 'peddlars made a continuing contribution' (Osborne, 1980, pp.61–8; Santink, 1990, p.56).

There is, it is true, abundant, albeit non-quantifiable, evidence of the major role that itinerant trading played in rural areas throughout the whole of the nineteenth century (Benson, 1985; Benson, 1990, pp.49–53). It was a form of selling that was able to meet many of the needs of the large proportion of the population (68 per cent in 1891 and 55 per cent in 1911) that continued to live in the countryside. The country pedlar brought news and excitement to isolated farming families: 'for a brief hour, the drab farm kitchen was transformed into a miniature bazaar of Araby' (Johnson, 1959, p.31). The country pedlar purchased the family's surplus dairy produce: indeed it has even been claimed that 'The farm woman's financial emancipation came with the arrival of the country peddler with his democrat loaded with empty crates and cases. He bought eggs and old hens and, for the first time, a bit of money found its way into Veronica's pockets' (Woywitka, 1978, pp.26–7; also Benson, 1876, p.30; Johnson, 1959, p.31). But primarily, of course, pedlars sold to rural families those manufactured goods and processed foods and drinks that could not be produced on the farm. Tea was a particular speciality; pedlars, claimed the *Canadian Grocer*, were able to 'presume upon the general inclination among the people to regard them as experts in judging, blending and preparing tea' (*Canadian Grocer*, 8 July 1892; also 8 February 1895, 6 May 1910).

There is more evidence still that in Canada, as in England, 'the pedlar's trade developed into an urban rather than a rural occupation: in a sense, the pedlar followed his customers into the towns' (Alexander, 1970, p.65; also Zucchi, 1980, pp.32–3). Although the evidence, once again, is essentially impressionistic, there are a few quantitative data that can be employed. The census of 1911 shows that, in the 26 Canadian cities with populations of 15,000 or more, there were enumerated 2,275 hawkers and pedlars, a figure which at 2.95 per thousand of the occupied population was a full 150 per cent higher than that for the country as a whole (Benson, 1985, p.78; also *Retailer*, January 1916).

In all events, there seems little doubt that itinerant trading survived because it was able to meet certain of the retailing requirements of the increasing proportion of the population (32 per cent in 1891 and 45 per cent in 1911) that found itself in the growing towns and cities. The pedlar brought his fruit and vegetables to the consumer's door and proved, it was claimed, 'a great convenience to the general public' (*Echo*, 16 July 1892; also *Independent*, 9 March 1901). The pedlar charged low prices (often for poor-quality stock) and was sometimes able to play upon his nefarious reputation by implying that his low prices could be explained by the fact that he was selling stolen or smuggled goods (*Canadian Grocer*, 27 May 1902). More generally, the pedlar found that he was able to move into districts without shops, and/or trade when existing shops were closed. Everywhere the 'early closing' movement of the late 1880s and early 1890s provided new possibilities and opportunities; thus as soon as the grocers in the Spring Gardens area of Halifax agreed in 1887 to close at 8 p.m., the pedlars moved in and began to sell tea, coffee, sugar and onions in the evenings (*Canadian Grocer*, 11 April 1889).

It is clear that itinerant trading survived too because it was a form of retailing which, much more than market selling, was able to meet the employment needs of some at least of the growing urban population. Cheap and apparently easy to start, it provided work and income for the young and the old, the sick and the injured, the unemployed and those involved in industrial disputes. For example, during the course of a dispute at London in 1882, one member of the Cigar Makers' International Union 'stayed out one week, then found out he could not live on $4 per week; but he can peddle plaster images when he cannot get a chance to make himself solid with the bosses' (Forsey, 1982, p.231; also *Butler's Journal*, August 1990). In turn-of-the-century Edmonton, remembers one visitor from the country, 'there used to be those, the blind and the crippled, almost every block, every corner there would be one of those . . . selling pencils or something' (Silverman, transcript 118, p.28).

Itinerant trading provided work and income too for a significant minority of working-class immigrants: the Chinese on the west coast; the Italians in Ontario; and the Jews, it seemed, almost everywhere. Italian immigrants seemed to have taken virtual control of the fruit and vegetable trade of central Canadian cities such as Hamilton and Toronto (Benson, 1985, p.81). By the turn of the century Jewish pedlars were active in large cities such as Montreal where, it was complained in 1905, they had 'established themselves almost irrevocably' (*Canadian Grocer*, 11 August 1905). By 1916 Jewish pedlars were entrenched so firmly in Toronto that

600 who made their living by selling rags offered to pay 10 dollars each to the local Red Cross if it would agree to stop collecting rags as a means of raising money (Speisman, 1979, p.73). Indeed by 1911 over three-quarters of all the hawkers and pedlars recorded in the census were foreign-born, compared with less than one-third of the population as a whole (Census, 1911, II, p.445; VI, p.31).

Whatever the precise balance between rural and urban selling, the press, oral sources and autobiographical evidence suggest, and the census returns confirm, that itinerant trading remained a good deal more common than has generally been allowed. The provincial press provides some guide to public irritation with itinerant sellers. The Toronto *Globe* explained in 1910, 'the voices of the street hawkers have become so much of a nuisance as to suggest the necessity of suppressing their calls and constraining them to resort to other methods of commending their wares to the public' (*Globe*, 7 July 1910). The trade press provides a fascinating insight into shopkeeper dissatisfaction. The *Maritime Merchant* complained in 1904, 'the Departmental store can only pester the public with catalogues and circulars. The itinerant vendor pesters them in person' (*Maritime Merchant*, 21 April 1904). A trader from Pickering, Ontario, explained a few years later: 'It makes the long-suffering merchant muse upon the possibility of finding an article in the trade that he can sell; it seems to him as if his existing stock were a permanent institution – come to stay, in fact' (*Canadian Grocer*, 7 January 1910; also *Retailer*, August 1917). The census returns provide a more systematic, if less compelling, indication of the scale of the itinerant trade. They suggest that between 1871 and 1911 the size of the permanent (or semi-permanent) core of full-time (or nearly full-time) hawkers and pedlars increased almost five times: from 666 to 3,248. They reveal, more surprisingly, a growth in the size of this permanent/semi-permanent core compared with the size of the Canadian population: in 1871 there were 1.8 hawkers and pedlars per 10,000 of the population; in 1911 there were 4.5, an increase of 150 per cent (Census, 1871–1911).

It would seem then that the adaptability of the itinerant trade, like the resilience of the semi-permanent market, remained an important, if easily overlooked, feature of the Canadian retailing system. In fact it may be that the relationship between these forms of selling and fixed-shop retailing was less competitive, and more complementary, than the complaints in the trade press – and the assertions in the historical literature – would lead one to suppose.

Nonetheless the attempt at historiographical revision must not be taken too far. For the outstanding feature of the nineteenth- and early twentieth-century Canadian retailing system was neither the resilience of the market nor the adaptability of itinerancy. It was the growth, and increasing domination, of the fixed-shop form of selling.

6.5 Country general stores

Of course, fixed shops had existed in both countryside and town since the very beginning of the period. Indeed the country general store – warm, inviting and ever-open – remains part of the mythology of the Canadian frontier: 'Everything you have heard about the old-fashioned store held true', recalls the daughter of an

Alberta homesteader (Nelson, 1989, p.10; also Olson and Pybus, 1982, p.19; Lindell, c.1970, p.52). Nonetheless, generalisation is difficult. 'It may be doubted,' admits Ian Drummond, 'whether any country general store could be regarded as "typical".' He believes however that 'the inventory of one such establishment will give some idea of the texture of Ontario commerce' towards the end of the nineteenth century. 'In March 1880 Henry Elliott's general store at Hampton, a small village near Brooklin, held an inventory that was valued at $1,802.95.' It did not sell food but

There were stocks of cloth, canvas, patterns, articles of clothing, trimmings, notions, boots, rubbers, locks, door knobs and other hardware, knives, mouse traps, cutlery, jewellery, combs, farm tools, nails, seeds, glue, borax, camphor, various farming chemicals, drugs, paper, books and envelopes. Elliott was also an agent for sewing machines, pianos and organs, which he was quite prepared to sell on the instalment plan. Furthermore, he took subscriptions for newspapers, and he lent money. As he explained in an advertisement, he was in a position to provide mortgage funds at 6 per cent; he would place funds for others, and he was an insurance agent (Drummond, 1987, p.276).

Unfortunately a country general store such as this is easier to describe than it is to define. However, any working definition would need to identify two key characteristics: that, like Henry Elliott's store, it should sell a wide variety of goods, and that, like Elliott's store, it should operate either in a rural community or in a settlement with less than a thousand inhabitants (Cf. Census of Merchandising, 1930, p.x).

The survival of the country general store is scarcely to be doubted. Indeed its continuing importance constitutes a recurring theme in the trade directories, retail journals, provincial newspapers, personal reminiscences and published autobiographies of the late nineteenth and early twentieth centuries (see, e.g., *Kindersley Clarion*, 2 September 1910; *Retailer*, 1915–18 *passim*; Olson and Pybus, 1982, p.19). Moreover the decline of this form of selling in the years following the First World War was less catastrophic than many people seem to imagine. The compilers of Canada's first Census of Merchandising and Service Establishments discovered that even in 1930 the country general store accounted for over eight per cent of all recorded sales – the proportion ranging from four per cent in industrialised Ontario to 24 per cent in unspoilt Prince Edward Island (Census of Merchandising, 1930, pp.x, xix; Drummond, 1987, p.302).

The survival of the country general store is to be explained by its ability to satisfy the demands of the rural population both as consumers and, to a lesser extent, as producers. It is well known that country stores met the needs of rural consumers in several different ways. They gave credit, they stayed open long hours, and they provided a popular meeting place for those living in small, isolated communities – it was said that in winter they attracted so many visitors that 'He will be a blessing to the store-keeper who will invent a stove that will eject loafers as well as emit heat' (*Canadian Grocer*, 25 October 1895; also 27 January 1905; *Retailer*, August 1916). More importantly, country stores made available those manufactured goods and processed foods which were not produced locally and which very often could not be purchased (or purchased as cheaply and conveniently) from competing retail outlets. Thus these stores carried a wider range of stock than a seasonal fair, a semi-permanent market or an itinerant trader; and they offered a more convenient form of shopping than a distant department store or a slow mail-order service. The implications were not lost upon one early twentieth-century Alberta retailer: the country storekeeper, he suggested, should advertise low prices on items that customers required immediately, and so were unlikely to purchase by mail order (*General Merchant*, 5 November 1929; also *Retailer*, July 1917).

It is less well known perhaps that country stores also met the needs of rural producers by helping them to supplement their agricultural incomes. This the stores did in two ways. They performed a useful, albeit, declining, role in the purchase of local produce. For despite increasing competition from wholesalers and commission houses, they continued to accept agricultural produce either for immediate resale or for transshipment to urban merchants. It was said in Saskatchewan, for example, that rural shopkeepers provided 'a ready market for eggs, butter, and the products of the soil' (*Retailer*, December 1916; also *Cotton's Weekly*, 1 April 1909; *Canadian Grocer*, 8 July 1910, 12 September 1913; Santink, 1990, pp.18–19).

Country stores also performed a useful, and continuing, role in the provision of non-agricultural employment and income. An examination of the available newspaper and oral evidence confirms that it was by no means unusual for farming families to open small general stores. For instance, it was reported that during the late nineteenth century many Quebecois *habitants* were encouraged by commercial travellers from Montreal and Quebec City to begin shopkeeping – often, it must be said, with predictably disastrous results (*Retail Merchants' Journal*, November 1903). Prairie homesteaders too turned to shopkeeping as one way of augmenting their (often meagre) farm incomes. Two examples from early twentieth-centry Saskatchewan will make the point. In 1905 a homesteader with experience of bakery work in Ontario began to sell small quantities of bread from his home at Hanley, some 40 miles south of Saskatoon (Saskatchewan Archives Board, A144, p.2). A few years later a newcomer from Quebec who had travelled west with very limited resources (his 'most valuable possession was his axe') decided to set up a small country store on his homestead at Arborfield, near Prince Albert (Saskatchewan Archives Board, A282, p.1; also A75, p.5).

Such anecdotal evidence will not satisfy those accustomed to approaching the history of retailing through licensing records, trade directories and census enumerators' returns. Nonetheless such evidence suggests, and there seems little reason to doubt, that the survival of the country general store, like that of the itinerant trade, owed something at least to the resilience, not just of consumer demand, but also of producer need and of retailer supply.

6.6 Urban specialist stores

The urban specialist store – quiet, dignified and increasingly sophisticated – was far removed from the country general store. Yet the problems it poses to historians of retailing will not be unfamiliar to those conversant with the rural trade. For it too remains part of the mythology of Canadian history. It too is difficult to define precisely, yet easy enough to recognise in practice. The urban specialist store was situated in a town or city with a thousand or more inhabitants, catering largely to a middle-class clientele, and trading in a narrow range of goods: groceries perhaps, or drugs, furniture, clothing, or boots and shoes.

The final decades of the nineteenth century saw considerable changes in the market position of such stores. They grew more common, and began to locate in the suburbs as well as in city centres (Savitt, 1985, p.1, 580; Wiesinger, 1985, p.119). It has been found, for example, that between 1871 and 1894 the number of grocers in Toronto grew from 77 to 794 (Santink, 1990, p.52). It has been found that although the population of Kingston increased scarcely at all between 1891 and 1901, the number of retail grocers listed in the city directories grew from 18 to 96, an increase of over 430 per cent (Wiesinger, 1985, p.112). Moreover many of these shops were opening in the suburbs, and many too were adopting more modern methods of selection and display. Kingston's *Daily British Whig* explained in 1909,

the corner grocery of years ago is not what is demanded in the present day of those who cater to the wants of the residential portion of such a city as Kingston. One of the neatest groceries in the uptown district is that of H.M. Stover. This store, located at 109 Alfred Street, is [a] bright and attractive looking shop filled with a well selected stock of staple and fancy groceries, canned goods, teas, and coffees (Wiesinger, 1985, p.117).

The success of urban specialist shops, like the survival of country general stores, owed most of course to the vitality of consumer demand. The crucial development was the growth of urban prosperity and the desire of the middle class to enjoy the benefits of mass production and distribution without foregoing the advantages of convenience and attention. By the end of the centry middle-class customers expected to be able to browse at attractive window displays and then order their goods by telephone; they took it for granted they would enjoy personal service, free home delivery, and generous credit facilities (*Canadian Grocer*, 11 April 1895, 6 October 1905; *Globe*, 7 January 1914; Martin, 1987, p.362; Pike, 1989, pp.40–41; Walden, 1989, pp.293–6, 305).

However, as in other countries, the success of urban specialist shops also owed something to the collective efforts that their owners made to maintain, and where possible to enhance, their competitive position (Bliss, 1972). They formed retail sub-committees on local Boards of Trade (*Maritime Merchant*, 21 October 1915). They formed their own broadly based retail associations. The Retail Merchants' Association of Canada was established in 1896 and went on to amalgamate, in 1905, with the Quebec Retail Merchants and the Ontario Retail Merchants' Association and, in 1913, with the Retail Merchants' Association of Western Canada. These associations spawned their own specialised groups: the Ontario Retail Merchants had a Grocers' Section; the Quebec Retail Merchants had two: one for grocers and one for shoe dealers (*Canadian Grocer*, 10 March, 4 July, 24 November 1905, 29 January 1915; *Labour Gazette*, March, April 1906; *Retailer*, September 1916, July 1917). The grocers in particular developed their own independent organisations: by the end of the period both Ontario and British Columbia had its own provincial Retail Grocers' Association, while grocers in towns and cities from Toronto to Montreal, from Sarnia to Saint John, were represented locally by their own specialised associations (*Canadian Grocer*, 28 November 1889, 25 October 1895, 4 May 1900, 10 February 1905, 26 August 1910, 25 April 1913).

These associations sought, with varying degrees of success, to sustain the competitive position of 'the legitimate retailer' (Retail Merchants' Association, 1914, p.2). They attempted to reduce the burden of bad debts. The assessment of customer credit worthiness proved such a problem that, according to the *Canadian Grocer*, 'Lack of ability to collect debts is responsible for more commercial failures than lack of capital' (*Canadian Grocer*, 2 August 1895). Thus the Brandon Retail Grocers' Protective Association was formed in 1902 precisely in order to protect its members against bad debts, and three years later the Retail Merchants' Association of Western Canada agreed that its members should attempt to sell for cash only – a restriction which it accepted would have to allow 30-day accounts to be treated as cash (*Labour Gazette*, July 1902; *Canadian Grocer*, 6 October 1905). When even such modest strategies proved unsuccessful, organisations compiled blacklists of bad risks or, like the Eastern Townships Branch of the Retail Merchants' Association, attempted to make it less expensive to recover small debts in the circuit courts (*Labour Gazette*, March 1906; also *Canadian Grocer*, 6 October 1905; Bliss, 1972, p.177).

Retailing associations were more successful, it seems, in removing restrictions placed upon their members' freedom of action. For instance, in 1879 the butchers of Kingston gained the right to sell fresh meat from shops throughout the city, rather than just in the market area or the shambles (Wiesinger, 1985, pp.78–80, 83). A quarter of a century later the master bakers of Windsor successfully petitioned the city council to allow them to sell a smaller size of loaf in order to compete with the bread that was arriving each day from London and Toronto (*Labour Gazette*, February 1905; also *Dunnville [Weekly] Chronicle*, 13 June 1913).

The associations were sometimes successful too in supporting attempts to restrict the freedom of action of their competitors. They objected, for example, to the 'guerilla trade' of farmers and urban pedlars. The Retail Merchants' Association of Canada dismissed farmers' markets as 'ancient history, because they were not working under natural laws' (*Globe*, 6 February 1914). The Association, together with Boards of Trade and Grocers' Associations across the country, campaigned for pedlars to be compelled to give full weight, to provide good quality and, most important of all, to pay much higher licence fees (Benson, 1985, p.80; Bliss, 1972, p.177). The associations had other grievances besides. They objected to the door-to-door selling by certain manufacturers and wholesalers, to the price-cutting of the department stores, and to the threat posed by the mail-order houses (*Cotton's Weekly*, 26 August 1909; *Canadian Grocer*, 15 November 1895; *Retailer*, 1915–18, *passim*). They complained about what they regarded as the unfair competition of small suburban groceries and/or general stores, which they referred to dismissively as 'seven cent' stores (*Canadian Grocer*, 8 July 1892). Indeed it is well known that throughout the 1880s and 1890s they organised 'early closing' campaigns designed to counteract the small shops' practice of remaining open for working-class and lower-middle-class business until late in the evening (Toronto Trades and Labour Council Minutes, 16 April 1886; Bliss, 1972, pp.175–7).

The success of such collective action is not easy to assess. On the one hand, it probably did something to reduce the burden of bad debts, and it certainly helped to increase the costs of urban peddling. On the other hand, it created new opportunities for pedlars and small suburban shopkeepers to exploit, and so did something to encourage the very competition that it was designed to undermine (*Retailer*, February, July 1916, February 1918; Bliss, 1972).

6.7 Suburban groceries-cum-general stores

There is little doubt that the late nineteenth-century expansion of urban specialist stores was matched by an expansion of suburban groceries-cum-general stores. These stores took many forms: from the lock-up unit in a purpose-built block, to the converted front room of a workman's house. Most often however these stores were small, depended largely upon family labour, stocked a wide range of basic goods, and catered primarily for a working-class and lower-middle-class clientele. Unfortunately the size, location (and frequent impermanence) of these shops means that their importance is impossible to assess in any systematic fashion. Fortunately, however, something of their significance may be gauged from the available qualitative evidence, the strength and consistency of which is too compelling to be ignored. For it seems that, in the larger cities at least, the final two decades of the nineteenth century witnessed a considerable increase in the number, and the importance, of suburban groceries-cum-general stores. Once again a small number of cases must serve to make the point. For example, it was felt by the trade press as early as 1889 that the number of small, working-class grocers in the cities was increasing at too rapid a rate (*Canadian Grocer*, 19 July 1889). Ten years later a visitor from New York was struck so forcibly by the large number of small stores in Toronto that he wrote a letter to the *Canadian Grocer* commenting upon what he had seen (*Canadian Grocer*, 1 June 1990; also *Voice*, 2 October 1897).

The expansion of the suburban grocery-cum-general store, like the survival of the country general store, is to be explained primarily by its capacity to meet the varied needs of its potential customers – who were members in this case chiefly of the working class and the lower middle class. Like his rural counterpart, the suburban shopkeeper had no option but to advance credit to his customers during the long Canadian winter. Indeed the grocer often had to offer such facilities for as long as six months at a time, only to find that he was accused, not unnaturally, of being 'a dictator to the families who had to live on his good will' (*Labour Gazette*, January 1906; also December 1905; *Canadian Grocer*, 11 April 1890).

Like its rural counterpart, the suburban store provided a convenient meeting place for members of the local community. It probably did so most often in areas with large immigrant populations, where the successful shopkeeper might provide his compatriots with a *poste restante* service, and act as a local agent for banking and steamship companies (Zucchi, 1980, p.23). But whether the storekeeper welcomed it or not, the suburban store functioned in nearly all communities, it seems, as a place where local people tended to congregate: 'The only customers I had were a few school children and rough young men and boys, and these would take possession of the place, and I was powerless to prevent it' (*Butler's Journal*, February 1891).

However, the major function of the suburban store, like that of its rural counterpart, was to make available the food and manufactured goods that could not be purchased as cheaply or conveniently from other retail outlets. Indeed it is ironic that on many occasions suburban stores, like suburban pedlars, benefited, rather than suffered, from the attempts that were made by specialist retailers to undermine them by the elimination of late night opening. For example, when early closing was introduced to Kingston in 1892, it was discovered that several corner groceries were among the stores able to enhance their competitive position by declining to adhere to the new hours of trading (*Canadian Grocer*, 11 March 1892). Suburban stores benefited in a similar way from the attempts that were made to regulate the sale of intoxicating liquor. The law that alcoholic drink should be served only with food in late nineteenth- and early twentieth-century Montreal meant that it was easy for shopkeepers in the poorer areas of the city to gain an advantage over their more law-abiding competitors: their shops 'are groceries in name only', it was claimed in 1889, 'but their principal trade being in liquors and then keeping only a few groceries in order to comply with the technical requirements of the law' (Royal Commission on the Relations of Labor and Capital in Canada, 1889, 4, p.412; also *Canadian Grocer*, 20 January 1905).

The expansion of the suburban grocery-cum-general store, like the survival of the country general store, also owed a good deal to the need of members of the local population to supplement, or replace, their existing sources of income. In the growing towns and cities they did this, not by selling their produce to the local store, but (as in the countryside) by opening stores of their own. It is well known that it was common for working-class (and other) immigrants from Asia and continental Europe to open small shops designed to serve the members of their local communities. One labourer-turned-shopkeeper arrived in Canada from Italy in 1911 when he was fifteen years old:

I never knew nobody. I land Montreal. I work, and stay three months. Then I go to Toronto, and I stay a year. Then I go to Whitby. Then back to Toronto. Then I come over to Hamilton, and I work in the steel plant for six months . . . From there I went to Calgary for the threshing. I stayed in a caboose and I worked in the threshing. I came back [to Hamilton] with four hundred dollars, and I bought a little store on C . . . Street (Synge, 1976, p.42; see also *Canadian Grocer*, 4 July 1913; *News Advertiser*, 17 December 1910; *Province*, 17 December 1910, 16 February 1911, 30 October 1912).

Such occupational mobility, culminating in small-scale shopkeeping, was far from unusual in immigrant communities. Indeed it has been found that in areas like the Mile End district of Montreal, where the size of the Italian population more than doubled between 1911 and 1916, the number of Italian grocery stores open for business also more than doubled over the same period (Ramirez and Del Balzo, 1980, pp.79–80).

It is less well known perhaps that working people from Britain and Canada also remained attracted to the idea of small-scale shopkeeping (*Maritime Grocer*, 15, 26 January 1893; Census, 1931, x, p.xxvi). It is certainly not fully appreciated that working people of all nationalities were able to turn their dreams into some sort of reality. 'A large number of the industrial classes having inherited small legacies are induced to embark in the "grocery and provision business" with a view to the profitable employment of their disposable capital' (*Canadian Grocer*, 19 July 1889). 'I built a shop of rough lumber, with two living rooms above and so got started', recalls a Manitoba carpenter. 'Later I built a larger shop, with a glass front to the street, which eventually became a general store' (Lindell, c.1970, p.91).

A still larger number of working people were forced into shopkeeping by sickness, unemployment, old age or widowhood (see Benson, 1990, pp.83–96). For example, it has been found that, during the 1860s and 1870s in Montreal, 'Women running their own businesses constituted between 15 and 20 per cent of widows officially reporting an employment' (Bradbury, 1989, p.91. Also *Echo*, 4 July 1891).

Whatever the motivation of working-class shopkeepers, a surprisingly large number of families managed to save the (admittedly generally small) amounts of money that they needed to rent or purchase suitable premises and stock. Indeed it was suggested by that best informed of all contemporary trade journals, the *Canadian Grocer*, that in the early years of the twentieth century nearly half the small retail stores in the Dominion had been bought by working people with the money that they had managed to save from their wage-earnings (*Canadian Grocer*, 1 December 1905; also 19 July 1889, 6 April 1900; Benson, 1876, pp.25–6, 31).

6.8 Conclusion

The discussion in this chapter of fairs, markets, pedlars and small fixed shops raises issues that are of considerable significance. For it suggests that the conventional history of nineteenth- and early twentieth-century Canadian retailing is misleading in at least two important respects. It is misleading in so far as it implies that non-fixed-shop forms of selling proved unable to withstand the changes brought about by industrialisation and urbanisation. For, while it is true that the outstanding development in retailing during this period was the growth, and increasing domination, of fixed shops, this does not mean that markets and itinerant trading collapsed into obscurity. Indeed it has been seen that the relationship between fixed-shop and non-fixed-shop forms of selling may well have been less competitive, and more complementary, than has usually been recognised. The conventional history of Canadian retailing also seems misleading in so far as it perpetuates an uncritical acceptance of a simple demand-led model of retail change. For, while it is clear that changes in consumer demand were the primary determinant of retail development, it does not follow that other factors can therefore be discounted. Indeed it has been seen that continuities in retailer supply were also of considerable significance: the survival both of itinerant selling and of rural and urban general storekeeping owed a good deal to the desire of local residents to supplement, or replace, their existing sources of income.

References

Alexander, D., 1970, *Retailing in England During the Industrial Revolution*, Athlone Press, London

Bank of Montreal, 1956, *The Service Industries*, Royal Commission on Canada's Economic Prospects, Ottawa

Benson, J., 1985, Hawking and peddling in Canada, 1867–1914, *Histoire sociale (Social History)*, 18 (35): 75–83

Benson, J., 1990, *Entrepreneurism in Canada: A History of "Penny Capitalists"*, Edwin Mellen Press, Lewiston, Queenston and Lampeter

Benson, W., 1876, *Life and Adventures of Wilson Benson, Written by Himself*, published privately, Toronto

Bliss, M., 1972, The protective impulse: an approach to the social history of Oliver Mowat's Ontario, in D. Swainson (ed.), *Oliver Mowat's Ontario*, Macmillan of Canada, Toronto

Bradbury, B., 1989, 'Surviving as a widow in nineteenth-century Montreal', *Urban History Review*, 17: 148–60
Butler's Journal, Fredericton, 1890–1, 1894
Calgary Daily Herald, 1913
Campbell, B.A. and Doyle, P.E., 1940, Public markets in Quebec city, *Economic Annalist*, 10: 44–6
Canada Farmer, Toronto, 1864–5
Canadian Grocer, Toronto, 1889–90, 1892, 1900, 1905, 1910, 1913, 1915
City of Hamilton, 1870, By-laws
Census of Canada, 1871–1911, 1931
Census of Merchandising and Service Establishments, 1930
Cotton's Weekly, Cowansville, 1909
Czuboka, M. (ed.), ND, *They Stopped at a Good Place: A History of the Bonsejour, Brokenhead, Garson and Tyndall Area of Manitoba 1875–1981*, Bonsejour-Brokenhead Historical Committee, Beausejour
Daily World, Vancouver, 1899
Drummond, I.M., 1987, *Progress Without Planning: The Economic History of Ontario from Confederation to the Second World War*, University of Toronto Press
Dunnville [Weekly] Chronicle, Dunnville, 1896, 1913
Echo, Montreal, 1891–2
Forsey, E., 1982, *Trade Unions in Canada 1812–1902*, University of Toronto Press
Friesen, G. and Potyondi, B., 1981, *A Guide to the Study of Manitoba Local History*, University of Manitoba, Winnipeg
General Merchant, Toronto, 1929
Globe, Toronto, 1910, 1914
Hamilton Spectator, Hamilton, 1900, 1919, 1922, 1926–7
Independent, Vancouver, 1901
Johnson, G., 1959, The Syrians in western Canada, *Saskatchewan History*, 12: 31–2
Kelly, K., 1971, Wheat farming in Simcoe county in the mid-nineteenth century, *Canadian Geographer*, 15: 95–112
Kelly, K., 1978, The development of farm produce marketing agencies and competition between market centres in eastern Simcoe county, 1850–1875, *Canadian Papers in Rural History*, 1: 67–88
Kindersley Clarion, Kindersley, 1910
Labour Gazette, Ottawa, 1902, 1905–6
Lindell, L., c.1970, *Memory Opens the Door to Yesterday*, L. Lindell, Eriksdale, Manitoba
Maritime Grocer, 1893
Maritime Merchant and Commercial Review, Halifax, 1893, 1904, 1915
Matthews, W.T., 1985, 'By and far the large propertied interests': the dynamics of local government in six upper Canadian towns during the era of commercial capitalism, 1832–60, PhD thesis, McMaster University
Matthews, W.T., 1987, Local government and the regulation of the public market in upper Canada, 1800–1860: the moral economy of the poor?, *Ontario History*, 79: 35–44
Napanee Beaver, Napanee, 1880
Nelson, F., 1989, *Barefoot on the Prairie: Memories of Life on a Prairie Homestead*, Western Producer Prairie Books, Saskatoon
News Advertiser, Vancouver, 1910
Olson, G. and Pybus, V., 1982, *By the Old Mill Stream: A History of the Village of Holmfield*, Holmfield History Book Committee, Holmfield
Osborne, B.S., 1980, Trading on a frontier: the functions of markets, peddlers, and fairs in nineteenth-century Ontario, *Canadian Papers in Rural History*, 2: 59–81
Province, Vancouver, 1910–12
Pike, R.M., 1989, 'Kingston adopts the telephone: the diffusion & use of the telephone in

urban central Canada, 1876–1914', *Urban History Review*, 18: 32–48

Pyle, J., 1971, Farmers' markets in the United States: functional anachronisms, *Geographical Review*, 61 (2): 167–97

Ramirez, B. and Del Balzo, M., 1980, *The Italians of Montreal: From Sojourning to Settlement, 1900–1921*, Editions du Courant, Montreal

Regina Leader, 1887

Retailer, 1915–18

Retail Merchants' Association, 1914, *First Annual Convention*

Retail Merchants Journal,, Toronto, 1903, 1905

Roy, P.E., 1980, *Vancouver: An Illustrated History*, Lorimer, Toronto

Royal Commission on the Relations of Labor and Capital, 1889

Saskatchewan Archives Board, Saskatoon, transcripts of interviews

Santink, J.L., 1990, *Timothy Eaton & the Rise of His Department Store*, University of Toronto Press

Savitt, R., 1985, Retail trade, *The Canadian Encyclopedia*, Vol. 3, Hurtig Publishers, Edmonton

Silverman, E., Oral history collection, University of Calgary

Smart, P.J., 1987, To hawk or not to hawk: A study of street hawkers in Hong Kong, PhD thesis, University of Toronto

Speisman, S.A., 1979, *The Jews of Toronto: A History to 1937*, McClelland & Stewart, Toronto

Synge, J., 1976, Immigrant communities – British and continental European – in early twentieth century Hamilton, Canada, *Oral History*, 4: 38–51

Toronto Trades and Labour Council Minutes, National Archives of Canada, 1886

Van Hoorn, L., 1973, The Hamilton central market: an economic anthropological study, MA thesis, McMaster University

Voice, Winnipeg, 1897

Walden, K., 1989, 'Speaking Modern: Language, Culture & Hegemony in Grocery Window Displays, 1887–1920', *Canadian Historical Review*, 70: 285–310

Wiesinger, J.P., 1985 [?] The evolution of market trading in Kingston, Ontario, unpublished thesis Department of Geography, Queen's University, Ontario

Woywitka, A.B., 1978, A pioneer woman in the labour movement, *Alberta History*, 26: 10–16

Zucchi, J., 1980, *The Italian Immigrants of the St John's Ward, 1875–1915: Patterns of Settlement and Neighbourhood Formation.* Multicultural History Society of Ontario, Toronto

Part III: The rise of large-scale retailing

Part III
The rise of large-scale retailing

The rise of large retail organisations forms a critical evolutionary stage in the distribution systems of many industrialising countries during the late nineteenth and early twentieth centuries. Comparative studies of these developments are minimal and obviously beset by problems of definition as discussed in Chapter 1. Indeed, while many of the major department store organisations have had their biographers, and the issues and ethics surrounding co-operation have attracted a wealth of national and international study, there remains, even leaving aside the definitional problems, considerable scope for further research.

Chapters 7–10 attempt in their different ways to explore and address some of the most critical issues in the rise of large-scale retailing. Of particular significance is the question of how important these developments were, and the impact that they had on the established retail systems of different economies. This is a common theme that runs through all the chapters, and relates in part to how, and from what perspective, change is measured. The preoccupation in these chapters is very much with assessing the pace of change and the relationship between established retailers and the newer large organisations. Surrounding these issues are other important changes, such as the transformation of work practices, and restructuring of shopping centres, and the nature of shopping habits.

Chapter 7 focusses on the detailed development of co-operative retailing in Britain, and adds a significant dimension to the study of large-scale retailing by highlighting both the socio-political and commercial processes behind such organisations. It also shows how vulnerable co-operative retail societies were to competition from capitalist retail organisations, a fact previously neglected in those few studies that had considered the relationship between co-operative stores and established shopkeepers as being a one-way impact to the detriment of the latter. This is certainly the strongly held view contained in the contemporary German literature, with traditional retailers seeing consumer co-operatives as an element of unfair competition that would ultimately destroy their livelihoods (Chapter 9). However, in Britain Martin Purvis suggests that the failure rate of co-operative stores was probably just as great as that found among other retailers.

Clearly co-operative stores were just one element of the transformation of British retailing during the nineteenth century, other powerful forces being associated with department stores, multiple shop organisations and mail-order selling. During the period before 1914 most growth related to department stores and multiples, as Chapter 8 demonstrates. The department store appears to represent a common pattern of growth in many different economies and certainly the evidence from the three case studies of Britain (Chapter 8), Germany (Chapter 9) and Canada (Chapter 10) is that the growth of such stores was already well underway during the 1880s. Common business methods and stages of development can also be strongly identified in each of the three countries. Such a pattern is far less evident with the growth of multiple retailers. Britain witnessed very early developments of such organisations when compared with Germany and still more so when compared with Canada. In the latter country, for example, the growth of multiples was confined to the period after 1900 (Chapter 10) compared with rapid growth in Britain during the 1880s. Developments in Canada were no doubt hampered by a lack of large urban centres, though the rural communities provided an excellent market for mail-order selling.

In each of the countries under consideration the measure of impact inflicted on the established retail system by the new developments is extremely difficult to gauge. Part of the problem concerns the image of rapid decline created by traditional shopkeepers in the wake of large, capital-intensive retailers. In all three countries shopkeepers present a picture in their trade journals of massive impact, with large numbers of small independent retailers being forced out of business through intense price competition. The reality does not, however, always measure up to such images since in Britain, Germany and Canada the total retail system continued to expand in spite of the growth of large-scale retail organisations. Such a fact was apparently either unknown or considered untrue by many of the contemporary independent shopkeepers, whose response to retail change was to ask for government protection or to move towards creating self-help organisations.

It is in response to the rise of large-scale retailing that marked differences begin to emerge between the three economies. In Britain and Canada the pressure did lead to a call for some form of protection for independent shopkeepers, but this never materialised. As an alternative retailers relied on self-help and established trade protection societies. In contrast the traditional retailers in Germany formed part of a more powerful socio-political group, that for some little time attracted government help with laws governing co-operatives and department stores. Even these, however, were deemed to be inadequate by most German shopkeepers who then led the way in the formation of new retail organisations.

Chapter 7
Co-operative retailing in Britain
Martin Purvis

7.1 Introduction

Collective or co-operative activity is far from new (Kropotkin, 1902). Even the more specific idea of jointly purchasing in bulk, so eliminating middlemen to reduce costs and promote a better service, defies attempts to identify its origins precisely. So to note that early references to joint-purchasing schemes survive from the eighteenth century is not necessarily to accord them any primacy. However, during the nineteenth century the idea of the formally constituted co-operative retailing society gained increasing currency. Societies proliferated in Britain and their example helped to encourage co-operation in other countries, including the rather ineffectual developments in Canada and the more solid achievements in Germany discussed in Chapter 9 of this volume (see also BPP, 1886, LXVII, pp.463–505). British co-operatives were among the most successful in establishing themselves as an important component of national retail provision. Yet their precise significance is difficult to calculate in the absence of reliable statistics for overall retail trade. There is little basis for refinement of Jefferys' estimate that the co-operative share of total retail sales rose from 2–3 per cent in 1875 to 6–7 per cent by 1900 (Jefferys, 1954, p.18).

The co-operative achievement can be stated with greater certainty in absolute terms. By 1913 there were around 1,500 independent local retail societies in Britain; in aggregate the custom of 2.9 million members and their families generated an annual turnover in excess of £85 million (BPP, 1914, LXXVI, p.510). Local societies were also associated as members of co-operative federations providing services such as banking and insurance, and extending the principle of joint-purchasing to the supply of their own stores through the English and Scottish Co-operative Wholesale Societies. But the importance of co-operation rests on more than the scale of its business. Acknowledged as an important new component of retailing (cf. Chapter 8 of this volume), it was active in the promotion of morality in trade, supplying basic goods of decent quality and full weight at fair prices to a largely working-class body of customers (Padberg and Thrope, 1974, pp.13–18; Winstanley, 1983, pp.33–49). This reforming zeal was given particular impetus by the unique identity between the store and the consumer that was the basis of co-operative retailing. For many, co-operatives were important not as just another shop but as their 'own shop'; a retailing operation financed and owned by its customers as shareholders, who benefited both from conventional returns on invested capital and from dividends proportional to the value of their custom. Individual societies cherished their independence as local democracies with members sharing in the shaping of policy decisions. Co-operatives were thus part of the development of collective activity by working people that characterised nineteenth-century Britain. Non-conformist religion, trades unions, friendly societies and working men's clubs were among the counterparts of co-operation, but many other labels were attached to the groupings through which workers pursued their own material, social, political and moral goals (Baernreither, 1889; Gosden, 1961, 1973; Crossick, 1978; Clarke, Critcher and Johnson, 1979; Ashplant, 1981). Indeed in many instances these were not separate ends (Yeo, 1986, p.338).

The activities of co-operative societies themselves were various. While retailing was central to the success of British co-operation, it did not define the limits of its aims or operations. Co-operation was seen by its more visionary supporters as contributing to their programmes of comprehensive social, economic and political transformation. Even more sober assessments acknowledged that co-operation could not be reduced to a narrowly economic purpose; just as contemporary ideas about respectability and self-help cannot be defined only in terms of the careful regulation of spending and saving (Kirk, 1985, pp.174-240). Thus it was proclaimed that 'The social and educational influences of co-operation are more important than its pecuniary benefits'; and the hope that co-operation 'will have a humanising and elevating influence upon home, and trade and society' was appended to its promotion of 'economy and good living' (*Co-operator*, 15 January 1866). Many consumers' societies expended resources upon housing, health care, education and recreation for their members, reinforcing the importance of the local co-operative within its community. Co-operation was also seen as providing workers with experience of democratic self-government that, together with its beneficial effects upon their financial position, would qualify them for Parliamentary enfranchisement. Moreover, it contributed to the widening of horizons for women, particularly from the 1880s onwards with the growth of the Women's Co-operative Guild. Intended originally as a means of strengthening social ties between local groups of co-operators, the Guild developed a larger campaigning role on issues such as suffrage, divorce law reform and state provision of health care (Joyce, 1980, pp.115-16; Gaffin and Thoms, 1983).

Ideologically motivated enthusiasm for the wider purpose and achievements of co-operation could reinforce the ties to 'our shop' that were formed by the basic act of purchasing at the local society's store. Some were total in their loyalty: 'My father used to . . . say . . . "I want nothing on my table but co-op" ' (Age Exchange Theatre Company, 1983, p.35). The majority were less committed and less exclusive in their dealings, being drawn to co-operation by its reputation for fair trade, the payment of dividends and, in some smaller communities, the absence of satisfactory alternatives. But all recognised the practical centrality of retailing to co-operation as the foundation of popular support for local societies and the chief source of finance for other activities. To treat co-operatives as just another retailer is to misunderstand their aims and methods. Equally it must be acknowledged that retailing was an important part of co-operation, and co-operatives were an element of growing significance within the system of retail distribution. The material that follows examines the development of co-operatives as retailers, charting their expansion over both space and time. Exploration of this achievement leads to consideration of the nature of local societies and their membership, and the composition and conduct of trade. To discover more precisely where retail co-operation succeeded and where it failed offers a perspective upon the appeal of co-operation to working people allowing us to consider it not only as part of the evolution of retail systems but also in the wider context of economy, society and polity in industrialising Britain.

7.2 Early co-operation

To see the establishment of the Rochdale Pioneers society in 1844 as initiating co-operation is to underestimate the extent of earlier activity that was co-operative in nature, if not always so in name. Eighteenth-century initiatives included quite ambitious efforts to distribute flour, as well as the joint-purchasing of other foodstuffs and household necessities. Local groups of the latter kind were usually small and emphemeral, often leaving little trace of their existence. But references survive to activity in Scotland, particularly in the textile-producing communities of the western lowlands (Maxwell, 1910, pp.43–114). Comparable English groups included the Oldham Co-operative Supply Company of 1795 and subsequent associations formed at the Woolwich Arsenal and Sheerness dockyard, and by miners at Hetton-le-Hole, County Durham (Angus, 1979, p.17; Garnett, 1972, p.60; Brown, 1919, p.20; Welbourne, 1923, p.25).

Efforts to organise the co-operative milling and distribution of flour also seem to have been widespread, reflecting its dietary importance and the commercial and political uncertainties surrounding its supply. Early mills were associated with the naval yards at Woolwich and Chatham during the 1750s but others followed, particularly during periods of inflated prices and heightened fears of adulteration associated with the American Wars of the 1770s and the Napoleonic era. Many such schemes were extensions of existing friendly societies, often launched by skilled workmen in areas such as ports and dockyards, the East Midlands hosiery and lace districts, and around Sheffield, Birmingham and the Black Country (Tann, 1980; Jones, 1894, pp.33–9).

These early schemes were part of wider concerns about the condition of food supply, an issue of considerable importance. Co-operatives were thus related to a tradition which found other means of collective expression, in action such as food riots (Thompson, 1971; Stevenson, 1974). Direct involvement with trading largely superseded customary appeals to paternalistic protection as a means to defend material living standards and secure morality in trade; being seen as more appropriate to the circumstances of an industrialising state (see Chapter 4 of this volume). The self-help of co-operation was thus established as a means of combating the food supply problems of particular communities by the early decades of the nineteenth century. However, the principle subsequently gained greater currency and support in assocation with schemes to effect comprehensive improvements in the economic, social and political status of workers. Co-operative fortunes from the 1820s to the 1840s reflected links with the redemptive programmes of Owenite Socialists and Chartists (Harrison, 1969; Garnett, 1972; Jones, 1975; Briggs, 1959). The journals and conferences spawned by both groups promoted the principle of collective activity as a means to achieve reform (Hollis, 1970; Thompson, 1984, pp.37-56; Mercer, 1947). In particular, co-operative retailing was seen as a means of generating capital to initiate grander schemes of self-employment in industrial and agricultural production and ultimately to establish communitarian developments. Such a programme was first propounded by Owenite Socialists, but was later echoed by some Chartists. ((Brighton) *Co-operator*, October 1828; Harrison and Hollis, 1979, pp.197-204). Among the latter group co-operative retailing was also seen as furthering their immediate political ends in challenging the interests of the newly enfranchised shopocracy.

Such links broadened the appeal of co-operative retailing, promoting it as a means to larger ends rather than an end in itself. The chronology of co-operative development also reflected the rhythms of popular radicalism; growth during the late 1820s and decline by 1832 marked the passage of mass support for Owenite Socialism, revival around 1840 reflected links with the regrouping of Owenism in some localities and the rise of Chartism. But, although co-operation developed within this wider context, the importance of retailing *per se* by no means disappeared. Although proclaimed as a means of promoting comprehensive change, support for co-operation often reflected appreciation of its more immediate role in supplying pure goods at fair prices. It was also true that, when co-operatives failed, this reflected their deficiencies not merely as agents of reform but as retailers.

During the late 1820s and early 1830s co-operatives proliferated in England and lowland Scotland. They clustered in the Midlands, Sussex, Norfolk, Cumberland and central Scotland; but were most numerous in London and the textile districts of Lancashire and the West Riding (Purvis, 1986a, p.195, Map 26.3). By the early 1830s it was claimed that societies numbered around 700 (*Lancashire Co-operator*, 25 June 1831; *Crisis*, 27 October 1832). If such totals are accurate they suggest a national co-operative membership of just over 50,000, for surviving details show that most individual associations were small, often with a membership of between 50 and 100. Even the largest known societies, including those in Sheffield, Huddersfield, Burslem and Hastings, had only 200 to 250 members and weekly sales of around £100. At the other extreme were the 15 members of the Fortitude society of Manchester, with a weekly turnover of £1 (Purvis, 1987, pp.37-41).

The scale of societies, although sometimes reflecting deliberate restriction, was both a symptom and a cause of their weakness. It probably also meant that, although numerous, these early co-operatives formed only a small part of total retail provision. Surpluses generated by trading were limited; even the £127 raised in three months during 1831 by the Halifax society seems discouragingly modest compared with the thousands of pounds thought necessary to capitalise communities (*Lancashire Co-operator*, 6 August 1831; Garnett, 1972, p.180). Such circumstances led some to abandon co-operation altogether, while others succumbed to pressures to divide surpluses for immediate distribution among society members.

The limited scale of individual associations also hindered their commercial vitality as traders. Particular difficulties were reported in the largest urban centres where there were often several separate co-operatives struggling within a substantial private retail sector. As Manchester Owenites noted on giving up storekeeping: 'we are no enemies to trading societies . . . but we much doubt their practicability in large towns where there is so wide a field for competition' (*Lancashire and Yorkshire Co-operator*, September 1832). While the failure of stores in Manchester, London, Liverpool, Birmingham and Leeds led the co-operative downturn by 1832, societies endured in some smaller centres, not least because they offered a locally valuable service as retailers. Decline during the second quarter was significant but not total. Thus standard accounts mislead in effectively discounting any co-operative survival during the mid 1830s and ignoring its revival around the end of the decade (Cole, 1944; Pollard, 1960; Bonner, 1970).

The extent of co-operative activity during the mid-1830s is unclear. But surviving societies were probably most common in the West Riding and central Scotland (Purvis, 1986b). Moreover, there were additional foundations; initially few, but rising around 1840 during which year reference to over 40 new stores can be found. Well over 100 societies are recorded as being established in the years immediately preceding the foundation of the famous Rochdale Pioneers' society of 1844 (Purvis, 1986b; Purvis, 1987, pp.57–8). Many added to the established societies in Yorkshire and Scotland but the revival also embraced Lancashire, London, parts of the Midlands and the north-east (Purvis, 1986a, p.195, Map 26.3).

Relatively few individual societies were enduring; those that survived were usually small village stores in parts of northern England and Scotland. Some were perhaps not intended to be permanent, others failed to establish themselves as retailers or fell foul of the fluctuating fortunes of Chartism and Socialism. Yet initiatives during these years maintained the continuity of co-operative activity and influenced subsequent developments in a number of ways. Some reactions followed from the vulnerability of early co-operatives; in north-east England, for example, failure generated disillusionment which contributed to a regional hiatus in co-operative activity largely unbroken until the late 1850s. By contrast, in parts of Lancashire, the West Riding and central Scotland, a continuing tradition of successful co-operation, rather than the example of the Rochdale Pioneers alone, helped underpin progress during the second half of the century. Moreover, it was during these years that basic tenets of 'modern' co-operation, such as open membership, the selection of committee members by election, and dividends on purchases, were increasingly publicised and adopted. Indeed some now forgotten Chartist stores seem to have been more advanced in their methods than the authors of the initial rules of the Rochdale Pioneers (Purvis, 1986b, pp.212–14).

7.3 Co-operative expansion during the latter half of the nineteenth century

The turnover of co-operative foundations and failures remained high around mid-century. But the number of extant societies increased to a temporary peak of around 300 during the early 1850s (*Journal of Association*, 28 June 1852; Maxwell, 1910, pp.43–114; Purvis, 1990, p.317). These societies reflected co-operative interest from a number of different quarters. The continuing vitality of co-operative traditions in the textile districts of northern England and in central Scotland, still to an extent separate from each other, ensured that those areas accounted for around half the recorded societies (Figure 7.1). Some of the stores scattered elsewhere

Figure 7.1 The distribution of co-operative societies, c.1851–2

followed the leads set by their northern counterparts, but there were other forces generating new activity. Societies in London reflected the involvement of the Christian Socialists, a metropolitan group of mainly middle-class reformers who promoted co-operation as a means of alleviating moral and material poverty among workers. Christian Socialists supported co-operative initiatives in both retailing and production, often seeing the former as serving the latter. Stores were planned to provide outlets for craft producers and generate funds for the extension of self-employment among workers. The reforming vision inspiring these ambitions seems akin to earlier British co-operative programmes, but followed more directly from the external influence of co-operative workshops in continental Europe (Raven, 1920, pp.55–8; Backstrom, 1974, p.29). However, the Christian Socialist emphasis on production as the prime sphere for co-operation had little lasting impact. Their influence was limited by the social remove of the group from the majority of co-operators with consequent overtones of patronage; and by their geographical separation from activity in northern England and Scotland which was more focussed upon practical retailing. As members of the metropolitan middle class the Christian Socialists were, however, well placed to contribute in another way to co-operative development. Their involvement in the drafting and passage of the Industrial and Provident Societies Act of 1852 yielded lasting benefit in establishing a specific legal status for co-operatives.

This Act helped consolidate the position of the more successful established stores, some of which were developing as significant operations; societies in Bacup, Ripponden and Rochdale each recorded annual sales of over £10,000 around 1852 (*Christian Socialist* 8 November 1851; *Journal of Association*, 28 June 1852). A rough balance between foundations and failures kept society numbers stable during the mid-1850s but between 1857 and 1863 the total for England and Wales rose from around 200 to over 600 (Purvis, 1990, p.317). Comparable figures for Scotland are not readily available, but foundations during these years numbered over 100 (BPP, 1867–68, XL, pp.756–7, 1060–1; BPP, 1872, LIV, pp.388–96; Maxwell, 1910, pp.115–226). Explanation of the timing of this upsurge remains tentative but interest in co-operation as a means of improving the lot of workers increased as a reaction to the renewed failure of efforts to win concessions in the workplace and in Parliamentary representation. Perceptions of the significance of retailing may also have been sharpened by fears of increased food prices associated with political upheavals and the threat of war in Europe. A more direct stimulus was the publication of new material proclaiming co-operative achievements. A history of the, by then substantial, Rochdale Pioneers' society issued in 1858 was frequently quoted as an inspiration for initiatives elsewhere (Holyoake, 1858). There was also increased attention to association in popular journals such as *Reynolds's Newspaper* and a revival of a specifically co-operative press. Moreover, enthusiasm once generated could become self-reinforcing, with successes sparking further emulation (Purvis, 1990, pp.325–6).

The initial pace of proliferation of societies was not sustained and the peak national foundation rates of the early 1860s were never repeated. But society numbers increased steadily until the mid-1870s when the national total peaked at over 1,300. This figure was not exceeded during the following years of general depression, but growth resumed in the decade from 1884 to 1893, carrying the number of societies to well over 1,500. During the latter years of the period up to the First World War new foundations were increasingly offset by the amalgamation of existing societies, so that the new peak of over 1,770 reached in 1911 was whittled back to nearer 1,500 by 1913 (BPP, 1872–1914, Reports of the Chief Registrar of Friendly Societies upon industrial and provident societies for the year ending December 1871 to December 1913). During all of this, however, the foundations of long-term co-operative expansion were being laid, as national membership and sales increased. Indeed some societies founded between 1857 and 1861 grew to be particularly substantial; by 1901 survivors from these years formed 13 per cent of extant societies in England and Wales, but accounted for 35 per cent of trade (BPP, 1902, XCVI, pp.144–224).

The foundations of the late 1850s and early 1860s also shaped the geographical pattern of expansion, re-invigorating co-operation beyond its circumscribed distribution at mid-century (Figure 7.1). While northern and Scottish heartlands generated much fresh activity so too did other areas, particularly north-eastern England, the Midlands, London and South Wales. Indeed new societies were widely scattered, chiefly in urban centres (Purvis, 1990, p.326). Activity was unevenly distributed, but accounts such as Cole mislead in their under-reporting of efforts to establish co-operation outside industrial northern England and central Scotland (Cole, 1944). Between 1857 and 1861 over 80 societies were registered in the English Midlands, with a similar figure for London alone. In the rest of southern England the total of new co-operatives was over 60. Moreover, while foundation rates for the following five years fell in the established strongholds, they rose elsewhere, particularly in parts of the East Midlands and in the extra-metropolitan south-east (Purvis, 1990, p.324).

Figure 7.2 The distribution of co-operative societies, 1901

Such activity testifies to contemporary interest, but it also highlights the difficulties of translating enthusiasm for the idea of co-operation into successful trading societies. Success was far from universal: only around 40 per cent of societies established during the third quarter of the nineteenth century were still trading in 1901; many of the others failed while still young and weak. Thus the under-reporting of the upsurge of co-operative activity around 1860 reflects the variable fortunes of the new societies. Some associations outside the co-operative heartlands achieved enduring success – indeed around the turn of the century the Plymouth society had the second largest membership in Britain – but failure rates in southern districts were above the national average, sometimes markedly so. Over half the societies in northern England dating from 1857–61 were still trading in 1901; in other regions it was rarely more than a third, and failure rates topped 90 per cent in Wales, the West Midlands, and the south-east. In London only one society survived from the initial body of over 80; an extreme example of the difficulties experienced by co-operatives in the largest cities (Purvis, 1990, pp.322–3, 325).

Thus the pattern of co-operatives trading in 1901 (Figure 7.2) reflects a convoluted development process. Few societies survived from the first half of the nineteenth century, although their contribution to the Scottish total (11 per cent) was rather higher than the figure for England and Wales (4 per cent). Associations from the decade 1857–66 accounted for around a quarter of extant societies, but over a third of those trading in 1901 were less than 20 years old. These continuing foundations reflected a variety of impulses; some larger societies split either to give individual communities control over their own stores, or as a result of other internal tensions (Joyce, 1980, p.283). New societies were formed to trade in particular commodities such as fresh meat and coal that were not provided by their established neighbours. Elsewhere, there were efforts to extend co-operation into new localities, chiefly smaller centres including some agricultural villages. Societies were also newly established in towns which had previously experimented unsuccessfully with co-operation. Over 40 per cent of foundations in south-east England during the 1880s and 1890s were such re-introductions. The establishment of societies continued to reflect independent local initiative but, during the later decades of the century, co-operation fostered larger institutions and these also became involved in promoting new stores. From the 1880s onwards there were suggestions that the Co-operative Union and the English and Scottish Co-operative Wholesale Societies, as national federations to which the majority of local consumers' societies were party, should help to finance and plan stores in localities which had proved resistant to co-operation. The direct involvement of the federations in founding societies had only limited positive impact, not least because of the conflict between this means of extending co-operation and the traditional adherence to the principle of local autonomy (*Co-operative News*, 12 June 1880, 16 October 1880, 6 November 1880, 20 November 1880; Co-operative Union, 1880, 1888, 1890). However, the simple presence of supportive institutions as a source of wholesale supplies and general advice on business practice helped to encourage and sustain local initiatives, thus aiding co-operative extension.

The prevalence of new foundations in southern districts meant that these were the areas recording the greatest proportional growth of membership and sales in the decades immediately preceding the First World War. The high rates of growth were, however, a product of the limitations of the existing co-operative base in the south

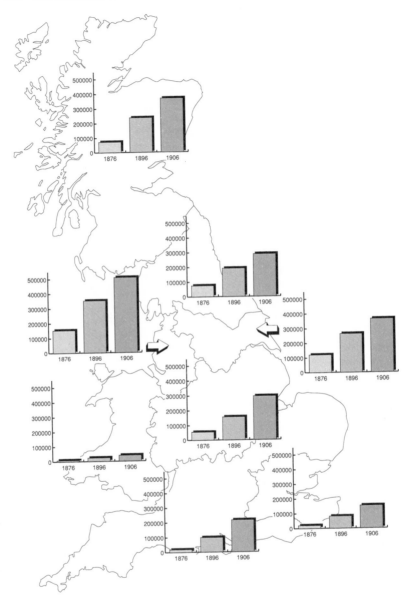

Figure 7.3 Regional membership of co-operatives, 1876–1906

and the disillusionment and delays associated with early failures (Figure 7.3). Despite the exhortations of co-operative leaders, membership levels remained relatively low in most southern counties till the end of our period (Figure 7.4). By contrast, membership was predictably common in areas of northern England and

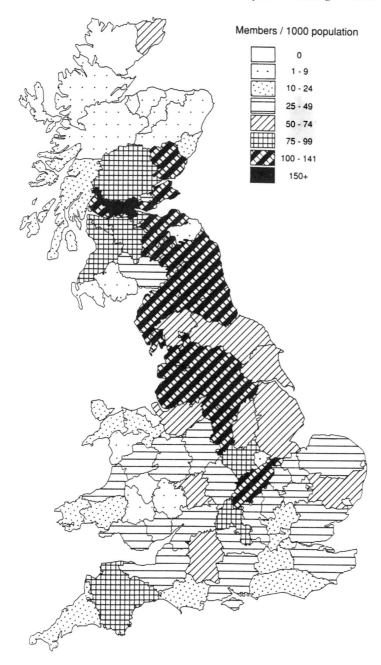

Figure 7.4 Co-operative membership by county as a proportion of total population, 1911

central Scotland which had major industrial and mining centres. Perhaps less expected was its strength in Northamptonshire and Leicestershire, and in parts of the Scottish borders, based upon well-established societies in footwear and textile producing districts. Yet co-operation remained weak in some areas including South Wales and the West Midlands where manufacturing industry and mining were important elements within the regional economy.

There were also significant variations in co-operative achievements at a local scale. Thus the strongest individual societies claimed near total domination of particular retail markets. This was true of smaller centres with limited retail provision but also of some larger towns, especially those with a predominantly working-class population. Crewe, Bolton and Oldham were among the centres where the co-operative share of retail trade was stated to be around 75 per cent by the 1890s and 1900s (Chaloner, 1950, p.265; Peoples, 1909, pp.183, 409; BPP, 1893–4, XXXIX Part I, p. 85). Such claims exist in isolation. However, a more comprehensive overview of localised variation in co-operative strength can be derived from the distribution of membership. Within Lancashire, for example, there were contrasts between the relative weakness of Merseyside and the coalfield of the south-west, and the activity in the south-east of the county. There was also variation within the textile districts; thus in 1901 the areas around Rochdale and Bury recorded significantly higher proportional levels of co-operators among their populations than did Blackburn or Manchester (Purvis, 1990, p.322).

7.4 The commercial and social context of co-operative development

The outline of development presented here differs from previously published accounts in stressing the sheer number of societies formed and their widespread distribution. Most larger and middle-sized towns saw some experimentation with co-operation in the years up to 1914, and the idea penetrated into rural areas. Yet this approach also indicates that co-operatives, in common with many of the smaller private entrants into retailing, often found it difficult to establish successful stores (Blackman, 1967; Winstanley, 1983, pp.41–2; Benson, 1983, pp.98–127). This sometimes reflected the inexperience of those promoting local societies. Moreover, the books, journals and personal contacts which promoted initial interest often dwelt more on the rectitude of co-operative principles than the practicalities of storekeeping. The establishment of co-operative wholesaling societies during the 1860s, followed during the 1870s by the Co-operative Union as an advisory body on legal and administrative affairs, offered the prospect of more substantial support for retail societies. But there was also concern that the creation of national organisations would engender unwelcome uniformity of operations and threaten to erode local autonomy. Ultimately, however, even the most comprehensive advice could not guarantee success where unfavourable socio-economic and commercial circumstances hampered the attraction of mass support.

Appreciation of co-operation and its importance to particular communities was widespread but this should not obscure the diversity of opinion. One Lancashire artisan held forth in 1886 that 'it is the co-operatives that has ruined our trade. . . . The co-operative is the cause of the depression and nothing else . . .' (BPP, 1886,

XXII, Appendix Pt II, p.76). Private shopkeepers whose trade was threatened, and employers who felt challenged by any independent organisation among workers, might be expected to have displayed least sympathy with co-operation. Certain employers discouraged co-operative membership and particularly the holding of co-operative office. In some instances such hostility reflected pressures from private traders; several railway companies, including the Midland and the North British, seem to have acted against co-operators in the face of threats from private wholesalers and producers to use alternative means of transport (*West Durham and South Northumberland Co-operative District Record*, March 1891; Co-operative Union 1894, 1895, 1896). In smaller workshops, it was suggested, personal identification between masters and men fermented anti-co-operative pressures; there were 'men who keep aloof from the movement, not because they do not see its value and . . . justice, but because they will not do violence to their feelings by acting in opposition to their employer . . .' (*Co-operative News*, 23 October 1875). Such craft workers may also have been open to pressure from shopkeepers, as important customers for their output. In smaller centres employers and shopkeepers sometimes also owned a significant share of local property and there were reports, from as late as the Edwardian era, of the refusal of premises to co-operatives on the developing Dukeries coalfield (Waller, 1983, pp.89–90).

Some of the crudest attempts to block co-operation came from smaller entrepreneurs whose income was supplemented by truck and other dealings in household necessities. Even during the 1870s there were instances, involving trades such as footwear and hosiery, of co-operators being refused work unless they dealt at shops in which their employer had an interest (BPP, 1871, XXXVI, p.44, 1098). There were also direct challenges to co-operative trade. Greatest attention has been paid to efforts to co-ordinate anti-co-operative sentiment from the 1880s onwards. Traders' defence leagues attempted to induce suppliers to refuse co-operative custom and to influence consumers by spreading allegations of overcharging and misman-agement (Winstanley, 1983, pp.83–8). But individual shopkeepers had long challenged particular local societies. A simple response was the temporary reduction of prices to undercut the stores. The abandonment of credit and a switch to ready-money dealing sometimes allowed price reductions to be sustained. Some private dealers imitated the attractions of co-operation including dividends and other bonuses on purchases (Purvis, 1987, p.413). Such activity rarely damaged a society that was locally established, but may have undermined some that were still small and weak.

Yet middle-class opinion was not uniformly anti-co-operative. Some entrepre-neurs, including the Quaker iron-masters Fox and Head who helped establish the Middlesbrough society in 1867, echoed the Christian Socialist ethos in supporting co-operation as a means to encourage desirable characteristics of thrift and hard work among their employees (Co-operative Union, 1901, p.36). Private traders, too, varied in their reaction. Some perceived little challenge to their own profitability, perhaps because past failures led to under-estimation of co-operative potential; or because expanding consumer demand allowed continued growth by both new and established retailers. More substantial shopkeepers may have felt that their most remunerative business was with middle-class consumers who were unlikely to patronise co-operatives. Some such dealers supplied workers 'second hand' by providing the stock for small working-class shopkeepers and may initially have regarded co-operatives as similar ventures. Certainly some societies recorded offers of wholesale supplies from their larger private neighbours in the grocery and provisions trade (Durham Record Office, D/Co/Da 1). Perceptions of co-operation also varied between retailers in different sectors. Dealers in foodstuffs and household necessities faced the most direct challenge; in London there were protests that the 'middle class co-operatives' formed by civil servants and military personnel threatened more lucrative trades in fancy goods but there was little comparable threat in the provinces (BPP, 1878-9, IX, pp.1-431). Indeed some retailers entered into agency agreements with co-operatives. The private trader aimed to increased custom by offering discounts or dividends to society members who were thus offered an increased range of goods on favourable terms. Early agreements usually covered fairly basic items such as meat and clothing, but as these were increasingly sold by co-operatives themselves later agencies involved products such as paints and wallpapers, jewellery, pianos, bicycles and even dentistry (Purvis, 1987, pp. 445-6).

Because of their singular constitution, co-operatives received particular attention, but their fortunes were also influenced simply by the presence of other shopkeepers. While societies might see themselves as separate from competitive commerce, they had to acknowledge the constraints imposed by a rival private sector. Prevailing competition levels influenced the need for, and ease of entry into the market of, any new retail outlet. The benefits of dividend on purchase and the ideological attractions of advancing the cause of workers and consumers as against that of private business were widely appreciated. But the appeal of co-operation and its chances of commercial success were greatest where existing retail provision was deficient. In smaller and younger industrial centres societies benefited from the absence, or even progressive erosion, of private provision. In larger industrial towns, co-operatives developed as part of a general expansion in retailing associated with rising populations and consumer demand (Scola, 1975; Wild and Shaw, 1979; Shaw, 1982).

Once established, co-operatives as a collective effort were often better placed to expand than some of their rivals for working-class custom, particularly the many small private shopkeepers operating general stores from front-room premises. Indeed by the 1870s there were claims that co-operatives in towns such as Rochdale and Oldham were acting as market leaders setting price levels for other traders (Co-operative Union, 1876, p.16). In such circumstances societies gained a degree of freedom to establish levels of prices, surpluses and dividends most attractive to consumers. Co-operators generally favoured generous dividends rather than especially low prices, perhaps because of fears that the small immediate savings of price cuts would be frittered away, while accumulated dividends could pay for more substantial items such as clothing and furniture, or accrue as a painless means of saving (Co-operative Union, 1876, pp.13-16). Certainly dividend levels increased over time; by 1896 over 30 per cent of co-operators in England and Wales received at least three shillings in the pound, more than was paid by any society in 1862 when dividends were recorded as typically around one shilling (Co-operator, October 1862; BPP, 1898, LXXXVIII, p.740). The value of dividends to individuals obviously varied, but it was suggested in 1887 that annual figures of £10-20 were common (BPP, 1887, XIII, p.606). Members also received a financial return in the form of interest upon their share holdings in a society. Such success fuelled allegations from private traders that these benefits were financed by overcharging

(Wilkinson, 1886). The limited available evidence reveals no consistent pricing discrepancies between co-operative and private stores (BPP, 1903, LXVIII, pp.433–70). However, Rowntree discovered that in late Victorian York only six out of twenty staple dietary items were sold at below average prices by the town's society (Rowntree, 1902, pp.103–4). Such findings suggest that the enthusiasm for price-cutting proclaimed by some co-operatives during the 1850s and 1860s subsequently faded (Purvis, 1987, pp.373–4, 388–9). They seem consistent also with concerns voiced during the 1890s that the pursuit of dividends inflated prices beyond the means of poorer consumers, thus debarring them from the advantages of co-operation (Co-operative Union, 1891, pp.13–17). As a remedy, it was suggested that dividends and price levels be reduced and special stores be established in poorer urban districts selling basic goods in small quantities at low prices. However, even the few societies, principally that at Sunderland, which responded to these proposals abandoned the experiment in the face of the disapproval of most existing co-operators who continued to regard dividends as an important symbol of success (Darvill, 1954, pp.172–89).

In such circumstances low dividends were a sign of weakness, a reflection of an inability to generate the necessary surpluses. Indeed the very success of the strongest co-operatives may have hampered developments elsewhere by raising expectations that could not generally be met. As a London delegate to the 1876 Co-operative Congress bemoaned 'They might in a southern society make dividends of 1s. 3d. or 1s. 6d.; and some body might get hold of a Bacup balance sheet, showing a much larger dividend, and they at once attributed the smallness of their own dividend to bad management, and didn't believe the explanations of their own committee' (Co-operative Union, 1876, p.17). In truth low dividends and high failure rates testify to co-operative difficulties in penetrating the more competitive local retail markets. Some societies were unable to outgrow such initial weakness because of the limitations of capital, membership and turnover that were inevitable given the small-scale of many co-operatives established as independent local societies. Hence the limited success in urban southern England where relatively stable consumer demand was more likely to be met by existing retailers.

Major cities were also difficult territory. Revenue and dividends were squeezed by a combination of high costs, including wages, rates, rents and building land, and price competition that reflected the sheer number of shops, markets and itinerant traders. Co-operatives generally lacked the capital resources, impressive central premises and entrepreneurial flair that allowed other retailers, principally successful new multiples to make an immediate impact upon large and competitive markets (Mathias, 1967, pp.96–8; Chapter 8 of this volume). Their problems were particularly acute where independent initiatives by several groups within a large city led to the foundation of a series of small and undercapitalised societies individually offering to uncommitted consumers very little incentive in the form of dividends, prices or quality of service. Fragmentation was a handicap in Liverpool and Birmingham, and special difficulties in London spawned calls from the 1870s onwards for metropolitan co-operation to be reconstructed creating fewer but stronger societies. London was an obvious target for those who during the 1880s and 1890s called for the involvement of the Co-operative Union and the Co-operative Wholesale Society (CWS) in the creation of new retail societies in areas where success had previously proved elusive. But the attempt launched in 1894 to unite efforts throughout the capital, in the People's Co-operative Society, proved short-lived. The society was liquidated after only five years and its eleven stores established as separate societies (Redfern, 1913, pp.195–6; Webb and Webb, 1921, pp.22–3). The policy of providing outside financial support for new stores was controversial as a breach of co-operative traditions of local autonomy and was never widely adopted. It was also self-defeating in undermining the development of a spirit of local initiative in the management of a society, and local identification of the membership with their 'own' store, which were important in the achievement of long-term success.

The record of co-operation in London highlights the necessity of social and communal foundations for success. The development of a handful of effective societies by the last decades of the nineteenth century suggested that metropolitan markets could be penetrated. But these were sustained by workers whose circumstances were more akin to those of provincial industrial districts than they were typical of metropolitan experience. Several enduring London societies were associated initially with the workforce of industrial operations on a scale relatively rare in the capital: Price's candle works in Battersea, the government armaments factory at Enfield, railway workshops in Stratford and the Woolwich Arsenal. These were the counterparts of the factories, mills and mines that fostered many co-operatives elsewhere.

Successful co-operatives were often established within the context of pre-existing groupings. Some originated among the members of other institutions, including friendly and temperance societies, trades unions and religious congregations. But the collective identity of those initiating local co-operatives was frequently rooted in a common occupation or workplace. Experience of working together, a residential community that mirrored the composition of the workforce, comparable income and expenditure patterns, all fostered shared values and aspirations, and these could promote shared appreciation of co-operative principles and practice. Indeed Crossick's study of workers associated with the Woolwich Arsenal stresses their support for co-operation as an expression of artisanal values of respectability, specifically a desire for morality in trade and thrift in expenditure (Crossick, 1978, pp.165–73).

The circumstances of Woolwich perhaps over-emphasise the extent to which co-operation was the preserve of a working-class élite, and a means of asserting that élite identity. The under-representation of semi-skilled and unskilled workers found among Woolwich co-operators was not universal. The Darlington society, for example, had a membership in which engineering and metal trades were well represented; nearly 40 per cent of some members admitted during the late 1860s and early 1870s were labourers or assistants, participating in the society alongside more skilled and affluent workers (Purvis, 1987, pp.532–3). Elsewhere co-operators were found among all grades of textile workers, not a group regarded as particularly skilled or highly paid. However, traditions of collectivity were well entrenched in the workplace and in the residential community, supporting long-standing co-operatives and other popular institutions (Joyce, 1980). But even where manufacturing employment among women was common, female participation in other extra-domestic activity was limited. Although shopping and household management were regarded as female tasks, women formed only a small minority of co-operative members during the nineteenth century; custom and the inferior legal status of married women's property dictated that male family members were recorded as co-operators.

Contemporaries identified particular trades – engineers, railwaymen, skilled factory workers – as model co-operators on the basis of assumptions about their income, intelligence and respectability (*Co-operator*, December 1864, 15 January 1867; *Co-operative News*, 10 April 1875). Thus the Leicester society reported that in establishing new stores: 'Our policy in selecting the branches has been to fix on those districts where large proportions of . . . the *elite* of the working class live' (*Co-operator*, 4 June 1870). Success, however, was not automatic. Also, groups such as agricultural labourers were sometimes dismissed as lacking the characteristics necessary for co-operation. Yet there were instances of independent village stores and the extension of the activities of urban societies (in, for example, Banbury, Ipswich and Lincoln) into their rural hinterlands (Co-operative Union, 1879, pp.43–6; Co-operative Union, 1895, pp.13–17). Indeed efforts at Banbury to recruit members from surrounding rural areas were reflected in the report of 1874 that agricultural labourers made up over half the society's membership of 850 (Crossley, 1972, p.16; *Banbury Co-operative Record*, June 1872).

However the experiences of some workers did reduce their chances of involvement with co-operation. The poorest, while not totally excluded, were generally under-represented in the membership. Casual labour, particularly common in the largest cities and ports where co-operation was invariably weak, lacked stability of association in work and regularity of income. High levels of residential mobility and indeed a philosophy of life in which present uncertainties took precedence over prudent provision for the future also worked against co-operation (Stedman Jones, 1971). By contrast, although artisans in the small workplaces of the metropolis and other centres, including Birmingham and Sheffield, may have espoused respectability and collectivity, sustaining a rich associative life of trade-based societies, they were rarely strong co-operators. Alternative foci of association, and the many distractions of a city, doubtless drew attention away from co-operation, but the requirements for its success also differed. Many trade clubs and friendly societies were organised on a different scale and basis from most enduring co-operatives. The former included bodies whose operations depended less on formal organisation than on trust and familiarity among a few dozen members drawn together by the tightly circumscribed bonds of the individual trade or workshop. The viability of the latter rested more on the emergence of a leadership with some formal commercial skills, and the recruitment of the hundreds of members necessary to sustain retail trading. During the last third of the nineteenth century over 80 per cent of co-operatives with a maximum recorded membership of under 100 ended in failure (calculated from the annual reports of the Chief Registrar of Friendly Societies upon industrial and provident societies, BPP 1863–1902).

7.5 The operation of co-operative stores

Co-operation was a distinctive element within the retail expansion of the nineteenth century and also contributed to wider changes in the conduct of trade. Enthusiasm for co-operation partly reflected the failings of private retailing; lack of provision was often compounded by suspicions of adulteration, overcharging and profiteering (Purvis, 1987, pp.366–410). Co-operatives, often formed in reaction against breaches of morality in trade, helped to reduce the numbers of small private shopkeepers; the example of, and competition from, co-operatives combined with the larger new private retailers and increasing legal regulation of trading to encourage general improvements in standards (Burnett, 1966, pp.190–213). Other changes in retail practices such as the introduction of pre-packaged branded goods also reduced opportunities for fraud. Co-operatives stocked early proprietary products including Keiller's marmalade, Epps' cocoa and Hudson's soap powder. Moreover, from the 1870s onwards, the CWS, as a major supplier to stores, developed its own branded products ranging from biscuits to boot-polish (Redfern, 1913, pp.72–82, 169–87, 239–92).

Co-operatives were chiefly suppliers of foodstuffs and other household items in mass demand. Indeed some initially sold only a handful of items; small stocks of goods such as flour, tea, sugar and candles could be obtained with an initial subscribed capital of a few pounds. Most societies' subsequent sales also rested on a fairly narrow range of foodstuffs. Among the 142 societies surveyed in 1882–3, around one-third of sales by value was accounted for by flour, butter and sugar alone. The addition of cheese, coffee, tea, bread, potatoes, bacon and hams, pork, dried fruit and tobacco brought the total to nearly half the turnover (CWS, 1884, pp.534–46). But co-operators generally displayed little early enthusiasm for some cheaper alternatives to traditional staples; it was perhaps consistent with an under-representation of the very poorest consumers among the membership that margarine accounted for only 1 per cent of trade in the CWS butter department in 1887 (BPP, 1887, IX, p.124).

Although contributing relatively little to the value of trade, exotic items such as rice, nutmegs, lemon peel and ginger were sold alongside the staple foodstuffs and household goods (Northamptonshire Record Office, SL 396; Durham Record Office, D/Co/JH 1). But entry into food trades other than groceries and provisions was initially uncommon. Dealing in perishables involved greater risks of loss and required resources and specific expertise for the purchasing, storage and preparation of stock. Some societies did sell fresh meat, indeed a few were established specifically for this purpose and there were also attempts to develop butchering by groups of local retail co-operatives. However, while cured meats were widely sold, by 1887 only 32 per cent of English and Welsh co-operatives traded in fresh meat. Dealing in other perishables such as greengrocery, fish and milk was still less common (Co-operative Union, 1887). Such items, traditionally the preserve of the market rather than the shop trade, were not widely sold by co-operatives until the twentieth century.

Co-operatives most frequently extended their stock to include drapery, footwear and hardware. Sometimes, particularly during the first half of the century, stocks included the output of co-operative members or that of producer groups; subsequently conventional wholesalers and the CWS were the chief suppliers. A stock-taking record compiled in 1839 for the society at Ripponden details cloths including silk, flannel, serge, checks, ginghams and linen. Among other items listed were handkerchiefs, stockings, thread, buttons, pots, nails, brushes and broom handles (Calderdale District Archives TU 57/3). Few contemporaneous societies would have matched this but during the latter half of the century an increasing range of dry-goods was stocked. By 1887 over 70 per cent of societies for which data are available sold drapery and footwear; more than half dealt in hardware and ironmongery (Co-operative Union, 1887). Higher value and luxury goods were initially sold chiefly by the 'middle-class co-operatives' in London and some other cities from the 1860s onwards (Hood and Yarney, 1957). But increasing numbers of conventional societies were dealing in furniture and jewellery by the final decades of the century; indeed some larger co-operatives developed their central premises as department stores. Circulars such as that produced by the Darlington society in 1885 advertising washing and sewing machines, furniture and carpets testify both to the expansion of co-operation and changing patterns of consumer expenditure (Durham Record Office, D/Co/Da 117). There is some evidence of an increasing lower middle-class element among co-operators (Smith and Walton, 1985), but workers were also purchasing consumer durables. This partly reflected rising real incomes, but co-operation itself contributed to trade expansion. Accumulated dividends could be spent on larger items and co-operative 'clubs' allowing payment for expensive items by instalments grew in popularity. Some larger societies also sold goods on hire purchase by the early years of the present century (Wilson, 1908, pp.132–8).

Innovations such as payment clubs and hire purchase were opposed by some co-operators as a threat to the principle of dealing for ready-money only. However, in practice the co-operative stand against credit trading and the associated problems of indebtedness was widely compromised throughout the nineteenth century. By 1901 nearly three-quarters of societies were granting credit (BPP, 1902, XCVI, pp.246–9, 290–1). Even where credit was officially outlawed by local societies, it was sometimes allowed by individual shopkeepers and assistants (Durham Record Office, D/Co/Da 10). It seems that co-operative practice was, perhaps of necessity, more accommodating of the needs of consumers than stated principles might suggest. But most did attempt to regulate credit, often insisting on the settlement of debts before further adding to the account and linking the total availability of credit to the member's assets as share holdings in the society.

Expanding businesses required larger premises, and successful societies generated the capital required to improve their accommodation and equipment. The smallest groups began trading, often during evenings only, in any premises that could be obtained, including the homes of members. Those with greater initial resources, reflecting a larger membership or capital derived from other sources such as the friendly society which loaned £100 to the infant Bishop Auckland co-operative (Durham Record Office, D/Co/BA 1), aspired to rent and stock a store from the outset. The acquisition of suitable premises was, however, sometimes problematic. In smaller communities property could be concentrated in the hands of interests hostile to co-operation, and in the largest centres attractive premises prominently sited to attract passing trade were beyond the means of small co-operatives. Such difficulties and the enforced acceptance of inferior accommodation contributed to co-operative failures (BPP, 1887, XIII, pp.583, 597–600, 604–5; Bishopsgate Institute Library, Edmonton Co-operative Society, 1889). But societies which surmounted such initial difficulties usually constructed or purchased their own stores; increasing the capacity of central premises, developing chains of branch stores and equipping vans to serve less densely populated areas.

Co-operatives were thus multiple retailers, but unlike the national chains of outlets developed by the largest of their private counterparts, the stores owned by individual societies were grouped in their own particular locality (cf. Chapter 8 of this volume, and Mathias, 1967). By 1861 the Manchester and Salford society had six stores, the Leeds society ten and the larger of Stockport's societies five (*Co-operator* February 1861, April 1861, August 1861). The opening of branches became increasingly common during the later decades of the nineteenth century so that nearly one-third of all co-operatives in England and Wales had two or more outlets by 1900. The 1,171 societies about which details are available operated 3,491 stores. Among these were 68 co-operatives with ten or more branches, the chief being Leeds with its 80 stores (Co-operative Union, 1900). Investment was not confined to the provision of shop premises; larger societies constructed their own warehousing, stables, butchering facilities, milk depots, bakeries and tailoring workshops (Wilson 1908, Appendix, Section 2). These last reflected the processing and productive activities carried on by co-operatives to stock their stores. By 1901 over half of societies reported some significant productive activity ancillary to their retailing (BPP, 1902, XCVI, pp.246–9, 290–1).

The increasing scale and complexity of co-operative retailing required a growing sophistication in operating methods. The initial volunteer shopkeepers were replaced by an increasingly professional staff. This reflected a separation between the role of the committee elected from among the membership of consumers, and that of the paid employees. It was noted from Crewe that in running the store during the 1850s 'nothing was too rough or too dirty for members of the committee to do' (quoted in Chaloner, 1950, pp.253–4). However, such direct involvement soon ended as the functions of the committee and its specific officers such as a society's president, secretary and treasurer became those of management. Although theoretically subject to the will of the membership as a whole, the committee had considerable powers to shape policy on such matters as the conduct of trade, staffing, premises, investments and participation in wider co-operative ventures. Under such supervision the routine operation of stores was undertaken by paid managers and assistants. Initially employees were recruited from the private retail trade, but societies also trained their own workers, hoping to create a staff sympathetic towards co-operative principles. Some attempts were made to accord employees a special status by including them in the division of trading surpluses. However, this principle was not widely adopted; as late as 1913 only around 160 co-operatives, chiefly smaller southern societies, paid a bonus to their employees (BPP, 1914, LXXVI, pp.394–439).

The needs of co-operatives as employers reflected in part the varying scale of their operations. While the store at Budleigh Salterton in Devon recorded an annual expenditure for 1913 of only £7 in wages and salaries, the substantial St Cuthbert's society of Edinburgh paid out £157,854 (BPP 1914, LXXVI, pp.426–7, 430–1). For all but the smallest societies the organisation of their employees reflected the departmental and branch structures of growing co-operatives, and a division of labour between those processing, selling and distributing stock, and those responsible for financial operations. Thus by 1878 the General Manager of the Blaydon co-operative in County Durham was responsible for a staff that included separate departmental managers for drapery, butchery, provisions, grocery, shoes, hardware and tailoring in the society's central store, managers working at the several branch stores, countermen and salesmen, milliners, shoemakers and butchers, warehousemen and cartmen, clerks and cashiers (Durham Record Office, D/Co/B1 2). The distinction between sales assistants serving customers with goods, and cashiers dealing with financial transactions, was widely adopted, and was perhaps especially appropriate to co-operation where all sales had to be attributed to individual consumers to allow calculation of entitlement to dividend. Certainly the centralisation of cash and dividend check systems was advocated by the Co-operative Union when advising local societies. Thus the *Co-operative Managers' Text Book* of 1908 details various means of handling cash and recording transactions. Indeed this text as a whole reflects a desire to promote efficiency in co-operative trading with chapters covering the workings of individual retail departments and other matters such as insurance, purchasing of stock, leakage, depreciation, stocktaking and the increasing body of legislation which regulated retailing (Wilson, 1908).

Table 7.1 Co-operative retail societies: size distribution by membership, 1862 and 1901

England and Wales 1862

Membership total	No. of societies (% of total)	No. of members (% of total)
0–99	46.8	10.6
100–199	25.2	14.8
200–299	9.6	9.6
300–499	7.7	11.8
500–999	7.5	21.6
1000–2999	2.3	15.6
3000–6999	1.0	15.9
7000–13999	–	–
>14000	–	–

England and Wales/Britain 1901

Membership total	No. of societies (% of total)		No. of members (% of total)	
	E & W	GB	E & W	GB
0–99	13.8	12.9	0.6	0.6
100–199	16.4	16.3	1.9	2.0
200–299	12.1	13.2	2.4	2.7
300–499	15.7	15.6	4.9	5.1
500–999	16.7	17.0	9.2	10.0
1000–2999	15.9	16.2	21.4	22.2
3000–6999	5.7	5.5	21.2	21.6
7000–13999	2.6	2.2	20.0	18.3
>14000	1.1	1.0	18.3	17.4

Sources: BPP, 1863, XXIX, Reports of the Chief Registrar of Friendly Societies for the year ending 31st December 1862, Industrial and provident societies; BPP, 1902, XCVI, Reports of the Chief Registrar of Friendly Societies for the year ending 31st December 1901, Industrial and provident societies

The various facets of co-operative extension were encapsulated in the growing national totals for membership and financial transactions, and in the changing size distribution of societies. By the turn of the century co-operatives were typically much more substantial operations than they had been even 40 years earlier (Table 7.1). Although small societies with under 200 members remained relatively common (in absolute terms they were more numerous in 1901 than 1862), the intimate personal sense of local community which they sustained was increasingly unlikely to be the experience of the average co-operator. By 1901 less than three per cent of British membership was accounted for by these smallest societies. Most now belonged to societies with thousands of members; indeed the 30 largest societies, each with a membership of more than 10,000, accounted for over 26 per cent of total membership (BPP, 1902, XCVI, pp.144–223, 266–85). By 1913 there were 61 such societies, representing nearly 40% of all co-operators (BPP, 1914, LXXVI, pp.394–439). Societies also grew financially, with the largest co-operatives establishing themselves as considerable commercial undertakings.

For the year 1913 the Leeds and Barnsley co-operatives both reported sales of over £1 million, but the largest turnover in Britain was the £1.7 million of the St Cuthbert's society of Edinburgh. Business of over half a million pounds was recorded by 16 societies, chiefly in northern England but also including Glasgow St George's, Derby, Plymouth, Stratford (London) and Woolwich Royal Arsenal. A further 59 societies each reported sales of between a quarter and half a million pounds. The assets of such societies were also substantial. Totals recorded for the combined value of stock in trade, buildings, fixtures and land, investments and other assets were over £100,000; Leeds, Bolton and Edinburgh St Cuthbert's had assets of over £1 million. These were, of course, the very largest elements of a size distribution of co-operatives that still extended down to the five smallest operations with annual sales valued in tens of pounds and with almost no fixed capital. During 1913 over 30 per cent of societies had sales of less than £10,000 and a further 20 per cent fell in the range £10,000–24,999 (BPP, 1914, LXXVI, pp.394–439).

Successful co-operatives offered testament to the power of collective effort, building from modest beginnings. One such was the Leigh society; claimed to have been initiated on a subscription of 37 shillings in 1857, it had annual sales of £498,544 and assets valued at £241,154 in 1913 (BPP, 1914, LXXVI, pp.398–9; Boydell, 1907, p.92). Indeed, within a few decades, societies could pass from an initial scarcity of capital to an almost embarrassing abundance. Some efforts were made to reduce capital surpluses by lowering the traditionally generous rates of return paid to shareholders, or by restricting the accumulation of holdings by individuals. Financial success founded upon retailing led many societies to expand into other activities, usually as a positive move to extend their services to their members, but sometimes driven as much by a desire to utilise capital otherwise surplus to requirements. Some societies invested money outside the co-operative sphere; one option was the purchase of railway shares, ostensibly in the hope of gaining the influence to ensure a better service from the companies concerned. But it was more common to devote money to co-operative provision in education, welfare and housing for particular localities. The broader co-operative vision of working-class self-improvement placed considerable stress on the value of education. An increasing number of societies made some concrete provision in this field; although sometimes encountering resistance from dividend-hungry members. Co-operatives provided libraries and reading rooms; they also sponsored classes for both juveniles and adults in academic and technical subjects, and in the principles of co-operation. In 1884 268 societies, among the 1,234 for which data are available, allocated a total of £19,030 to education. By 1901 624 societies, from a total of 1,549, were spending £67,354 (BPP, 1884–5, LXXII, pp.420–3, 450–1; 1902, XCVI, pp.246–9, 290–1). Many societies also devoted rather smaller sums to the support of charitable institutions, often in the form of subscriptions to local hospitals which would have yielded the return of entitlement to treatment for nominated members (Co-operative Wholesale Society, 1884, pp.78–91). A request for information on co-operative housing circulated by the CWS in 1884 prompted positive replies from 96 societies which had devoted a total of £685,000 to building houses themselves or advancing funds to their members to allow them to buy or build (Co-operative Wholesale Society, 1885, pp.134–41).

The CWS was itself funded initially by local retail societies as shareholders. Established in England in 1863 and followed by a Scottish counterpart in 1867, the CWS was a response to the desire to extend co-operative principles to the wider sphere of wholesaling and ultimately manufacturing, and to more immediately practical imperatives that followed from fears of discrimination against co-operatives by some private suppliers. The wholesale societies never became exclusive suppliers to local retail societies; such a suggestion of centralised control of stocking and conduct of trade would have been firmly resisted. Certainly during the 1870s and 1880s many retail co-operatives continued to deal with a range of suppliers in addition to the CWS: millers, wholesale grocers and provision dealers in their own immediate vicinity, sugar refiners on Clydeside and Merseyside, metropolitan tea and coffee dealers, and manufacturers such as Reckitt's, Keiller's and Colman's. Some maintained contracts with several different suppliers of the same item, switching between them in an effort to get the best deal. However, the wholesale societies themselves achieved substantial expansion. The CWS, initially supplying only 54 societies, chiefly clustered in the vicinity of its base in Manchester, could claim to be one of the largest trading and manufacturing operations in late Victorian Britain. By 1913 its plant included a network of distributive premises in major English centres, factories producing textiles, clothing, footwear, furniture and foodstuffs, and purchasing depots for provisions in Europe, North America and Australia (Co-operative Wholesale Society, 1901, pp.5–10; Redfern, 1938, p.538). Consumers from 1,168 member societies generated an annual turnover of £31.37 million and further sales of £8.97 million were reported by the parallel Scottish CWS (BPP, 1914, LXXVI, p.458).

7.6 Conclusion

Judged only in material terms there was clearly more to co-operation than retailing alone; activity extended to spheres such as wholesaling, production, housing and education. The ideological horizons of co-operation – if not of all co-operators – also stretched far beyond storekeeping; there was a continuity of belief in the redeeming power of collective effort to transform a corrupt and competitive world into a more equitable co-operative commonwealth. Such an ethos seems far removed from the world of some private shopkeepers whose political vision was reflected more in the 'cheap government' philosophy of numerous Victorian municipalities (Hennock, 1973). But, as this chapter demonstrates, the practical focus of British co-operation was in retailing; it was principally as storekeepers that co-operatives were judged worthy of popular support. From storekeeping came the means to extend co-operation into other spheres, and through storekeeping co-operatives made their most significant contribution to the wider economic expansion of Britain in the years up to 1914.

Co-operatives enjoyed mixed fortunes; of all known societies only a minority were successful or even enduring. But throughout the contemporaneous private retail sector there was also continual turnover of establishment and failure of individual businesses. Co-operatives were not the only stores to encounter difficulties in penetrating competitive local markets, and the commercial circumstances of many societies were further complicated by association during the first half of the nineteenth century with the variable fortunes of Owenite Socialism and Chartism. But those societies which took root were often very successful, establishing co-operation as a retail force of steadily increasing significance from the mid-nineteenth century onwards. Some individual societies grew to be among the largest of all retailers; many more were of modest absolute size but of considerable significance as a major retail outlet for their own particular locality.

Co-operative development also testifies to the perseverance with which its supporters pursued their goal of establishing a successful store. In many localities an initial failure was eventually followed by the successful reintroduction of co-operation. Thus by the Edwardian period co-operation was expanding in areas which had previously proved resistant: the smaller towns of southern England, the remoter rural areas of Wales and Scotland, and, most substantially, through concentrated effort, in London, Liverpool and Birmingham. Such persistence itself suggests the appeal of co-operation: the principles of mutuality and the practical benefits that accrued to consumer members. Dividends, fair prices, full weight, and freedom from adulteration were important co-operative contributions to the lives of contemporaries, as well as to any retrospective survey of the evolution of British retailing. Appreciation of the practical benefits was part of a larger pride in the collective achievement of ordinary people. Enthusiasm for co-operation was reflected in the celebratory grandeur of the architecture of the larger stores and in the society histories produced in their hundreds to commemorate significant anniversaries.

References

Age Exchange Theatre Company, 1983, *Of Whole Heart Cometh Hope. Centenary Memories of the Co-operative Women's Guild*, London
Angus, R.N.S., 1979, The co-operative movement in Oldham, 1850–1900, unpublished MA dissertation, University of Lancaster
Ashplant, T.G., 1981, London working men's clubs, 1875–1914, in E. Yeo and S. Yeo (eds.), *Popular Culture and Class Conflict 1890–1914: Explorations in the History of Labour and Leisure*, Harvester Press, Brighton, pp.241–70
Backstrom, P.N., 1974, *Christian Socialism and Co-operation in Victorian England:*

Edward Vansittart Neale and the Co-operative Movement, Croom Helm, London
Baernreither, J.M., 1889, *English Associations of Working Men*, Swan Sonnenschein, London
Banbury Co-operative Record, June 1872
Benson, J., 1983, *The Penny Capitalists: A Study of Nineteenth Century Working-class Entrepreneurs*, Gill and Macmillan, Dublin
Bishopsgate Institute Library, Edmonton Co-operative Society, Minute Book, 1888–91
Blackman, J., 1967, The development of the retail grocery trade in the nineteenth century, *Business History*, 9 (2): 110–17
Bonner, A., 1970, *British Co-operation*, Co-operative Union, Manchester
Boydell, T., 1907, *Jubilee History of the Leigh Friendly Co-operative Society Ltd. 1857–1907*, Co-operative Union, Manchester
Briggs, A. (ed.), 1959, *Chartist Studies*, Macmillan, London
BPP, 1867–8, Return of the general statement of the funds and effects of the co-operative societies in Scotland for the year ending 31st December 1866, XL, 755–8; 1059–62
BPP, 1871, Royal commission on the truck system, XXXVI, 1–1196
BPP, 1872, Return giving particulars relating to industrial and co-operative societies in Scotland 1871, LIV, 388–96
BPP, 1878–9, Report of the select committee on co-operative stores, IX, 1–431
BPP, 1884–5, Reports of the Chief Registrar of Friendly Societies for the year ending 31st December 1884, Part B, Appendix G Industrial and provident societies, LXXII, 331–453
BPP, 1886, Second report of the royal commission appointed to inquire into the depression of trade and industry, Appendix II, XXII, 1–428
BPP, 1886, Reports by Her Majesty's representatives abroad, on the system of co-operation in foreign countries, LXVII, 429–570
BPP, 1887, Special report from the select committee on the butter substitutes bill, IX, 1–184
BPP, 1887, Minutes of evidence taken before the select committee on town holdings, XIII, 53–1009
BPP, 1893–94, Fourth report of the royal commission on labour, XXXIX Part 1, 1–1178
BPP, 1898, Fifth annual abstract of labour statistics of the United Kingdom, LXXXVIII, 695–920
BPP, 1902, Reports of the Chief Registrar of Friendly Societies for the year ending 31st December 1901, Part B, Appendix (L) Industrial and provident societies, XCVI, 139–352
BPP, 1903, Report on wholesale and retail prices in the United Kingdom in 1902, LXVIII, 1–512
BPP, 1914, Reports of the Chief Registrar of Friendly Societies for the year ending 31st December 1913. Part B Industrial and provident societies, LXXVI, 293–622
Brown, W.H., 1919, *A Century of Co-operation at Sheerness*, Co-operative Union, Manchester
Burnett, J., 1966, *Plenty and Want: A Social History of Diet in England from 1815 to the Present Day*, Nelson, London
Calderdale District Archives, TU 57/3, Ripponden Co-operative Society, stocklist 1839
Chaloner, W.H., 1950, *The Social and Economic Development of Crewe 1780–1923*, Manchester University Press
Christian Socialist, 8 November 1851
Clarke, J., Critcher, C. and Johnson, R. (eds.), 1979, *Working Class Culture: Studies in History and Theory*, Hutchinson, London
Cole, G.D.H., 1944, *A Century of Co-operation*, Co-operative Union, Manchester
Co-operative News, 10 April 1875, 23 October 1875, 12 June 1880, 16 October 1880, 6 November 1880, 20 November 1880
Co-operative Union, 1876, *Proceedings of the Annual Congress*, Co-operative Union, Manchester

Co-operative Union, 1879, *Proceedings of the Annual Congress*, Co-operative Union, Manchester
Co-operative Union, 1880, *Proceedings of the Annual Congress*, Co-operative Union, Manchester
Co-operative Union, 1887, *Co-operative Directory*, Co-operative Union, Manchester
Co-operative Union, 1888, *Proceedings of the Annual Congress*, Co-operative Union, Manchester
Co-operative Union, 1890, *Proceedings of the Annual Congress*, Co-operative Union, Manchester
Co-operative Union, 1891, *Proceedings of the Annual Congress*, Co-operative Union, Manchester
Co-operative Union, 1894, *Proceedings of the Annual Congress*, Co-operative Union, Manchester
Co-operative Union, 1895, *Proceedings of the Annual Congress*, Co-operative Union, Manchester
Co-operative Union, 1896, *Proceedings of the Annual Congress*, Co-operative Union, Manchester
Co-operative Union, 1900, *Co-operative Directory*, Co-operative Union, Manchester
Co-operative Union, 1901, *Congress Handbook*, Co-operative Union, Manchester
Co-operative Wholesale Society, 1884, *CWS Annual*, Co-operative Wholesale Society, Manchester
Co-operative Wholesale Society, 1885, *CWS Annual*, Co-operative Wholesale Society, Manchester
Co-operative Wholesale Society, 1901, *CWS Annual*, Co-operative Wholesale Society, Manchester
The (Brighton) Co-operator, October 1828
The Co-operator, February 1861, April 1861, August 1861, October 1962, December 1864, 15 January 1866, 15 January 1867, 4 June 1870
The Crisis, 27 October 1832
Crossick, G.J., 1978, *An Artisan Elite in Victorian Society: Kentish London, 1840–1880*, Croom Helm, London
Crossley, A. (ed.), 1972, *A History of the County of Oxford*, Volume X Banbury Hundred, Oxford University Press
Darvill, P.A., 1954, The contribution of co-operative retail societies to welfare within the social framework of the north-east coast area, unpublished M.Litt thesis, University of Durham
Durham Record Office, D/Co/BA 1, Bishop Auckland Co-operative Society, minute book, 1860–67
Durham Record Office, D/Co/Bl 2, Blaydon Co-operative Society, minute book, 1876–78
Durham Record Office, D/Co/Da 1, Darlington Co-operative Society, minute book, 1868–69
Durham Record Office, D/Co/Da 10, Darlington Co-operative Society, minute book, 1891–95
Durham Record Office, D/Co/Da 117, Darlington Co-operative Society, publicity announcement, 1885
Durham Record Office, D/Co/JH 1, Jarrow Co-operative Society, minute book, 1868–72
Gaffin, J. and Thoms, D., 1983, *Caring and Sharing: The Centenary History of the Co-operative Women's Guild*, Co-operative Union, Manchester
Garnett, R.J., 1972, *Co-operation and the Owenite Socialist Communities in Britain, 1825–45*, Manchester University Press
Gosden, P.H.J.H., 1961, *The Friendly Societies in England, 1815–1875*, Manchester University Press

Gosden, P.H.J.H., 1973, *Self-help: Voluntary Associations in the Nineteenth Century*, Batsford, London

Harrison, B.H. and Hollis, P. (eds.), 1979, *Robert Lowery, Radical and Chartist*, Europa, London

Harrison, J.F.C., 1969, *Robert Owen and the Owenites in Britain and America*, Routledge and Kegan Paul, London

Hennock, E.P., 1973, *Fit and Proper Persons: Ideal and Reality in Nineteenth Century Urban Government*, Arnold, London

Hollis, P., 1970, *The Pauper Press: A Study in Working Class Radicalism of the 1830s*, Oxford University Press

Holyoake, G.J., 1858, *Self-help by the People: History of Co-operation in Rochdale*, Holyoake, London

Hood, J. and Yarney, B.S., 1957, The middle-class co-operative retailing societies in London, 1864–1900, *Oxford Economic Papers* NS 9 (3): 309–22

Jefferys, J.B., 1954, *Retail Trading in Britain, 1850–1950*, Cambridge University Press

Jones, B., 1894, *Co-operative Production*, Clarendon Press, Oxford

Jones, D., 1975, *Chartism and the Chartists*, Lane, London

Journal of Association, 28 June 1852

Joyce, P., 1980, *Work, Society and Politics: The Culture of the Factory in Later Victorian Britain*, Harvester Press, Brighton

Kirk, N., 1985, *The Growth of Working Class Reformism in Mid-Victorian England*, Croom Helm, London

Kropotkin, P., 1902, *Mutual Aid: A Factor of Evolution*, Heinemann, London

Lancashire Co-operator, 25 June 1831, 6 August 1831

Lancashire and Yorkshire Co-operator, September 1832

Mathias, P., 1967, *Retailing Revolution: A History of Multiple Retailing in the Food Trades Based upon the Allied Suppliers Group of Companies*, Longman, London

Maxwell, W., 1910, *A History of Co-operation in Scotland: Its Inception and its Leaders*, Co-operative Union, Glasgow

Mercer, T.W., 1947, *Co-operation's Prophet: The Life and Letters of Dr William King of Brighton*, Co-operative Union, Manchester

Northamptonshire Record Office, SL 396, Long Buckby Co-operative Society, minute book, 1863–73

Padberg, D.I., and Thorpe, D., 1974, Channels of grocery distribution: changing stages in evolution – a comparison of USA and UK, *Journal of Agricultural Economics*, 25: 1–22

Peoples, F.W., 1909, *History of the Great and Little Bolton Co-operative Society Ltd: Showing Fifty Years Progress*, Co-operative Union, Manchester

Pollard, S., 1960, Nineteenth century co-operation: from community building to shopkeeping, in A. Briggs and J. Saville (eds.), *Essays in Labour History*, Macmillan, London, Vol. 1, pp.74–112

Purvis, M., 1986a, Popular institutions, in J. Langton and R.J. Morris (eds.), *An Atlas of Industrializing Britain 1780–1914*, Methuen, London, pp.194–7

Purvis, M., 1986b, Co-operative retailing in England, 1835–1850: developments beyond Rochdale, *Northern History*, 22: 198–215

Purvis, M., 1987, Nineteenth century co-operative retailing in England and Wales: a geographical approach, unpublished D. Phil. thesis, University of Oxford

Purvis, M., 1990, The development of co-operative retailing in England and Wales, 1851–1901: a geographical study, *Journal of Historical Geography*, 16 (3): 314–31

Raven, C.E., 1920, *Christian Socialism 1848–1854*, Macmillan, London

Redfern, P., 1913, *The Story of the CWS, 1863–1913*, Co-operative Wholesale Society, Manchester

Redfern, P., 1938, *The New History of the CWS*, Dent, London

Rowntree, B.S., 1902, *Poverty. A Study of Town Life*, Macmillan, London

Scola, R., 1975, Food markets and shops in Manchester 1770–1870, *Journal of Historical Geography*, 1 (2): 153–68

Shaw, G., 1982, The role of retailing in the urban economy, in J.H. Johnson and C.G. Pooley (eds.), *The Structure of Nineteenth Century Cities*, Croom Helm, London, pp.171–94

Smith, J. and Walton, J.K., 1985, Property, employment and the co-operative movement: the social structure of co-operation in Sabden, 1923, *Transactions of the Historical Society of Lancashire and Cheshire*, 134: 129–49

Stedman Jones, G., 1971, *Outcast London: A Study in the Relationship Between the Classes in Victorian Society*, Oxford University Press

Stevenson, J., 1974, Food riots in England, 1792–1818, in R. Quinault and J. Stevenson (eds.), *Popular Protest and Public Order: Six Studies in British History 1780–1920*, Allen and Unwin, London, pp.33–74

Tann, J., 1980, Co-operative corn milling: self-help during the grain crises of the Napoleonic wars, *Agricultural History Review*, 28: 45–57

Thompson, D., 1984, *The Chartists*, Temple Smith, London

Thompson, E.P., 1971, The moral economy of the English crowd in the eighteenth century, *Past and Present*, 50, 76–136

Waller, R.J., 1983, *The Dukeries Transformed: The Social and Political Development of a Twentieth Century Coalfield*, Clarendon Press, Oxford

Webb, B. and Webb, S., 1921, *The Consumers' Co-operative Movement*, Longmans Green, London

Welbourne, E., 1923, *The Miners' Unions of Northumberland and Durham*, Cambridge University Press

West Durham and South Northumberland Co-operative District Record, March 1891

Wild, M.T. and Shaw, G., 1979, Trends in urban retailing: the British experience during the nineteenth century, *Tijdschrift voor Economische en Sociale Geografie*, 70 (1): 35–44

Wilkinson, H.B., 1886, *Is Co-operation Beneficial to the Community?*, Heywood, Manchester

Wilson, R.J. (ed.), 1908, *The Co-operative Managers' Text Book*, Co-operative Union, Manchester

Winstanley, M.J., 1983, *The Shopkeeper's World 1830–1914*, Manchester University Press

Yeo, S., 1986, Socialism, the state, and some oppositional Englishness, in R. Colls and P. Dodd (eds.), *Englishness: Politics and Culture 1880–1920*, Croom Helm, London, pp.308–69

Chapter 8
The evolution and impact of large-scale retailing in Britain
Gareth Shaw

8.1 The historiography of large retail firms

The growth of large-scale retail organisations in Britain has been charted by a number of publications, ranging from those focussing on individual firms through to more generalised accounts. In terms of the latter the most influential has been the work of Jefferys (1954) which details the growth of multiple shop retailing, as well as commenting on department stores and consumer co-operatives. What Jefferys (1954, p.6) attempts to describe is the 'revolution of the distributive trades', a theme taken up by Mathias (1967) in the title of his book, *Retailing Revolution*. This tells the history of multiple retailing in the food sector through the experiences of the Allied Suppliers Group of Companies, though in essence the work is far more than a mere company history.

Significantly, both authors had access to company files and records either directly or indirectly. In Jefferys' (1954, p.444) case his work was based around a complete search of all the reference books and directories available, together with interviews of all multiple retail organisations with 20 or more branch shops, and postal questionnaire surveys from a sample of firms with between three and nineteen shops. In total he traced the records of some 1,132 firms with ten or more shops, the details of which provided much of the statistical information in his book. Given this background it is not surprising that Jefferys' book has acted as a primary reference point for others researching the growth of multiple retaililng. Thus, Fraser (1981, pp.116–17) in his examination of retail development was content to use all of Jefferys' estimates of multiple-shop firms, without attempting to collect any new information.

The substantive data base provided by Jefferys for multiple retailers is unfortunately lacking in the study of department stores and mail-order retailing. For these retail organisations, and particularly department stores, publications are more numerous but also rather narrowly based. The historiography of British department stores is somewhat dominated by individual firm histories, only briefly punctuated by more generalised perspectives. Lambert (1938) has told the story of Whiteley's store in London, Briggs (1956) covers the history of Lewis's; while in less academic formats Pound (1960) has examined the development of Selfridges, and Corina (1978) gives a historical view of Debenhams. These store biographies do not, as Samson (1981) has argued in an American context, make a well-rounded view of the historical development of department stores. Indeed, of these individual histories only Hower's (1943) study of Macy's in New York attempts a discussion of the general conditions surrounding the growth of these large stores.

In contrast to the fairly numerous biographies of department store organisations, only a handful of which have been referred to here, general approaches are more scarce. Pasdermadjian's (1954, p.viii) early work places department store evolution in a collective and international context, and claims to be 'based on one main approach, the historical approach'. Unfortunately, most historical details are based on experiences in France and the USA, with only patchy information on Britain. The only other general international perspective, written by Ferry (1960), suffers even more from a lack of any historical framework and often degenerates into a fragmented collection of somewhat limited store histories. The one co-ordinated study of British department stores is that by Adburgham (1981) which, despite its rather anecdotal style, gives an evolutionary perspective of fashionable retailing and the rise of department stores in London.

The final element of large-scale retailing is that of mail order, the historiography of which has not been researched in Britain. Pasdermadjian argues that mail-order selling evolved in very different ways in North America and Europe. In the former, large mail-order companies such as Sears, Roebuck and Montgomery Ward focussed on the expanding agricultural market west of the Mississippi during the years after 1870. The close relationship between the needs of the growing farm community and the rise of Sears, Roebuck has been discussed in considerable detail by Emmet and Jeuck (1950). In their words it is 'important in following the rise of mail-order selling to note the role of agrarian discontent, for it was this dissatisfaction – almost universally articulated in terms of middlemen's abuses – that did much to lead to accepting the intrusion of a new institution' (Emmet and Jeuck, 1950, p.18). In Britain the evolutionary pathway for mail-order retailing was closely bound with the growth of department stores, some of which according to Pasdermadjian (1954, p.32) 'made up to 25% of their sales through this means'. Detailed evidence of this is unfortunately missing and the most one finds are limited comments in department store biographies. Briggs (1956, p.130), for example, claims 'it was through their velveteen department that Lewis's built up the enormous mail-order section of their industry'. The only measure of its size is given for 1913 when Lewis's issued 50,000 copies of their mail-order catalogue and 'so many orders were received that stocks were exhausted' (Briggs, 1956, pp.112–13). In a similar way Adburgham (1981, p.233) states that in 1888 'Marshall and Snelgrove received about 1,000 letters daily' in their mail-order section. Given this close relationship, therefore, between mail-order selling and department stores in Britain, this chapter will discuss the two developments together. It will also focus on four key, interrelated issues in the historiography of large-scale retailing, namely: origins, evolution, growth trends and impact.

8.2 Origins and evolutionary pathways of large-scale retailing

Most publications on the origin and development of large-scale retail institutions have discussed the rise of multiple shops and department stores as quite different events. Very often the only common link perceived by commentators was the supposedly revolutionary nature of their development and the surrounding factors. On closer inspection, however, both these premises give a somewhat distorted picture of the origins and evolution of large retail firms. Thus, while it is true that department stores grew in different ways, both economically and geographically, from multiple retailers, there were also some strong common elements. Equally, while the growth of these retail forms in significant numbers did constitute something of a revolution in the distributive trades during the last quarter of the nineteenth century, both had much earlier origins.

Attempts by retailers to increase the size and scale of their operations during the nineteenth century followed two pathways. One way was to increase shop size and, more importantly, to widen the range of products sold, in the hope that more customers would be attracted. The other was to open additional shops in new areas. Jefferys (1954, p.32) considered these two pathways as quite separate strategies with the first 'followed by the drapers, mercers, furnishers and some food retailers'; while the second was followed by shops selling food, footwear and convenience goods. In reality the divisions were never clear-cut, in the sense that some department stores attempted to increase their number of shops and adopt strategies used by multiple retail organisations. Moreover, both forms of growth tended to share common business methods such as standardised work practices, central buying, cash sales, and sometimes control over product production. Very often it was the ability to adopt and operate such methods which controlled the pace of growth in different sectors as well as characterising the 'revolutionary' developments of the late nineteenth century. Indeed during the 1830s there is strong evidence that many progressive retailers and wholesalers, especially in drapery, had improved their performance by reducing the period for which credit was available. When questioned before a government committee on the improved performance of retailing one wholesaler was clear 'that the limitation of credit given by the retail trade [was] one part of the improved system of business' (BPP, 1833, Q 1389). Wholesalers appeared to have started the trend by reducing credit to retailers from 6–9 months to 3–4 months. This in turn led to more retailers introducing cash payments and 'ticketing', in other words the clear pricing of goods, particularly for those who sought customers 'among the lower and middling classes of people' (Select Committee, 1833, Q 1438). A consequence of these changes was that drapery wholesalers and retailers were 'turning stocks round oftener', while retailers were also 'holding less stocks', thereby freeing some of their working capital for store expansion (Select Committee, 1833, Q 1449 and Q 1365).

Within the limited debate on the origins and evolution of department stores much emphasis has been placed on when and where the first department store was created. Pasdermadjian (1954) supports the case of the Bon Marché in Paris, while Resseguie (1962) and Hower (1943) push the claims of North American stores, such as Stewart's Marble Palace and Macy's in New York. Such an argument is however rather futile since definitions vary and, more importantly, it tends to deflect research away from more promising themes.

In Britain there is evidence of large shops, or 'monster shops' as they were then known, as early as the 1820s in London and other large cities. As Alexander (1970, p.107) points out, most of these 'monster shops' were confined to the drapery trades, and one such London-based store was employing between 20 and 30 people by 1821. Evidence from government select committees points to an increasing concentration in large establishments, and shows that in Manchester in 1839 some shops had sales of over £1 million per year. The two most noted 'monster shops' were probably Shoolbreds of Tottenham Court Road, London, established in 1820, and Campbells of Glasgow. By the mid-nineteenth century both of these had annual turnovers of well over £1 million, with Shoolbreds employing 500 people, while Campbells had a workforce of about 300 (Alexander, 1970, pp.107–8). Shoolbreds also illustrates an early link between large-scale retailing and manufacturing during the 1850s, when James Shoolbred had a partnership with Henry Jecks Dixon, a carpet manufacturer in Kidderminster. The store not only provided some much needed capital for Dixon's expansion schemes before the partnership was dissolved in 1859 but also a ready outlet for the products (Bartlett, 1978, p.25).

These 'monster' shops of the early and mid-nineteenth century operated on the system of fixed prices, cash sales and a high volume of stock turnover. Such methods enabled them to offer lower prices, a policy very much directed at the lower middle classes and to people who attached importance to price differences. The growth of shop size was achieved almost exclusively through the process of buying up and amalgamating adjoining shop premises, a trend that was to continue throughout the nineteenth century.

A second, early origin of the department store is to be found in the development of so-called 'bazaars' during the late eighteenth and early nineteenth centuries. These were buildings managed by an individual who rented out counters to retailers. Many were aimed at the fashionable end of the trade such as the Royal London Bazaar in Liverpool Street where, in 1830, 'you may purchase any of the thousand and one varieties of fancy and useful articles' (Adburgham, 1981, p.18). The articles for sale would most probably have been millinery, lace and jewellery, sold from shop counters rented either monthly or quarterly. Such establishments afford two types of evolutionary links with department stores, one direct and the other more tentative through the general idea of collecting different goods under one roof. The firmer, direct link is provided by the Manchester department store of Kendal Milne, which originated as the Manchester Bazaar probably in about 1820. This sold fashionable items and insisted that the traders renting the counters put prices on all their goods (Adburgham, 1981). Some bazaars even survived into the late nineteenth century, as in the case of the Soho Bazaar on Oxford Street, London. The directory for 1880 shows that the Bazaar was advertising itself as a collection of 'trades of all kinds, both fancy and useful, under one roof' (*The Marylebone and St John's Wood Directory*, 1880, p.133). In all some 21 different businesses were listed as occupying stalls in the bazaar ranging from toys and books, through to millinery, jewellery, hardware, Chinese and Japanese goods.

While some retailers, especially within the drapery trades, sought scale economies through increasing the size of their shops, others expanded by adding more shops to their organisation. Evidence of multiple-shop developments is common during the early nineteenth century, although Alexander (1970, p.103) claims their share of trade was insignificant at this time. Most of these early multiple-shop organisations operated either in large cities or had an urban–rural dimension.

In the former, it was often a case of a retailer controlling two or three shops, one in the central shopping area and the others in more distant suburbs. From Alexander's information on Manchester and Liverpool it is possible to show that multiple-shop retailers increased from 16 to 127 in Liverpool, and 15 to 88 in Manchester between 1822 and 1851. In relative terms, however, such figures do not represent any increase, as the proportion of multiples in the two cities averaged 1.7 per cent of all retailers in 1822 and only 1.6 per cent by 1851. Clearly then, from this evidence, multiples were not making rapid progress in large cities before 1850, but merely keeping pace with retail expansion. Most of these small multiple retail firms were based within the grocery and provision trades and bakers, trades in which close proximity to consumers was important and where it was therefore worthwhile to open additional shops in new suburbs.

Evidence of multiple retailers operating in more than one city is extremely limited during the early nineteenth century and is confined to a few specialist, fashionable shops based in London who operated branches in spa towns. Rather more common was the case where food retailers based in market centres would open additional shops in surrounding villages. Those few larger firms that did attempt to develop outlets in a number of widely dispersed settlements at a national level very often failed, hampered in the main by slow and difficult transport. In this sense, the retail revolution ascribed to the growth of large-scale multiple retailers by Jefferys did have to wait until more favourable conditions arrived after 1850.

Retailing, like other aspects of economic change associated with industrialisation, exhibited change at different rates during the early nineteenth century. Large shops had arrived; these employed sizeable workforces and pioneered the ideas of fixed prices, standardised conditions of sale and central buying. Such developments were common, if not widespread, in major cities and focussed on the drapery trades since these benefited from factory production techniques found in the textile industries. As Alexander and Jefferys both show, in these different ways, the drapery sector was freed from processing problems and retailers could devote most of their energies to developing techniques of selling. In contrast, other parts of the retail system had yet to experience the impact of factory production technique. Consequently, food retailers especially could not transform their distribution methods fully. Attempts to develop large-scale multiples were hindered further by inadequate transport networks, limiting the ideas and benefits of multiple trading to intra-urban environments.

8.3 The growth of department stores

Jefferys (1954, p.19) stated that, 'in the middle of the nineteenth century it is fairly certain that no department store as defined in the modern sense existed in Great Britain'. His definition was of a large store with four or more departments selling different classes of goods, including women's and children's wear, although he also recognised so-called part department stores. In contrast to this view Adburgham (1981) shows how Kendal Milne (1836) of Manchester, Bainbridge (1841) of

Newcastle and Shoolbreds of London all fulfilled this definition by 1850. There was therefore a small, but significant, group of early department stores in Britain that arose before 1850 that were innovators even when compared with the more numerous 'monster shops'. Such stores do not however detract from the fact that during the period after 1860 the idea of the department store grew rapidly.

Unfortunately, the fragmented nature of department store records makes it impossible to give any meaningful figures as to the scale of growth at a national level. As a consequence we have considerable detail on the growth of individual stores but very little on common trends and patterns. Existing evidence suggests that two main phases of growth can be identified. The first we can term 'evolutionary', since it encompasses those stores that had early origins and evolved into full department stores over a longish period (Table 8.1). The second phase may be termed 'revolutionary' as it covers the fairly rapid growth of firms that from their foundations planned to operate as department stores. Table 8.1 gives an idea of the relative scale of these two phases, although it should be viewed with some caution because of its inadequate data base. In addition, the terms 'evolutionary' and 'revolutionary' are used in a relative context, since even in the second period some organisations took a considerable time to become full department stores.

Table 8.1 The growth phases of British department stores

'Evolutionary' phase (pre c.1860)

Debenhams (1778, London), Swan and Edgar (1812, London), Shoolbreds (1817, London), Peter Robinson (1833, London), Kendle Milne (1836, Manchester), Marshall and Wilson (Snelgrove 1848) (1837, London), Bainbridge (1838, Newcastle), Harrods (1849, London)

'Revolutionary' phase (post c.1860)

Whiteley (1863, London), Lewis's (1856, Liverpool – main expansion after 1860, e.g. Manchester, 1880; Sheffield, 1884; Birmingham, 1885), John Lewis (1864, London), Civil Service Supply Association Ltd. (1866, London), Peter Jones (1871, London), Army and Navy (1871, London), Bon Marché (1877, Brixton), Fenwicks (1882, Newcastle), Bobby's (1887, Margate, also Leamington Spa, 1904; Folkestone, 1906; Eastbourne, 1910; Torquay, 1913), Bourne and Hollingsworth (1894, London), Selfridges (1909, London)

Source: based on information in Adburgham, 1981; Jefferys, 1954; and Ferry, 1960

A more detailed and accurate picture of department store growth can only be gained by focussing on specific areas, where it is possible to collect adequate information. This can be done for London, where sufficient studies have already been undertaken on department stores, and from recent research on part of the West Midlands. These two perspectives will also provide a contrast between changes in London and those in provincial centres.

Shaw and Wild (1979) have already commented on the evolutionary pattern of department stores in London's West End. This shows how the ultimate aim of many of the early stores was to obtain an 'island' site or complete street block, by buying-up and moving into adjoining buildings. For example, the significant expansion of

Peter Robinson's West End store started in 1854 when two adjoining shops were acquired; further growth occurred in 1856 and 1858 when two other adjoining shops were taken over. The process was finally completed in 1860 when a further shop was purchased giving Robinson's a complete block of six shops (Adburgham, 1981, p.142). Other stores were taking a more radical line and rebuilding their sites completely, as in the case of Marshall and Snelgrove who extended their seven adjoining shops along Oxford Street back to form an 'island' site in 1876. The building of Selfridges in 1909 represented a final phase of department store development in London, with the construction of a large, purpose-built store.

These changes produced a strong concentration of department stores in London's West End, and in particular transformed Oxford Street (Figure 8.1). The dispersion of department stores was also encouraged by street improvement schemes, such as the Kensington Improvement Scheme of 1867, which by 1870 had widened the road and added new shops. Three of these sites were occupied by the large stores of Pontings, Derry and Toms, and John Barker's three-storey shop. Despite this spatial expansion of department store trading, the pattern of their development within London remained constant. The majority of stores once established did not change their locations, a feature that contrasts strongly with the situation in New York. There, department stores moved frequently in a series of northward movements along the main streets of Manhattan Island (Figure 8.2). Ferry (1960) has shown how this locational instability was conditioned by the geography of New York and the changing centres of its population.

Large stores were common outside London before 1850, and so too were full department stores, after the mid-nineteenth century. The growth of large stores in

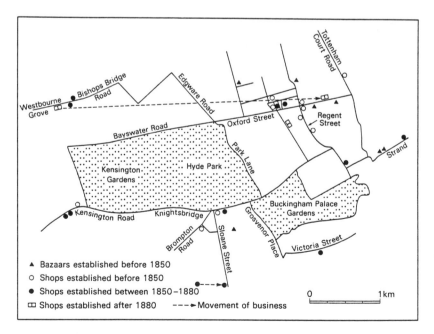

Figure 8.1 The evolution and distribution of department stores in London

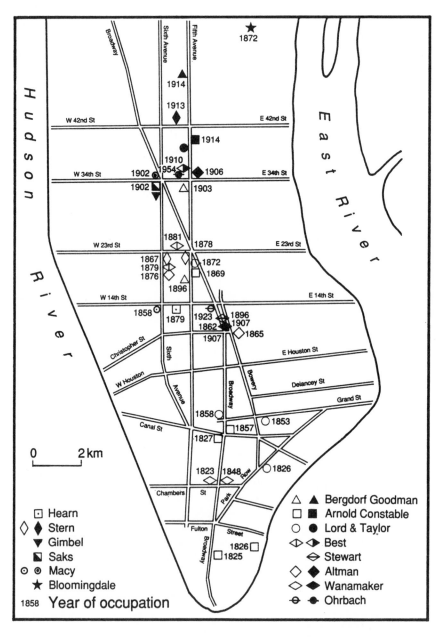

Figure 8.2 Patterns of department store evolution in New York (modified from Ferry, 1960) The first symbol for each store indicates its initial location, the second its final location

the provinces follows a similar pattern to that of London, often with only a slight time lag. In the Birmingham region for example, there were already some five department stores and eleven part department stores by the early 1870s. As Table 8.2 shows, their distribution within the regional settlement system was based to some extent on population levels and, in the case of Leamington, a large fashionable demand. By around 1910 the department store had pushed further down the settlement hierarchy and only the smallest centres had failed to attract such retailers (Table 8.2). As in London, the process of store enlargement was almost entirely through shop amalgamations, with the number of multi-fronted shops dealing in clothing increasing between 1870 and 1910 from 45 to 236 in Birmingham alone. Typical of such developments were businesses like Holiday and Lewis (later Holiday and Son Ltd) which was established in 1836 but by 1870 occupied numbers 25–30 New Street, Birmingham.

Table 8.2 Large-scale retailing and department stores in Birmingham and the West Midlands, c.1870–c.1910

Town	Multi-front shops[1]		Part department stores		Full department stores	
	c.1870	c.1910	c.1870	c.1910	c.1870	c.1910
Birmingham	45	236	4	9	2	8
Bridgnorth	–	1	–	–	–	–
Coventry	1	28	–	6	–	2
Kidderminster	3	9	2	–	–	1
Leamington	3	15	1	6	–	3
Lichfield	–	–	–	–	–	–
Nuneaton	2	6	1	1	–	–
Redditch	–	7	–	1	–	–
Stratford	1	6	1	2	–	–
Tamworth	–	1	–	–	–	–
Walsall	1	24	–	3	–	5
Wolverhampton	5	7	1	5	3	2
Worcester	1	17	1	4	–	4

[1] Multi-front shops refers to shops with more than one street address. Part and full department stores follows the definitions used by Jefferys (1954)

Source: directories and local newspapers

A more detailed example of this process of shop amalgamation is provided by that of Beatties in nearby Wolverhampton. In this case surviving records enable the growth of the store to be examined in detail between 1897 and 1909 (Figure 8.3 and Table 8.3). The firm initially acquired a freehold property on Victoria Street (Figure 8.3) for the cost of £4,750 in 1897. By 1900 the store expanded to adjoining land on Darlington Street purchasing the freehold of old offices at a cost of £1,050. At the end of 1902 further land and property were required as the store grew extremely rapidly. This time the demands were met by Beatties buying the freehold of four shops and warehouses along Victoria Street at a cost of £14,000. The final phase of

Figure 8.3 Shop amalgamation and site development: the evolution of Beatties, Wolverhampton

this pre-war expansion took place in the early part of 1903 when the freehold on two more properties along Victoria Street was purchased for £2,090. In the space of just six years the store had expanded from one shop front in 1897 to eight in 1903 at a total cost of £21,890 (Table 8.3). Unfortunately there are no figures of the shop's turnover in 1897, but by 1900 it was £44,000, and had grown to £70,000 by 1912, with a gross profit of £17,000. It would seem therefore that the store was investing considerably during this period in property and fixtures.

Table 8.3 The expansion and property acquisition of a provincial department store: Beatties, Wolverhampton, 1897–1903

Date	Details of property acquired	Cost (£)
1897	77 Victoria Street + brewhouse and yard	4,750
1900	6 Darlington Street; formerly a stable and converted into offices by previous occupants	1,050
1902	73a, 74, 75 and 76 Victoria Street; shops and adjoining warehouses, frontage 66' and area of 996 square yards	14,000
1903	72 and 73 Victoria Street; two shops and warehouse, area of 284 square yards	2,090
	Total property costs	21,890

Source: Beatties' Private Archive Volume I

The growth of large stores in Birmingham was also greatly influenced by the newly built Corporation Street which was the centre of Joseph Chamberlain's improvement scheme. Lewis's was the most prominent store attracted to the site, but other department stores also grasped the opportunities of building new shops. Indeed, one of the ideas behind the development of Corporation Street was to make 'Birmingham the metropolis of the midland counties' by improving its shopping facilities (Skipp, 1983, p.171).

This link between city centre development and the rise of department stores, as identified in South Kensington and Birmingham, was part of a wider recognition in many towns of the importance of improving shopping facilities. In the Midlands, for example, Coventry was seen to be lagging behind its neighbours and there were strong suggestions in the local press that the lack of modern shops (department stores) was losing the city trade (*Coventry Herald*, 1891). According to one female customer, 'the tradesmen of Coventry have for the most part been to sleep for the last twenty years', and newcomers to the city constantly ask 'where are the shops in Coventry, and after a brief experience they promptly go off to do their shopping in Leamington, Birmingham or London' (Lowe, 1903, p.92). The suggestion was that Coventry's failure to attract modern shops was because of the 'crooked and narrow character of the ancient streets' (Lowe, 1890–1, p.199).

A further factor in department store growth was the influence of fashionable centres and resorts. Early evidence has already been discussed showing how some London shops followed their fashionable customers to spa towns and watering places. For the department store these fasionable centres provided another market for expansion during the early twentieth century. Bobby and Company of London exploited this most successfully and developed stores in many of the fashionable resorts, including Leamington (see Table 8.1). Their store at Leamington was advertised as having 'exclusive departments devoted to gowns, costumes, wraps, blouses, furs, dresses and fancy drapery etc.' (*Spennell's Directory*, 1911).

8.4 Universal providers: the organisation and selling techniques of department stores

Department stores not only increased in number and gained a greater proportion of trade during the period 1880–1914, but also became larger and more complex organisations. It is impossible to obtain any accurate information on their numbers, although Jefferys (1954, p.21) estimated from his survey that the proportion of total retail sales taken by department stores was 1–2 per cent in 1900 and 2–3 per cent by 1915. For selected commodities, such as clothing and footwear, these figures increase to 5.5–7.0 per cent and 9.5–11.0 per cent respectively. Associated with these growth processes were organisational changes that operated both within the store, and between retailer, supplier and manufacturer. (Pasdermadjian 1954, p.34) suggests that the 'department store does not represent an exclusively retailing enterprise, but to a certain extent an integration of retailing with wholesaling, and in some cases even with manufacturing'. Such linkages allowed department stores to lower costs and enabled them to compete successfully with specialist retailers. Lewis's, for example, told their customers that 'they could save three profit margins – the factory profit, the middleman's profit and the specialised draper's profit' by shopping at the department store (Briggs, 1956, p.130).

The relationships between department stores, suppliers and manufacturers is somewhat complicated by changes over time, and variations in the different trade sectors. The latter point may be illustrated by the case of Lewis's, which decided at an early date to buy from the new style producers of footwear who were using machine techniques, rather than trying to make their own shoes. At the same time, however, by 1880 Lewis's claimed to have the largest tailoring establishment in England, employing some 300 tailors at their Liverpool store (Briggs, 1956, pp.44 and 130). Clearly, the economics of selling 'ready to wear' clothes were such that it paid department stores to carry out their own production processes. Indeed, many department stores appear to have had fairly substantive tailoring and dressmaking sections. In some stores emphasis was placed on other consumer items, such as furniture, as at Kendal Milne and Company in Manchester. At this store in the early 1890s there was a large cabinet factory occupying a seven-storey building, and an upholstering works with a combined workforce of 130 (*The Century's Progress*, 1892, p.19).

Towards the end of the nineteenth century some stores started to expand their interests in manufacturing by buying into the production stage of the distribution chain, and setting up plants away from their stores. Such a trend was far more prominent in North America, though some significant British examples do exist. Perhaps one of the earliest was the establishment in 1892, by William Whiteley, of a model village for his permanent workers, together with a farm and food processing factory on a 200 acre site at Hanworth, 12 miles south-west of his London department stores (Lambert, 1938, pp.223–9; Ferry, 1960, p.208). By 1894

Whiteley increased his interests in food production by purchasing an additional farm of 34 acres close to his Hanworth village. For many other British department stores, however, full control over large-scale manufacturing plants was only to be a significant growth process during the 1920s and 1930s.

As department stores expanded during the 1870s and 1880s almost all of them started to perform the operations traditionally associated with wholesalers, thereby lowering their purchase prices. However, as McNair (1931) points out, in absorbing these wholesale functions the department store also took on increased expenses, the control of which depended on improving their organisational skills. Increasingly department stores bought direct from producers and built up an important group of buyers whose skills at purchasing could have a strong influence on the success of the store. As more of the population became fashion conscious during the 1890s (see Chapter 2 of this book) the skills of these buyers were even more important in selecting the correct types of clothing materials and prints.

In some large store organisations the wholesale functions acquired predominant positions and retailing very much took second place. This was certainly the case at Debenhams, which developed an important wholesale trade during the 1870s, supplying both retailers and dressmakers with material. The organisation initiated the practice of supplying small quantities of material to dressmakers and even loaned them lengths of cloth to show to their customers (Corina, 1978, p.44). In addition, Debenhams had five wholesale departments, costumes, silks, gloves, ribbons, and tulles, with further sections opened for millinery, the success of which necessitated opening a new factory at Luton. By the mid-1880s Debenhams had moved into the export market and opened their first overseas warehouse in Brussels, to be followed by others in New York, Melbourne, Sydney, Johannesburg, Montreal, Toronto, Buenos Aires, Valparaiso, Montevideo, Paris, The Hague, and Copenhagen (Ferry, 1960, p.236).

In other large stores the mixing of retail and wholesale functions was less clear-cut than that within Debenhams, with both activities often occupying the same premises. Indeed, some stores even styled themselves on warehouses, though most of their business was through the retail trade. In these instances there was an attempt to convince customers that the store offered lower prices because it was buying and selling at wholesale rather than retail. One clear example of this is the business of John Noble of Manchester, who styled himself 'general warehouseman', and established a store in 1870 based on the policy of 'supplying the public direct at wholesale prices' (*The Century's Progress*, 1892, p.18). Such selling methods, he claimed, were exceedingly popular with the public 'who, naturally enough, like to make their purchases at a source of first supply, and thus avoid the added charges of the middleman' (*The Century's Progress*, 1892, p.18). Noble's business was also to become increasingly based on mail order, and by the end of the nineteenth century he was employing some 300 people and claiming that even 'ladies residing in the remotest hamlet of the United Kingdom, may supply all their wants in the way of drapery goods, as completely . . . as if they were to undertake the most toilsome shopping expedition round the largest establishments in London' (*The Century's Progress*, 1892, p.18). By the twentieth century Noble's was to develop into one of the country's major mail-order businesses, completely turning away from store-based sales. Other large mail-order firms grew at the turn of the century, with Great Universal Stores being formed in 1905 based around large warehouses in

Manchester. This organisation expanded rapidly in the inter-war period and moved into retailing by purchasing a number of clothing multiples (Edwards and Townsend, 1959, pp.297–8).

Unfortunately, few or no data exist from these early stores that operated mail-order selling, beyond a few general facts. From these it would seem that most department stores issued catalogues of their products to be used both as general advertising and, more specifically, as a medium for mail order. It would seem from surviving fragmentary evidence that two forms of mail-order accounts were operated by department stores. Beatties of Wolverhampton, for example, had a ledger account for some of their regular customers and a postal order account in 1913. But in their catalogue the store stressed their cash policy and 'customers who

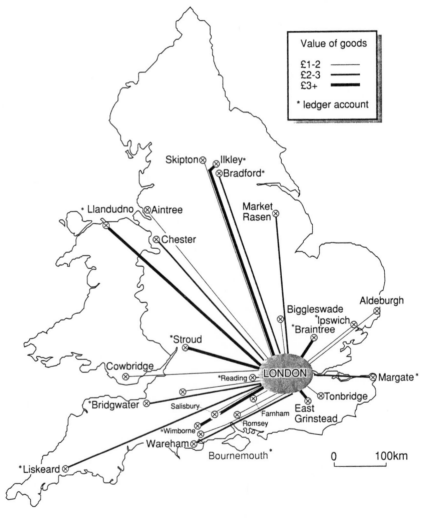

Figure 8.4 The location of provincial customers of Kingsbury's store in London, 1882

have not a ledger account . . . must enclose with order a remittance', although they also paid 'carriage on all Draper Parcels exceeding 5/- value to any address in the United Kingdom' (Beatties Private Archive, Vol. I, p.56).

Lack of customer records makes it difficult to say who used the mail-order or postal trade operated by department stores. Limited evidence from the bankruptcy records of one large London store dealing in drapery, silk, ladies and gentlemen's clothing and Berlin wool in 1882 does provide a small glimpse into the geography of this postal trade. The store, Kingsbury of Fulham Road, had over 100 small postal accounts of below £1 and a further 20 over £1 during the last year of trading. The latter, as Figure 8.4 shows, were scattered over a large area – including Ireland. In addition, the store had a ledger account totalling over £450; and although most customers were concentrated in the London area, some lived in more distant locations in the south and east of England, and at least one came from Yorkshire (Figure 8.4). Obviously, these data from the Kingsbury store are not fully representative of a true mail-order trade that was carried on by many department stores. Nevertheless, the case study does indicate that postal transactions had become significant for consumers and retailers alike by the 1880s.

Between around 1890 and 1914 most department stores began to expand their sales by restructuring their stores. This process took two common and often interrelated forms. The first was through the process of physical expansion and the re-building of store premises. For many organisations their formative years had been characterised by physical expansion through the amalgamation of adjoining premises (see Table 8.3). However, the pace of change after 1890, especially in London's West End, necessitated more drastic solutions in the form of completely new stores. Debenhams (Debenham and Freebody), for example, rebuilt their store at Wigmore Street in 1883, and completed a new building in 1907. This renewed search for more selling space was because of the second process operating in department stores, which was an expansion of customer services.

Despite William Whiteley's early claim of his store being a 'universal provider', it was only towards the end of the nineteenth century that department stores considerably expanded their range of services. The size and complexity of department stores at this time is difficult to grasp, simply because few of the store biographies have given any attention to such features. Some idea can, however, be gained by reference to the surviving records of Cockaynes, a provincial department store that grew from a drapers shop in Sheffield. The records show that the store employed some 519 permanent and 20 temporary staff by 1913, ranging from porters, carters and domestic servants through to 77 hand tailors, and 31 cabinet makers (Table 8.4). Of these staff only just less than 22 per cent were directly involved in selling goods in the store, the remainder being part of production and delivery services. Not all the staff worked on the premises, since even at this date the store employed outworkers in the bedding, cotton goods and gentlemen's outfitting departments.

The detailed information from Cockaynes of Sheffield also highlights another feature of department store organisation; the living-in of many staff. In the Sheffield store it would appear that even after 1900 some 80 female workers slept on the premises, while a further 54 were provided with meals but slept out. This practice of staff sleeping on the premises had started early in the large stores, though by the turn of the century many stores had abandoned the system. Indeed, the Shop

Table 8.4 The departmental structure and employment levels at Cockayne's store, Sheffield, c.1913

Number of employees	Description and classification of occupations
5 managers/salesmen 24 workroom hands	Making up, selling and fixing carpets and floor coverings
5 managers/salesmen 12 workroom	Making up soft furnishings materials
2 managers/salesmen 4 workmen and outworkers	Making up bedsteads and bedding, etc.
5 managers/salesmen 54 workrooms, porters	Selling, polishing, upholstering and fixing of cabinet furniture
1 manager, 12 carters, stablemen	Removal and storage of household furniture
1 manager, 1 foreman, 30 storekeepers, 10, 55 workmen	Decorating and painting
1 manageress 2 assistants, 12 workroom	Manufacture and sale of millinery
3 assistants	Sale of silk materials
1 manager, 3 assistants	Sale of dress goods, etc.
1 manageress, 4 assistants 5 workroom hands	Manufacture and sales of ladies' mantles, furs, etc.
1 assistant	Sale of mourning goods
1 manager, 8 assistants, 2 workroom, outworkers	Making up and sale of household linen and cotton goods
1 manageress, 6 assistants 77 hands, tailors	Manufacture and sale of ladies' dresses, costumes, etc.
1 manageress, 6 assistants, 7 workroom hands	Manufacture and sales of ladies' underclothing and baby linen
1 manager, 4 assistants, workroom, outworkers	Manufacture and sale of gents' outfitting goods
1 manageress, 3 assistants, 1 boy	Sale of foreign fancy drapery goods
1 manager, 4 assistants	Manufacture and sale of ladies' hosiery
1 manager, 8 assistants	Manufacture and sale of lace goods
2 assistants	Making up and sale of ribbons and light goods
1 manager, 5 assistants	Sale of haberdashery, trimmings and light goods
1 foreman, 31 cabinet makers, boys and assistants	Manufacture of cabinet furniture

Table 8.4   *(Cont)*

Number of employees	Description and classification of occupations
3 machine men, boys, etc.	'Preparation and Machinery of Timber for last mentioned process'
1 manageress, 3 waitresses	Restaurant
1 manager, 3 assistants, 1 carter, 1 boy	Sales of glass and china goods
2 travellers, 1 salesman, 13 foremen, workroom boys and assistants	Manufacture and sale and fixing of electrical machinery and appliances, house wiring, motor repairing and driving, lighting, heating, plumbing etc.
1 manager, 2 assistants	Sale and repair of ironmongery goods
3 assistants	Sale of toys
2	Cleaning of carpets by vacuum process
7 carters, 6 boys, 10 porters	

Source: South Yorkshire County Record Office, Acc. 492/B9/1

Assistants' Union was very much against the practice, complaining that the board and lodging and accommodation provided were often 'inferior and inadequate' (Departmental Committee on The Truck Acts, 1908, p.69). For the retailer, however, the system was defended at government committees on the grounds that it 'afforded a real protection against moral dangers', especially for the many young female assistants drawn to work in the large London department stores. In reality the reason why many retailers favoured the 'living-in' system was because it gave them increased control over their workforce and was economic for the long, unsocial hours worked by shop assistants (Whitaker, 1973). By the time of the 1908 Truck Committee many retailers had, however, abandoned the system. Such was the case at Debenhams which had stopped the practice in 1905 on the grounds that 'living-in tended rather to diminish the independence of the staff' and, since the system had been abandoned, 'the business was now better conducted, the assistants were physically superior, brighter and more energetic' (Departmental Committee on The Truck Acts, 1908, p.73).

   If some stores were slow to transform their labour relations, most needed little encouragement to expand their consumer services. From the Sheffield example shown in Table 8.4 it can be seen that, even in the provinces, department stores had acquired a full range of departments and had opened tea rooms and full restaurants. By 1900 most stores had strongly diversified away from their drapery backgrounds, adding furniture, household appliances, and toy departments. In most cases it was the major London stores that pioneered the opening of new departments and the selling of new consumer products. Smaller, provincial department stores were, however, quick to follow and most had developed a wide range of facilities by 1914. For these stores progress was not always easy as the records for Cockaynes of Sheffield show. In this store a number of new product lines were introduced between 1898 and 1914, as Table 8.5 illustrates, though not all of them brought immediate success. Thus, in 1898 the store listed 19 individual selling departments in its balance sheets, with the cabinet department producing the largest gross profits (Table 8.5). By 1914 the store listed 28 departments, and although the cabinet department still turned in the largest profit others had increased their share of total gross profits. In contrast, some departments, such as toys, had only just started to

Table 8.5 Gross profits on departments in Cockayne's store, Sheffield, 1898 and 1914

Departments	February 1898			February 1914		
	£	s	d	£	s	d
Carpets	1,032	5	6	1,207	5	6
General furnishing	1,715	6	7	1,203	3	6
Bedding	797	10	8	864	1	2
Cabinet	2,061	9	5	1,657	3	6
Removals	–			114	6	0
Decorating	43	19	4	57	10	6
Millinery	401	19	9	352	3	11
Silks	726	3	11	366	18	7
Stuffs	729	4	5	623	13	4
Mantles	1,584	15	7	1,354	11	5
Mourning	463	0	7	–		
'Cheap Ready-made-Costumes'[1]	–			383	4	10
Manchester	1,651	4	3	1,397	15	5
Costumes	1,016	6	9	867	11	3
Baby linen and underclothing	728	4	9	772	7	3
Gloves and outfitting	956	13	10			
Gents' and outfitting	–			993	4	1
Ladies' and outfitting	–			579	12	0
Berlin	285	5	4	285	17	9
Laces	498	17	4	1,003	2	6
Ribbons	152	1	5	168	0	10
Trimmings	629	10	8	351	8	1
Tea room/restaurant	23	13	6	14	16	7
Glass and china	–			568	7	0
Electrical	–			315	17	10
Ironmongery	–			474	15	11
Toys	–			49	11	0
Gents' boots and shoes	–			53	16	11
Ladies' boots and shoes	–			115	15	0
Paper and twine	–			6	5	5

Note:
[1] Replaced mourning department in 1913

Source: South Yorkshire County Record Office, Acc. 492/B

make a profit, and just a year earlier in 1913 it had been run at a loss. Similarly, the restaurant (formerly the tea room in 1898) was being operated as a customer service since profit levels were extremely small (Table 8.5). The situation in Sheffield and the expansion of Cockaynes may be compared with the growth of Broadbents, another provincial department store located in Southport. In this case Porter (1971) has provided a detailed account of the store's development, with the boom years of the 1890s witnessing a growth in Broadbents' trade in haberdashery, millinery and patent medicines.

As Jefferys (1954, pp.330–1) points out, every new service and department meant an increase in employment levels, and he estimates that by 1900 there were around 12 department store organisations with 1,000 or more employees (see also Lambert, 1938, p.140 for levels of employment in the 1880s). By 1914 further developments had increased employment levels even more, with Harrods having a workforce of 6,000 and Whiteley's 4,000. The department store had come of age, providing a significant shopping environment in most British towns and cities. It had also completed its first stages of growth based on store expansion, with future development being very much dependent on organisational changes and the amalgamation of firms.

8.5 The rise of large-scale multiples

The development of large-scale multiple retail organisations came at least a decade later than the establishment of department stores. Furthermore, unlike department stores, the multiples had few links with earlier attempts to establish multiple-shop trading; they were rather true products of a revolution in retail distribution. This revolution comprised three main, interrelated elements, which tended to operate at different rates within various retail trades – thereby conditioning the speed at which multiple-shop organisations developed. The first of these elements concerned new products and innovations in product manufacturing together with changes in distribution channels. The second was associated with improvements in product transportation and storage facilities, with the initial stimulus being provided by the expansion of the railway network. Finally, the availability of a concentrated mass market in the large urban centres provided a third element conditioning the growth of multiples. To historians such as Mathias (1967, pp.38–9) the multiples 'owed their life completely to the new urban society spawned by the process of industrialisation' and certainly most of the major firms had their roots in the industrial towns of the North and Midlands, or the largest consumer market – London. As Table 8.6 shows, of the 29 major multiples in the grocery, clothing and footwear trades established before 1890, only two had their origins outside London or one of the major industrial cities. These locations had two significant advantages, namely, large and concentrated levels of demand, together with good rail connections.

From his survey Jefferys (1954) suggested that two distinct phases of development could be identified in the rise of the multiples. The first was between the 1870s and the mid-1890s, with multiples developing chiefly in the footwear and grocery trades. He estimated, for example, that as early as 1880 there were some 277

Table 8.6 Original headquarter locations of early multiple retailers, 1870–1890

Location	Grocery	Clothing	Footwear	Total
London	5	2	3	10
Manchester	2	1	0	3
Glasgow	1	1	3	5
Newcastle	1	0	1	2
Liverpool	1	0	0	1
Leeds	0	4	1	5
Cardiff	0	1	0	1
Birmingham	0	0	2	2
Total	10	9	10	29

Source: based on information in Jeffreys (1954) and Mathias (1967)

multiple-branch shops in the grocery and provisions trade, with a further 500 in footwear retailing (Figure 8.5). Development in the second phase was characterised by the continuous spread of multiples in footwear and grocery, together with their growth in the meat trades, men's outfitting and clothing, women's wear and chemists' goods. Thus, by 1895 there were an estimated 1,253 branch shops in meat retailing and 502 in clothing (Figure 8.5). To these two growth phases identified by Jefferys can be added a third, which saw the development of variety chain stores after 1900. These were stores which retailed a wide variety of low-priced articles under one roof without any clear departments and operated over 10 branch shops, as with the multiples. Before the First World War their numbers were limited, although they grew from 22 branch shops in 1900 to 247 in 1915. In Britain this form of trading originated in the 1890s with the so-called 'Penny Bazaars' of Michael Marks in Leeds; although the giant North American variety chain of F.W. Woolworth opened its first branch shop in Liverpool during 1909.

As was mentioned in Chapter 1 there are problems in identifying multiple retailers. Jefferys adopted a figure of 10 shops to define a multiple-shop retailer, claiming there were 'significant economies of scale' at this size (Jefferys, 1954, p.465). In this respect the data gathered here follow this definition, at least when examining growth trends. However, it would be foolish not to recognise that there were many small-scale multiples, with between two and nine shops, that developed in the nineteenth century. Some of these became large-scale multiples (with over 10 shops) and are therefore covered in this discussion, others remained small and locally based – falling outside our discussion. This is acceptable here since it is the large-scale multiples that brought with them new methods of selling, and organisational changes.

These different growth phases are also indicative of the timing of changes in production and distribution techniques within the different retail trades. In the grocery and provisions trade, for example, it was the 'radical changes in volume and character of goods and in the type of demand', that led to widespread restructuring, and the rise of the multiples (Jefferys, 1954, p.129). Similarly, in the retail footwear trade, innovations in the production of footwear associated with Blake's sole sewer,

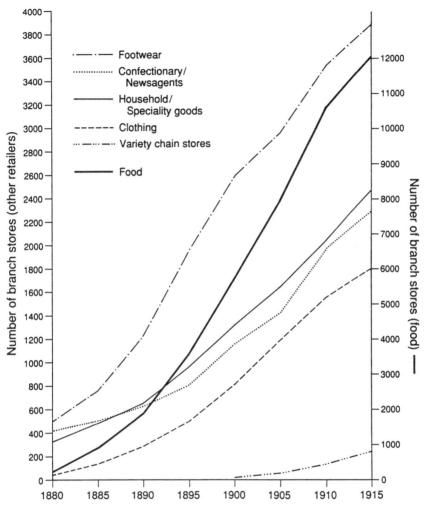

Figure 8.5 The estimated numbers of multiple retailers and variety stores in Britain, 1880–1915
Source: Jefferys, 1954

Crick's riveting process and the Goodyear welding machine combined to transform the distribution system. Between 1870 and 1880 new multiple-retail firms began to appear that dealt entirely in machine-made boots and shoes. These firms adopted vigorous and aggressive methods of salesmanship, with the predominant use of lower prices and cash sales. At a slightly later date the story was the same in the retail meat trade with new products producing radical changes in distribution methods. In this instance the arrival of the multiples was associated with two developments. The first was the widening of the supply areas as local meat supplies failed to match demand after 1870. This produced a growing trade in the importation of American live and dressed meat, and associated multiples to sell these products, which were shunned by more traditional butchers. Firms such as the American Fresh Meat Company opened shops during the late 1870s and 1880s (Shaw, 1979, p.37). The second and major impetus to the growth of multiples was the perfection of freezing techniques and the vast increase in imported frozen meat (see Chapter 2 of this volume).

The linkages between product innovation and the growth of multiples obviously varied from trade to trade, but some of the more detailed associations can be illustrated in the case of the grocery and provisions sector. In the period before around 1880 the grocery trade comprised a variety of different retail types, with the most prominent being the middle-class grocery. These traditional retailers had a completely different range of products from that of the small shopkeeper, whose numbers were increasing after the mid-nineteenth century. For example, in Manchester the number of shopkeepers increased by 48 per cent between 1834 and 1851, compared with a 38 per cent increase of more traditional grocers and tea dealers. The traditional shops would emphasise service and the use of credit for established customers, with the retailer stocking in depth on grocery and household lines. In contrast, the shopkeepers, orientated towards the working-class trade, would stock horizontally rather than vertically, stressing price and cash sales (Alexander, 1970).

Increasing working-class demand after 1870, together with new products such as margarine, exposed the inadequacies of the existing distribution and provided a massive stimulus for the growth of new firms (Hoffman, 1969). As Mathias (1967, p.40) points out, the founders of Scotland's major retail grocery multiples all established the first shops during the period 1870–1885, which also 'saw mounting working class incomes, low unemployment rates on average, and a leap in the value of imported foodstuffs'.

Jefferys (1954) in his study identifies two main types of multiple retailer within the grocery trade, a distinction he bases on their mode of origin. One group relates to the development of shops which originated as oil and colourmen, but switched to focus on cash sales, serving the growing working-class market. The second group were firms that specialised in the sale of a limited range of products, usually about three or four major lines, including margarine. It is this latter group, which includes such firms as Home and Colonial Stores, Liptons and Maypole Dairy, that expanded most rapidly as multiples throughout the national market.

In practical terms the establishment and expansion of multiple-retail firms was often a difficult managerial task, although the limited evidence collected by company histories suggests there were many pathways available for growth. The critical factor was very often that of finance, with the smaller multiple organisations being totally dependent on personal and family capital for investment programmes. Jefferys (1954, p.26) argues that the most difficult growth phase was from 5 to 35 branch shops, since at the lower size level such firms were not able fully to gain buying economies, while to expand they had to reduce prices and work on lower profit margins. The reinvestment of profits was the most common method of expansion before the 1890s, and this may have been a strong factor limiting the spread of regional multiples to a national market. In this sense the 1890s mark a watershed between the growth rates of family-run multiples and the expansion of limited companies that could issue shares to gain the much needed funds for new development projects. For example, the newly incorporated Home and Colonial

Stores Ltd of 1888 issued £150,000 ordinary shares and £70,000 of special preference shares to extend the new store programme, together with a further £90,000 raised on debenture stock in 1891 (Mathias, 1967, p.127). Such capitalisation schemes enabled the company to expand its branch shops from 107 in 1890 to 320 in 1897 and 500 by 1903. In addition, the company also developed

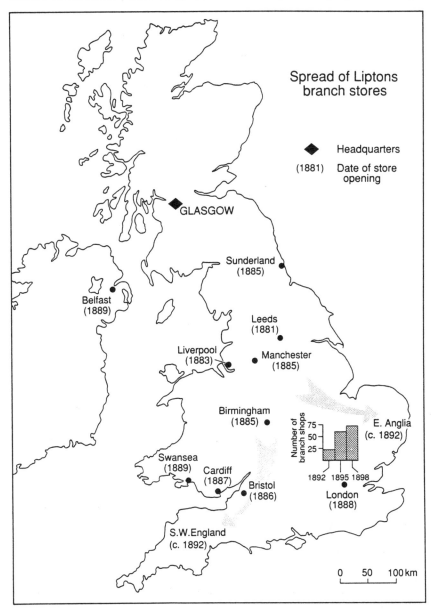

Figure 8.6 The geographical spread of Liptons stores after 1881

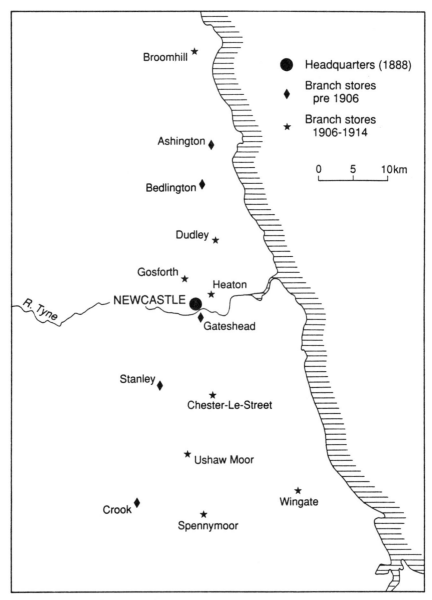

Figure 8.7 The development of the grocery firm of Broughs in the north-east of England, 1888–1914
Source: Mathias, 1967

its wholesale trade between 1904 and 1906 with a pilot venture on the international tea market, the success of which resulted in some 4,583 agents being appointed and a separate export department being established by 1910.

Large-scale multiples such as Home and Colonial Stores and Liptons owed their success not only to their trading methods but also to their ability to raise capital for store expansion. In 1900 Home and Colonial Stores were still very poorly represented in some northern regions; for example the company only had 10 branch shops in Lancashire compared with 200 in the London area. It responded to such geographical variations by opening more new shops in a determined effort to become a national force. In reality it projected in advance of trade through its store expansion programme, a strategy also used by other companies. Thus, Liptons expanded its market area away from its origins in Glasgow by opening branch shops in all the major regional centres during the 1880s. As Figure 8.6 shows, the geographical spread of Liptons stores was one of a swift movement from north to south starting in Leeds in 1881 and culminating in the entry into the London market by 1888. From these major regional centres the company was then in a position to open branch shops in the smaller settlements.

If Liptons and Home and Colonial Stores highlight one pathway of growth, other more locally and regionally based companies illustrate different methods. Figure 8.7 shows the geographical spread of the branch shops owned by Broughs, a north-east grocery firm. The first shop was opened by Joseph Brough at Newcastle in 1894. The business advertised itself as 'The Wholesale Cash Store', and like some of the early department stores stressed to the customer price savings through eliminating the middleman (Mathias, 1967, p.83). Business was firmly directed at the working classes, particularly the wives of miners coming into town weekly from the neighbouring villages. Products were sold at low prices and in small quantities. Before too long the store was sending out travellers to the mining villages, and then started to open branch shops in some of the more important local centres. From these village branch shops a more localised travelling trade was developed and so the firm expanded its coverage of the area surrounding Newcastle. In this case, unlike that of, say, Liptons, branch shop expansion followed the trade developed by travellers. Mathias (1967, p.82) calls the growth of Broughs 'the most singular style of trade', though it may well be a common pathway of expansion followed by many regional multiples constrained by limited capital.

8.6 The impact of large-scale retailing

The impact of department stores and multiple retailers may be examined in a number of different ways, including their effect on: other retailers, the behaviour and buying habits of consumers, the retail labour force, and the structure of commercial areas. One of these themes has already been addressed fully in Chapter 2, namely the relationship between the rise of conspicuous consumption and the growth of department stores. In addition, some limited attention has also been given to the impact which these new retail organisations had on work practices and the shop labour force. As we have shown, the practice of 'living-in' was certainly out of favour in many department stores during the early years of the twentieth century. At the same time these large retail organisations, especially the multiples, heightened the process of de-skilling the shop labour force as management practices standardised the work routines of most shop assistants. Such erosion of traditional skills was, it should be pointed out, occurring on a wide front as 'price competition, proprietary goods, pre-packaging all undermined the price and craft-consciousness' of the independent retailers (Crossick, 1986, p.154). In effect the traditional shopkeeping skills, concerning the knowledge and preparation of goods, had been significantly replaced by commercial ability. All retailers needed these new skills to survive, but for the multiples they were paramount. Perhaps it is not surprising that few records survive of the labour force of the multiple retailers since the upper management had little interest in their conditions of work before 1914 (Mathias, 1967, p.123).

Interesting though the issue of labour force change is, it is not the intention in this chapter to focus on such a theme, but rather to follow through other areas of impact. Of particular importance are the impacts which large-scale retailers had on other sectors of the trade, especially independent shopkeepers. According to contemporary commentators observing British business practices at the turn of the century, the 'retail trades appear to be the last stronghold of competition' (Macrosty, 1907, p.244). This may have been so, but the competitive structure of British retailing was intensely polarised between the large-scale organisations and the independents. There had been since the last decade of the nineteenth century a major shift towards highly capital-intensive retail methods, especially in the formation of new multiple-retail companies and department stores. As Table 8.7 shows, the capital of some of the largest organisations had reached massive proportions by 1905, with the London-based store of Maples having a capital of £2,620,000. At the other end of the scale it was, if anything, becoming easier to enter the retail trade. Would-be retailers found no barriers beset their entrance and often only small amounts of capital were needed to start-up in business. Crossick (1986) has highlighted one routeway of entrance into small shopkeeping, which was the practice of wholesalers and large, traditional grocers setting-up people as retailers by advancing them stock and money. If entry was relatively easy, then so was failure, with Macrosty (1907) estimating that at least 940 grocers failed in businesses every year.

Table 8.7 The capitalisation of large-scale retail firms, c.1905

Company	Trade	Capital (£)
Maple and Co.	Department Store	2,620,200
Whiteley's	Department Store	1,800,100
Harrods	Department Store	738,550
Liptons Ltd	Multiple, grocery	2,500,000
Home and Colonial	Multiple, grocery	1,200,000
Boots Ltd	Multiple, chemists	1,348,500
Eastmans	Multiple, meat	1,126,490
Nelson's	Multiple, meat	601,434

Source: Macrosty, 1907

These failures, and indeed the very intense period of price competition experienced after 1890 in British retailing, were firmly laid at the door of large-scale retailers. As Crossick (1986, p.153) points out, the 'quantitative impact of all these changes has not been satisfactorily measured', though there is little doubt that the impact of large retail firms was considerable. Furthermore, their effect on smaller independent retailers was not confined to the large urban centre, as many 'a country shopkeeper had reason to blaspheme the parcels post and cheap railway carriage for bringing his mammoth competitors to his very door' (Macrosty, 1907, p.235). While department stores used mail-order methods to extend their market, the multiples, as we have seen, set about opening branches in all types of settlements. For most multiples, price competition was all-important, though their main competitors were very often the co-operative stores. To the independent trader, especially those in grocery retailing, the combined assault of multiples and co-operatives was to force local price wars. In Glasgow for example, it was reported that one multiple retailer was selling Danish butter at 1s 2d/lb as against 1s 4d/lb, which was the lowest price at which an independent shopkeeper could make a 'decent profit' (*The Grocer*, 1906).

For their part, the multiples and department stores used every means possible to secure a market, including the widespread use of newspaper advertising. According to Mathias (1967, p.106), the importance of advertising was a lesson brought back by Thomas Lipton from his visit to America in 1869. One trade journal claimed that Lipton was 'an inveterate advertiser in the local press . . ., and it is to this publicity, no doubt, he owes much of his success' (*The Grocer*, 1880). He also used a variety of advertising stunts including parading giant cheeses through the streets in 1881, a promotion which culminated in distributing food to the poor for the Queen's Jubilee celebrations in 1887 (Mathias, 1967, p.106). Lipton may have been an extreme in his stunts, revelling as he did in the title 'King of the Dairy Provisions Trades', but in another sense he epitomised the policies of the national multiples (Mathias, 1967, p.98). One view is that such capacity for publicity acted as a double-edged sword; increasing consumer awareness while having a daily psychological impact on the independent traders as they read their newspapers (Crossick, 1986, p.154).

The pressure was not confined to the multiples as is shown by the evidence of Whiteley's department store and its competition with local trades. Lambert (1938, pp.74–102) provides a detailed account of the intense ill-feeling that developed between William Whiteley and the independent shopkeepers of Westbourne Grove, London. Every expansion of the department store, and there were many, was regarded with dislike and dismay by the local retailers, especially as they saw many of their fellow businessmen closing down. The dislike reached new heights when Whiteley introduced provision dealing into his range of services in 1875. The battle was played out in the local press, with the *Bayswater Chronicle* taking the local traders' view with headlines such as 'Wholesale Butchery in Bayswater – the Victims' (Lambert, 1938, p.75). Needless to say, this and other actions, such as street protests, made little or no impact on Whiteley. If anything they gave the department free publicity and indirectly showed consumers how much lower prices were in these large shops.

In response to these changes, and more especially the competition from the large-scale retailers, independent retailers attempted to organise themselves to fight against price-cutting. Attempts to erect legal barriers or to tax large shops were never accepted in Britain, unlike developments in Belgium, the Netherlands and Germany. Similarly, the organisation of independent retailers into retail buying groups did not occur until after 1950, unlike the early developments in the United States. There, small retailers had experimented with co-operative buying, buying exchanges, groups and even co-operatively owned warehouses, at least from 1890 (Barger, 1955, p.73).

The response in Britain was to form trade associations, or at least to use these associations to fight price-cutting. By far the most strongly organised were the chemists and druggists, who established 'The Proprietary Articles Trade Association' in 1896. The association had as one of its major aims 'to deal with extreme cutting of prices', and used its journal – the *Anti-Cutting Record* – to spread the word (Macrosty, 1907, p.249). By 1905 the association had a membership of 3,647 retailers and 214 manufacturers; and had established a protected list of proprietary articles which the manufacturers agreed only to supply to shops that would retail them at specified prices. There was also a 'stop list' of retailers who had persisted in cutting prices on protected goods and with whom members would not trade. Significantly it was the co-operative societies that stood against the association which, in 1905, had decided that the dividends paid out by the co-ops were like a bonus and therefore 'an illegitimate reduction of the protected minimum price' (Macrosty, 1907, p.252).

Other traders were not as well organised as the chemists and druggists, as the attempts by the grocers to form a national federation illustrate. Thus, the Federation of Grocers' Associations only accounted for 20 per cent of all grocers in 1906, making it impossible to fight price competition at a national level. Local associations attempted to impose some degree or order over prices, though most admitted that they were fortunate if they could keep retail prices moving in response to wholesale ones. Often independent grocers, through their local associations, tried to convince multiple retailers that there should be a minimum agreed price for certain key items, such as sugar. In most cases these local contacts and agreements appear to have had some success, giving the hard-pressed independents some brief respite. The debate over the price of sugar, for example, did reach a broader agreement with the establishment in 1904 of the Retailers' Sugar Association (London and Suburban) which not only published weekly sugar prices but also had some support from multiples.

At a more quantitative level it is difficult to gauge the impact of large-scale retailers on the overall number of shops. The scant evidence we have suggests that Britain's retail system continued to expand relative to the number of consumers through the years of intense competition. It appears that shop numbers increased continually not only throughout the nineteenth century but also up to 1914. Thus, in 1881 it is estimated that there were 154 shops per 10,000 people, in 1901, 175 and by 1911 the figure had risen to 196 per 10,000 (Shaw, 1978, p.29). On the face of it this evidence seems to bely any massive decline in retailing, although in reality three main factors were at work – though not all pulling in the same direction. First, there was the competition introduced by the large retail organisations that intensified after 1890 and served to reduce the market for independent traders. Second was the ease of entry into small-scale retailing, which gave a continual supply of new, hopeful entrepreneurs willing to try their hand at shopkeeping. Finally was the growth of population suburbanisation, and although this was not as significant as in the inter-war years, it certainly did provide new locational opportunities and markets for some retailers.

The complex interaction of these three trends is difficult to unravel, but a closer inspection of individual retail trades shows that a decline had set in by the period 1900–1910. Data obtained from surveys published during the mid-1930s, amid general fears of Britain being 'over shopped' and calls for restrictions on entry into retailing, show that for a range of settlements differential trends in shop growth were occurring (Ford, 1935; Ford, 1936; and Ford and White, 1937). For example, the number of grocers, a sector within which pressure from multiples and co-operatives was particularly great, declined by 10.7 per cent between 1901 and 1911 (Ford, 1935). If, however, grocers and shopkeepers are considered together, thus bringing in the very small retailers whose numbers were swelled by ease of entry, then the decline is less marked. In this case there is only a fall of 6.25 per cent between 1901 and 1911. Similar trends are also found in the meat trades and among drapers, both of which had experienced the rapid expansion of large-scale retailing. Conversely, those retailers operating in sectors without large firms seemed to experience an increase. Confectioners dealing in sweets, for example, increased their numbers between 1901 and 1911 by one-third (Ford, 1935).

Obviously, even from these figures it is still extremely difficult to attribute the decline to the impact of the multiples, given the other factors that were also operating. A further and more detailed analysis of shop changes at different levels of the settlement hierarchy was also undertaken by Ford and White (1937) for the West Riding of Yorkshire. This survey shows for the food trades that the rates of shop decline varied depending on the size of settlement (Table 8.8). If this is the case, it would seem that the intense price competition brought about by the multiples and the co-operatives, was a more important factor than suburbanisation processes – which after all should be at its most effective in the larger settlements.

Table 8.8 Retail change in selected food trades by settlement size in West Yorkshire, 1901–12

	Retail change in settlement with populations:		
Trades	Over 75,000	20,000–75,000	10,000–19,999
Grocers	–17.1	–4.0	–6.3
Grocers and shopkeepers	–12.1	–8.1	+2.0
Bakers	–34.5	+5.8	0.0
Butchers	–26.5	–6.2	+9.15

Source: modified from Ford and White, 1937

This may be illustrated by the situation in Hull, which experienced an increase in the number of independent grocers from 259 in 1880 to 467 by 1910, at the same time that large-scale multiples were expanding. Thus, in 1880 there was just one branch shop of a large multiple firm in the city, compared with 40 by 1910 (Shaw, 1976). Relative to population growth, however, independent grocers were decreasing; with the number of shops per 1,000 people falling by 5.4 per cent between 1891 and 1901, and by 4.6 per cent from 1901 to 1911. Though of a smaller order than those outlined by Ford, these figures from Hull would seem to confirm the trend outlined in Table 8.8; and suggest that in the very large centres like Hull (population 278,000 in 1911) the relative decline of independent grocers was occurring a decade earlier than in smaller centres.

References

Adburgham, A., 1981, *Shops and Shopping 1800–1914*, George Allen and Unwin, London, second edition

Alexander, D., 1970, *Retailing in England During the Industrial Revolution*, Athlone Press, London

Barger, H., 1955, *Distribution's Place in the American Economy since 1869*, Princeton University Press

Bartlett, J.N., 1978, *Carpeting The Millions: The Growth of Britain's Carpet Industry*, John Donald Ltd, Edinburgh

Beatties Private Archive Vol. 1

Briggs, A., 1956, *Friends of the People: The Centenary History of Lewis's*, Batsford, London

British Parliamentary Papers, 1833, Select Committee on Manufacturers, Commerce and Shipping, Minutes of Evidence

British Parliamentary Papers, 1908, Departmental Committee on the Truck Acts

Corina, M., 1978, *Fine Silks and Oak Counters: Debenhams 1778–1978*, Hutchinson Benham, London

Crossick, G., 1986, The Petit Bourgeoisie in Nineteenth-century Britain, in P. Thane and A. Sutcliffe (eds.), *Essays in Social History*, Vol. 2, Oxford University Press

Edwards, R.S. and Townsend, H., 1959, *Business Enterprise: Its Growth and Organisation*, Macmillan, London

Emmet, B. and Jeuck, J., 1950, *Catalogues and Counters: A History of Sears, Roebuck and Company*, University of Chicago Press

Ferry, F.W., 1960, *A History of the Department Store*, Macmillan, New York

Ford, P., 1935, Excessive competition in the retail trades. Changes in the number of shops 1901–1931, *Economic Journal*, 45:501–8

Ford, P., 1936, Decentralisation and changes in the number of shops, 1901–1931, *Economic Journal*, 46: 359–63

Ford, P. and White, G.V., 1937, Trends in retail distribution in Yorkshire (West Riding), 1901–1927, *The Manchester School*, 119–125

Fraser, W.H., 1981, *The Coming of the Mass Market, 1850–1914*, Macmillan London

Hower, R., 1943, *History of Macy's of New York 1858–1919: Chapters in the Evolution of the Department Store*, Harvard University Press, Cambridge

Jefferys, J.B., 1954, *Retail Trading in Britain, 1850–1950*, Cambridge University Press

Lambert, R., 1938, *The Universal Provider*, Harrap, London

Lowe, A., 1890-1 and 1903, *History and Antiquities of the City of Coventry*, author, Coventry

Macrosty, H.W., 1907, *The Trust Movement in British Industry: A Study of Business Organisation*, Longmans, Green and Co., London

Mathias, P., 1967, *Retailing Revolution*, Longman, London

McNair, M.P., 1931, 'Trends in large scale retailing' *Harvard Business Review*, 10: 30–9

Pasdermadjian, H., 1954, *The Department Store: Its Origins, Evolution and Economics*, Newman, London

Porter, J.H., 1971, 'The development of the provincial department store, 1870–1939', *Business History*, 13: 64–71

Pound, R., 1960, *Selfridge: A Biography*, Heinemann, London

Resseguie, H.E., 1962, Alexander Turney Stewart and the development of the department store, 1823–1876, *Business History Review*, 301–22

Samson, P., 1981, The department store, its past and its future: a review article, *Business History Review*, 4 (2): 26–34

Shaw, G., 1976, The geography of changes in retail trading patterns, unpublished PhD thesis, University of Hull

Shaw, G., 1978, *Processes and Patterns in the Geography of Retail Change, with special reference to Kingston-upon-Hull, 1880–1950*, University of Hull Press

Shaw, G. and Wild, M.T., 1979, Retail patterns in the Victorian City, *Transactions of the Institute of British Geographers*, 4

Skipp, V., 1983, *The Making of Victorian Birmingham*, Victor Skipp, Birmingham

Spennell's Annual Directory of Royal Leamington Spa, 1911, R. Spennell, Warwick

The Century's Progress, 1892 reprinted in 1989 as *Good Value & No Humbug: Manchester in 1892*, N. Richardson, Swinton

The Marylebone & St John's Wood Directory, 1880, Hutchings & Crowsley, London

Whitaker, W.B., 1973, *Victorian and Edwardian Shopkeepers*, David and Charles, Newton Abbot

Chapter 9
Large-scale retailing in Germany and the development of new retail organisations
Gareth Shaw

9.1 Identifying the large-scale retailer

In June 1914 members of federal, state and local government, together with representatives of major retailing groups, came together to design an officially sponsored survey of German retailing. Unfortunately, because of the war the work was never undertaken, but the meeting tells us much about the political importance attached to retailers in Germany, an importance that clearly never existed within Britain. The meeting also represented the culmination of a massive outpouring of contemporary concern over the 'health' of German retailing and more particularly the retailers themselves, who formed part of the important so-called *Mittelstand*. As recent social historians have explained, this term has no direct English equivalent and represents far more than the 'middle class', covering an ideology which saw society as a natural, fixed social hierarchy (Gellately, 1974, pp.8–9; Pilbeam, 1990, pp.14–15). From our perspective, this threat to the existence of a part of the German *Mittelstand* produced a wealth of literature on the economic difficulties of independent retailers in the face of competition from large new retail organisations.

Any investigation of the evolution of large-scale retailing therefore starts with the advantage of having available a number of contemporary surveys and reports. These range from regional and national studies of the size of the retail system (Adlmair and Bahnbrecher, 1909; Schmoller, 1919) through to more specific contemporary examinations of department stores, mail-order selling and co-operative retailers (Lux, 1910; Wiener, 1911; Staudinger, 1908; Cassau, 1925). In this respect there are some fairly detailed assessments of the evolution and potential impact of certain sectors of large-scale retailing, with department stores probably being the best represented. Unfortunately, in all of this literature little concern is given to the definition of these large organisations, and in the case of department stores and multiples no accepted national definitions existed. Indeed, the definition of department stores varied within official statistics between each of the main German states, depending on the type of special tax imposed on these organisations (Gellately, 1974, p.42).

Unlike the situation in Britain, however, it is possible to utilise census data in Germany, since this at least gives employment levels in different trade sectors and, more importantly, by size of firm. Schmoller (1923), for example, made use of such data to indicate the rise of large retail organisations (*Grossbetrieb*), using the definition of those firms employing 50 or more persons. Such firms increased from 250 in 1882 (the first census date for which data are available) to 1,000 by 1907. But of course these general figures, as Gellately (1974, p.41) points out, cover all large-scale retailers and, more importantly, they also include under the census heading *Warenhandel* wholesale firms. Given these difficulties it is possible to make a more detailed examination of these census data within particular trades to give some indication of the growth of large-scale retailing. This is attempted in Table 9.1, which shows that large firms (those employing over 50 people) were especially important in textiles and drapery, with 88 firms employing between 51 and 100 people while a further 29 had workforces of over 100 in 1895. Clearly, these figures highlight not only the growth of large, specialist drapery shops but also the size of department stores, which had their roots within the textiles and drapery trades.

Table 9.1 The structure of Germany's distribution system, 1895

Size of firms (no. of employees)	Selected trade sectors (number of firms)					
	Grocery		Textiles/draper		Chemists/druggists	
1	82,929	55.0%	25,192	43.3%	1,594	30.8%
2	39,539	26.2%	12,543	21.6%	1,178	22.8%
3–5	23,380	15.5%	13,925	23.9%	1,612	31.2%
6–10	3,784	2.5%	4,191	7.2%	495	9.6%
11–20	894	0.6%	1,583	2.7%	212	4.1%
21–50	185	0.1%	576	1.0%	65	1.3%
51–100	17	0.01%	88	0.2%	9	0.1%
100+	5	0.003%	29	0.05%	1	0.02%
Total	150,733		58,127		5,166	

Source: Der Handel in Reichsgebeit, 1895

Set against the contemporary concern over the fate of the independent retailer and the rise of large, capital-intensive retail organisations is a virtual absence of any recent investigations on the evolution of Germany's retail system. Historical geographers and economic historians have very largely bypassed recent German retailing as an area of study in favour of the recent situation in Britain, France and North America. Those assessments that have been made are almost entirely focussed on the political interplay between large-scale retailing and the shopkeeper elements of the *Mittlestand*. Gellately (1974) has provided the most far reaching and comprehensive review, with more recent discussions coming from Blackbourn (1984) and in a broader context from Pilbeam (1990).

From these studies and, more importantly, the earlier accounts it is possible to trace the evolution of large-scale retailing in Germany and at the same time recognise significant features that distinguish its retail system from those in Britain or Canada. As is to be expected, all the major retail forms are represented, including: co-operatives (*Konsumvereine*), department stores (*Warenhäuser* or *Kaufhäusser*), mail order (*Versandgeschäfte*) and multiple retailers (*Handelsketten* or *Filialen*). However, in addition, we can recognise in Germany the development of other retail organisations, especially retail buying groups, which made their appearance at a much earlier date than in Britain. As will be shown in this chapter, large-scale retailing in Germany had to evolve in a very difficult political environment, and certainly one in which public policy towards retailing exercised a fairly early control.

9.2 The rise of consumer co-operatives

As in Britain, the idea of co-operation had fairly early beginnings with societies being established in Chemnitz in 1845, Berlin in 1848, Hamburg in 1852 and Magdeburg in 1864. These, however, were not the real foundations of consumer co-operatives which underwent a transformation and period of most rapid growth after 1890 (Gellately, 1974, p.38). During the early phases of development the influential forces behind the ideals of co-operation, people such as Victor Huber and Hermann Schulze, believed consumer co-operatives were of less importance than co-operative credit societies and the purchasing societies of artisans. So much so that after the first year of founding a central organisation (*Allgemeiner Verband der auf Selbsthilfe beruhenden deutschen Erwerbs – und Wirtschaftsgenossenschaften*) in 1864, consumer co-operatives only represented 8.4 per cent of the total number of member societies compared with 83.5 per cent for co-operative credit societies (Cassau, 1925). Even though other consumer societies existed outside the organisation (*Allgemeiner Verband*), these were small in number and in the mid-1860s there were probably only about 97 consumer co-operatives. Furthermore, the early development of co-operation in Germany was very much associated with the middle classes, and in particular the setting-up of co-operative credit societies. These, as Gide (1921, p.26) points out, 'are the most conservative of all forms of co-operation', bringing together not only the liberal and bourgeois parties but also small traders. Quite naturally the small traders thought very little of the creation of distribution societies which they declared were aimed at their very extermination. This fear of consumer co-operation by the small traders who were members of the so-called 'Schultze-Delitzsch' movement was to lead in 1903 to the explosion of consumer co-operatives, as the movement (General Association) decided in favour of small-scale retailers. The split was brought to full conflict after 1894, when 47 autonomous consumers' co-operatives founded the Wholesale Society of German Consumers' Co-operatives Ltd (*Grosseinkaufsgesellschaft deutscher Konsumvereine* mbH) (Hesselbach, 1976, p.46).

Consumer co-operatives were also established outside the Schulze-Delitzsch movements by the Christian consumers' co-operative movements, which were more closely associated with trade unions and the working classes. These were, however, established quite late, with the first recorded society being established at

Mönchen–Gladbach in 1900. By 1902 the General Union of Christian Trade Unions were recommending 'the foundation of consumers' co-operatives as an important means to improve the economic situation of workers' (Hesselbach, 1976, p.48).

As Table 9.2 shows, there were two periods of growth: the first during the 1890s when the Allgemeiner Verband increased its member societies from 198 in 1888 to 638 in 1901; the second after the establishment of a new organisation (*Zentralverband deutscher Konsumvereine*) in 1903. In both cases common factors producing the stimulus for more rapid growth can be identified. One group of factors was associated with changes in consumer demand and more especially the attitudes of the urbanised working classes. In both periods of growth the foundation of consumer co-operatives appears to have been strongly related to levels of industrialisation. For example, the industrialised areas of Saxony already had some 16 consumer co-operatives before 1869, compared with only one in the less industrialised Bavaria (Gellately, 1974, p.41). Furthermore, during the first phase of major expansion in the 1890s only 13 co-operatives were established in Bavaria and with only limited growth after 1903 the penetration of consumer co-operatives remained extremely low up to 1914. This link between co-operative stores and industrialisation led to widely differential growth rates, both regionally, and by size and type of settlement.

Table 9.2 Estimated number of consumer co-operative societies and membership

	Societies	Membership
1864[1]	38	7,700
1888[1]	198	172,931
1901[1]	638	630,785
1903[2]	639	575,449
1913[2]	1169	1,633,644

Note: all these figures refer to 'reporting organisations'

[1] Figures based on membership of Allgemeiner Verband
[2] Figures based on Zentralverband deutscher Konsumvereine

Source: based on Gellately, 1974

Saxony was one of the early centres of co-operative development, with over a half of its 10 largest societies (those with annual turnovers over 10 million marks in 1913) being established before 1890. By comparison, in the newly industrialised areas of nineteenth-century Germany, such as Rhineland and Westphalia, most large societies had their foundations after 1895 (Table 9.3). Within the industrial centres of the Ruhr, co-operative retail societies grew rapidly, catering to the growing working-class demand. Furthermore, the later periods of foundation and the concentrations of demand within Rhineland–Westphalia created good conditions for the growth of large societies and associated production units. So much so that by the immediate pre-war period Rhineland–Westphalia had 47.5 per cent of its co-operative membership in societies with turnovers of five million marks per annum, compared with 36.7 per cent in Saxony. At the other end of the scale, regions such as Thuringia and Bavaria were more characterised by small-scale co-operative societies. In Thuringia, for example, in 1913 there were no societies that had annual turnovers of five million marks and 15.4 per cent of members belonged to co-operative societies with turnovers of less than 100,000 marks. The very small-scale nature of consumer co-operatives in Thuringia is further illustrated by the fact that 63.5 per cent of its societies had just one shop, compared with 30.9 per cent in Rhineland and Westphalia (Table 9.4). In Thuringia the co-operative movement was relatively early and somewhat scattered in its development, with attempts to create larger societies being hampered by its hilly nature and difficult transport links.

Table 9.3 The establishment of the largest consumer co-operatives

Co-operative region	Number of societies	Period of foundation						
		1860s	1870s	1880s	1890–4	1895–9	1900–5	After 1905
Bavaria	6	–	–	2	1	–	3	–
Central Germany	6	–	–	–	3	–	3	–
North-west Germany	18	1	–	4	2	2	7	2
East Germany	5	1	–	–	1	1	2	–
Rhineland and Westphalia	13	–	–	–	–	4	9	–
Saxony	10	2	1	3	2	2	–	–
Silesia	6	–	–	1	1	–	3	1
South-west Germany	13	3	2	–	1	1	6	–
Thuringia	11	–	4	2	–	1	3	1
Würtemberg	5	3	–	–	1	–	1	–
Total	93	10	7	12	12	11	37	4

Source: after Cassau, 1925

In the very large cities the co-operatives had few early successes, and had to battle against multiple retailers, department stores and other large-scale organisations. However, from the late 1890s onwards co-operative retailers made greater inroads into the cities. Hamburg had the largest Society (*Produktion*) with 267 shops in 1913, compared with only 152 in Berlin, and 101 in Köln. The industrial centres of the Ruhr also had large societies: in 1913, Essen had 141 stores, Dortmund 94, Bochum 78 and Düsseldorf 72 (Table 9.5). While much of the early interest and idealism about co-operation came from the middle classes, it was in the working-class areas that consumer co-operatives spread. By the early years of the twentieth century between 66 and 75 per cent of all members were working class or salaried employees (Cassau, 1925, pp.111–12). Around these average membership levels marked variations do occur which in turn tell much about the character and spread of this form of retailing in Germany. At one extreme is Rhineland–Westphalia, where over 80 per cent of the membership was working class, while in more rural Würtemberg there was a large proportion of middle-class members.

Table 9.4 The characteristics of co-operative membership, 1913

Co-operative region	Number of reporting societies	Percentage with: less than 250 members	1 shop	central warehouse
Bavaria	96	36.5	57.3	14.6
Brandenburg	100	16.0	36.0	28.0
Central Germany	130	39.2	56.9	16.9
North-west Germany	169	49.7	51.4	18.9
Rhineland and Westphalia	42	14.2	30.9	47.6
Saxony	173	6.9	36.4	23.1
Southern Germany	116	39.6	49.1	23.3
Thuringia	211	45.9	63.5	8.1
Würtemberg	88	40.1	57.9	30.7

Source: modified from Cassau, 1925

Other factors that conditioned the spread and adoption of consumer co-operation were concerned with the competition from large-scale multiples and stores supported by large industrial establishments, especially within the textile and footwear trades. These latter firms, such as Salamander, Mercedes and Bata, were subsidised with industrial capital and as Cassau (1925, p.57) points out 'many a co-operative society's manager had an anxious time of it to keep on a level with the industrial store'. More generally in terms of the provisions trade, the competition came from the large multiple organisations which, in the late nineteenth century, had a strong foothold particularly in south-west Germany and some of the very large cities. According to Hirsch (1925) and Cassau (1925) these multiple shops were serious competitors and responsible for retarding the growth of consumer co-

Table 9.5 Co-operative societies with 50 shops or more in 1913

Society	Number of shops	Society	Number of shops
Hamburg	267	Bielefeld	81
Berlin	152	Bochum	78
Essen	141	Düsseldorf	72
Dresden	136	Chemnitz	61
Köln	101	Kiel	60
Leipzig	101	Nuremberg	58
Dortmund	94	Barmen	57
Münich	83	Erfurt	50
Frankfurt	82		

Source: modified from Cassau, 1925

operatives in some regions. Similarly, the fact that co-operative stores did not always flourish in rural areas was partly due to the more conservative attitudes of consumers, and also because of the development of other forms of co-operation, especially the agricultural credit societies.

The growth of consumer co-operation was also directly influenced by organisational changes. The first major one was the formation of the Hamburg Thrift and Co-operative Society (*Produktion*) in 1899, which linked production with retail distribution and introduced the idea of co-operative stores controlling their own products (Cassau, 1925, p.9). Furthermore, as Gellately (1974, p.40) argues, the establishment of these ideas 'opened-up the possibilities for closer collaboration with both the trade union movement and the SDP (Social Democrats)'. This in turn provided an added political impetus for the spread of co-operative stores, as did the repeal of the anti-socialist laws in 1890. The second major organisational change was the break-up of the *Allgemeiner Verband*, partly brought about by the Hamburg society, and its replacement by the *Zentralverband deutscher Konsumvereine* in 1903. This new central organisation was born from a growing working-class membership demanding more emphasis on consumer co-operation as opposed to credit co-operatives. In response the *Zentralverband* set about encouraging more co-operative stores, many of which were influenced by the model established by *Produktion* in Hamburg.

The majority of German co-operative stores were based initially within the provisions trade and to this core were gradually added other retail products, such as bakeries, manufactured goods and, much later, meat. Naturally, the pace and style of change varied depending on the size and location of the society. For example, the village society stores were forced to trade in anything they could and so from an early date they may have sold household and manufactured goods. A closer inspection of retail trade within co-operative stores reveals that in many cases two very different periods of experimentation and development can be identified. In the case of bakeries, societies began such trade in the 1860s and by the mid-1870s it was being strongly recommended to all stores. At a later date, during the 1890s, some societies, such as *Produktion* in Hamburg, had started bread making on a large factory basis which involved considerable capital investment. In addition, the *Produktion* society constructed large flour mills, as did the societies at Münich and Leipzig–Plagwitz. The retailing of bread, especially fresh bread rolls, was so important to the German co-operatives that many of the large societies established special shops to sell bread. In addition, in the cities, co-operative stores operated a home delivery service for fresh bread rolls, supplying those members who lived within the immediate neighbourhood of the stores (Cassau, 1925, p.62). The importance of these bakeries may be gauged by the fact that they accounted for between 7 per cent and 19 per cent of turnover by 1920.

Another trade area which follows the two-stage process of experimentation, and then later development, is that of textile goods. In this case there was much more of a break between the early period of experimentation during the 1870s and when textile goods were more successfully introduced between 1890 and 1900. Such processes are best observed in the large urban-based societies located in middle-sized towns, where the sale of textiles constituted a substantial new business during the late nineteenth century. In regions such as Prussia the growth of large stores selling food, household goods and textiles was greatly retarded by the 'department store tax', and growth of stores retailing textiles was largely on a very small scale (Cassau, 1925, p.71). The influence of village societies on the sale of textile goods may be seen in the Thuringia Union, where 88 per cent of societies traded such goods by 1913. Despite the fact that legislation restricted the growth of very large, department-style co-operative stores in some regions, these larger units were established by some societies. For example, the Elberfeld society developed market hall type stores or very large stores selling a wide range of food and manufactured products, and according to Cassau (1925, p.72) appeared to have been influenced by stores such as Potins in Paris.

One trade area in which co-operative societies had very mixed fortunes was in the butchering and sale of meat. Early disappointments, such as the failure of the Magdeburg fleshmeat co-operative in the mid-1870s, led to a general misgiving about this particular retail sector. Thus, the *Journal for Co-operative Affairs* (1875, p.233) stated 'So far as the slaughtery trade is concerned, the consumers' societies can only be recommended not to enter into this branch of business'. It was only after 1900 that the very large societies engaged in this trade to any extent. For some of these the developments were forced on them through circumstances, as in the case of the Leipzig–Plagwitz Society which felt obligated to take over the slaughter house of the failed Connewitz society. For the very large societies the increasing consumption of meat by the working classes proved to be a decisive factor. This was certainly the case for *Produktion* in Hamburg which developed its own slaughtering and butchering units in 1903 when surveys showed that 50 per cent of total household expenditure of the working class went on bread and meat (Cassau, 1925, p.67).

9.3 Department store chains and mail-order selling

The evidence from Germany is that department stores had similar origins to those developed in Britain, with most of the original businesses growing from the textile and drapery trades. There are also obvious similarities between the internal organisations of German and British stores, with a strong emphasis being placed on scale economies, low mark-ups and high turnovers. For example, Askar Tietz, an early department store owner, claimed his success was due to two main factors. One was avoiding the extra cost of the middleman by ordering direct from the factory; while the other was passing on a part of such savings to the customer by only having a small mark-up on products (Gellately, 1974, p.43). These ideas are the common ground of early department store trading and allowed such stores to develop very quickly during the second part of the nineteenth century. If these are common threads that tie together the international growth of department stores, as Pasdermadjian (1954) has argued, in the case of Germany there are also some unique features that set it aside from Britain.

One of these differences relates to the timing of department store growth, which in Germany was very much rooted in the period after 1880. There were certainly some large shops developed before that time, but most appear to have been specialised retailers, selling clothes and textiles. Some of these firms destined for large-scale growth appeared to link together from the very outset manufacturing and retail functions. This may be illustrated in the case of the Grünfeld family from Upper Silesia, who started with a small textile shop and combined workshop in 1862 (Mosse, 1987, pp.119–20). By 1864 larger premises had been acquired and more expansion took place following substantial military orders during the Austro–Prussian war of 1866. The business then grew in two different ways: one was through the early development of mail-order selling from the mid-1870s, while the other involved the growth of large shops. This second pathway of expansion culminated in the opening of a large store in Berlin during 1889 offering a wide quality range of goods to consumers.

The shops developed by Grünfeld were large textile and drapery retailers and not full or even part department stores. These later developments were associated with entrepreneurs such as the Tietz family or the Wertheim brothers, whose origins lay in the haberdashery business. Both of these organisations began life in Stralsund, north Germany, and, while that was probably something of a coincidence, the fact that they were both Jewish was not. As Mosse (1987) points out, there appears to be a strong relationship in Germany between the development of department stores and Jewish entrepreneurial skills. Indeed, in addition to the Tietz and Wertheim's stores, two other large stores were run by Jews in Berlin, namely Berthold Israel and Hermann Gerson (Mosse, 1987, pp.189–90). There appear to be two main reasons for this link. The first is that Jewish businessmen were heavily involved in the textile and retail trades, this involvement ranging from petty trading through to the foundation of large textile firms such as Goldschmidts of Berlin (Mosse, 1987, p.45). It was from such backgrounds that large shops and then department stores developed. Secondly, many of the Jewish retailers who went on to develop the early department stores in Germany had links with the United States, and no doubt were quickly exposed to the new retail methods already developed there. Georg Tietz and F.V. Grünfeld both spent time in America enabling them to observe at first hand the use made of advertising, new equipment and organisational methods. Such quick knowledge of advanced selling practices must certainly have given these firms an advantage in the German market.

In Germany therefore the department store appears to have grown in a limited form during the 1880s and been given a further rapid boost in the 1890s by the importation of techniques from America and probably to a lesser extent Paris. It is perhaps this ability to adopt and quickly to modify new techniques for the local market that ensured that department stores grew rapidly from the mid-1880s onwards. As Figure 9.1 shows, by 1889 department stores had developed in at least 13 different areas, with Berlin and nearby Potsdam and Spandau accounting for 10, or 19 per cent, of the recorded stores. It is not clear from the limited evidence whether these large shops were in fact full department stores; as Gellately (1974, p.42) quoting an early study by Mataja (1909) states, 'There appears to have been no example of a founding of a department store before 1890.' Here we are back with the problems of definitions and the difficulty in stating precisely when large textile and drapery retailers became full department stores. Certainly, Tietz was using some of the techniques associated with the department store during the 1880s, though the number of retail lines was still fairly restricted.

The pattern of development is probably typified by the Wertheim family who in 1885 moved their retail business from Stralsund to Berlin, where they established a specialist clothing and fashion shop. By 1894, 'this had become a modest

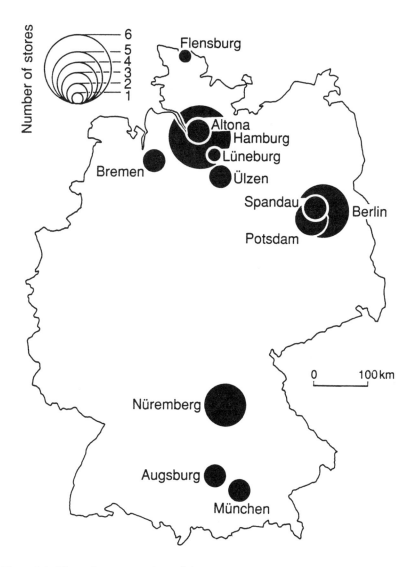

Figure 9.1 The main concentrations of department stores in Germany, 1880–1890

department store', which was then transformed two years later when a very large new store was constructed (Mosse, 1987, p.191). Growth continued into the twentieth century and by 1909 the family firm had become a joint stock company with a capital of 5 million marks, as well as diversifying into banking and real-estate.

By 1906 a special survey of German department stores found that there were some 200 in existence, with the oldest having their origins in the mid-1880s (Wernicke, 1907). Of these, 45 per cent were located in Prussia and just under 21 per cent in Bavaria. A further more detailed survey of the 90 Prussian department stores revealed that 30 per cent were located in the Berlin region, while only 14 per cent had moved down the urban hierarchy to settlements with populations of less then 50,000 people (Lux, 1910). From the records of those stores liable for the special store tax in Prussia it can be seen that the number of very large concerns fluctuated between 1901 and 1913. Thus, in 1901 there were 109 firms paying the tax, 73 in 1903, 90 in 1906 and 126 by 1913 (Gellately, 1974, pp.43–4). Leaving aside the large number in 1901, which was probably associated with changes in the tax law, Prussia, like the rest of Germany, witnessed a constant growth in department stores (Table 9.6).

Table 9.6 The growth of department store trading in Prussia, 1905/6–1911/13

Store size by annual turnover (marks)	Number of stores 1905/6	1911/13	Total turnover (million marks) 1905/6	1911/13
Less than 400,000	22	65	7	22
More than 400,000	68	61	169	274
Total	90	126	176	296

Source: modified from Gellately, 1974

A further major distinctive feature concerning department store development in Germany is the fairly early establishment of department store chains (Pasdermadjian, 1954, p.65). These were not found at such early dates in Britain, and rarely at all in France, and their development in Germany would seem partly to explain the rapid spread of department stores. By the 1890s, for example, Hermann Tietz operated three stores in the Berlin area, two in fashionable Karlsruhe, and individual stores in Köln, Strassburg, Stuttgart and Hamburg. At the same time his brother Leonhard was expanding his retail empire in Berlin and another relative, Oskar Tietz, was operating department stores in München. It is not clear why these chains developed so quickly in Germany, but access to ready capital through the Jewish control of banks and textile manufacturing may have been the reason. In addition, firms like Tietz and Wertheim were family based, with a number of brothers working together, which may have also facilitated the opening of a number of department stores. Another example is the Jewish firm of Schocken and Sons which had established full or part department stores in the following cities before 1914: Zwickau (1901), Oelsnitz (1904), Lugau (1907), Ave (1909), Planitz (1910), Meissen (1912), Frankenberg (1913), Zerbst (1913), Cottbus (1913), Freiberg (1914), (Fuchs, 1988, p.233). Certainly, this system gave the retailer both store and organisational economies of scale allowing mass selling on an extremely large basis.

As in the case of the Grünfeld organisation, many of the large stores operated mail-order selling, which was given a strong boost in Germany through early innovations in the postal system and an efficient rail service. The former introduced the 50-pfennig tariff on packages of 5 kilograms in 1874 and, more importantly, the cash on delivery system in 1878 (Gellately, 1974, p.44). According to a contemporary commentator – Sombart (1903) – it was cash on delivery which was the greatest boon to mail-order selling, and these transactions increased from 3.9 million deliveries in 1880 to 13.4 million in 1900; with a further dramatic increase to 61.8 million by 1910 (Hirsch, 1925). From these statistics it is possible to pinpoint the main growth of mail-order selling in the period after 1900. Many of the customers were drawn from Germany's still fairly large rural population which, as was shown in Chapter 2, was becoming increasingly drawn into the use of new, large-scale retail organisations.

An example of the relationship between mail-order selling and store growth may be provided by the case of Stukenbrok's store in the market centre of Einbeck, north Germany (Plümer, 1982). The original business was based on the retailing of textile goods in 1888, although Stukenbrok was also extremely interested in the construction of bicycles, the technical improvements in which led to him producing large numbers by 1890. Supply soon outstripped local demand and expansion of the business could only be maintained by developing mail-order selling. The first catalogue was published in 1893; by 1901 around 100,000 catalogues were being circulated, this rose to 500,000 in 1907 and 1 million by 1915. Alongside this rapid increase in mail-order trade the sales of bicycles leapt from a mere 28 in 1890 to a peak of 22,000 in 1906.

Unlike in other countries, such as Britain, where no historic official statistics exist on multiple retailers, it is possible in Germany to use some census data at least by 1907. At that time the national census collected information on firms with more than one outlet, of which there were 12,166, with two shop outlets or 2.5 per cent of retail concerns, out of a total of 481,294 firms. Significantly, even at this time there were a mere 1,452 firms (0.3 per cent) with three or more shop outlets, most of which had less than ten shops and operated at local and regional levels. Unfortunately, it is not possible to examine the origins and trends in these multiple retail organisations using census data; indeed, analysis of their growth is sadly lacking in the work of economic historians.

9.4 Responses to the growth of large-scale retail organisations

In Germany, as in the other countries under consideration in this book, it is extremely difficult to disentangle myth from reality when it comes to assessing the competitive impact of large retail organisations. Within the recent literature no statistical or trade assessments have been made concerning the changing numbers of independent retailers in the face of new retail methods, since attention has focussed almost entirely on the socio-political problems of the so-called *Mittelstand* (Crossick and Haupt. 1984; Pilbeam, 1990). Within these studies, myth and reality are very often mixed together as much of the evidence of economic impact is taken from the contemporary account of independent retailers and their trade associations. These accounts naturally paint a gloomy and despairing picture of the effect of large-scale retail developments, aimed as they were at attracting political attention.

Furthermore, given the social and political importance of the *Mittelstand* in Germany and in turn its link with shopkeepers and artisans, the problems of bias, and overstatement, are extremely strong. To obtain a more balanced and, it is hoped, a more accurate view, five different sets of evidence can be examined. These are: a review of the political rhetoric used by the independent shopkeepers, the accounts of contemporary observers, an assessment of changes in retail structure, the response of the state and, finally, the response of retailers themselves.

The majority of independent shopkeepers were in no doubt about the impact of the new retail organisations. Thus, consumer co-operatives were seen as 'the gravediggers' of the *Mittelstand* (Zimmermann, 1903), and it was thought that their trade practices 'very greatly threatens and burdens retail trade' (Gellately, 1974, p.117). To the shopkeepers of Hamburg department stores were viewed in semi-conspiratorial terms, and as organisations that used 'unfair advertising to get the public to enter the store at all' (Gellately, 1974, p.91). At a discussion among independent retailers in Hamburg's 'Verein gegen Unwesen im Handel und Gewerbe' the general consensus was that department stores were dangers to society, representing as they did *Grosskapital*, unfair competition, worker exploitation, and a direct attack on the *Mittelstand*. During the 1870s, distrust of consumer co-operatives often moved from rhetoric to direct action, as in Ingolstadt during 1876, when no society could be established for fear of any local founder receiving notice to quit his dwelling – so strong was the opposition (Cassau, 1925, p.173).

Set against these impassioned statements of the independent retailers we have only very limited evidence on the changing number of shops and their trade composition. During the period of the initial development of large retail organisations Germany's retail system continued to expand. For example, in 1872 there were some 529,459 retail and wholesale businesses (*Handelsbetriebe*), by 1882 this figure had increased to 616,836 and grown again in 1895 to 777,495. Obviously, these data measure more than retailers, enumerating as they do all those businesses involved in distribution. Nevertheless, they present a picture of an expanding distribution system, though without indicating the status of small, independent shopkeepers. Indeed, the whole question of just how many retailers there were in Germany is extremely difficult to answer in any precise way. Contemporary commentators such as Sombart (1903) estimated that in Saxony there were some 256 traders (*Händlerschaft*) per 100,000 population in the 1860s and that the ratio had increased to 637 traders per 10,000 population by 1897. For Germany as a whole Sombart found similar increases from one trader per 54 inhabitants in 1882 to one trader for every 30 people by 1907 (Gellately, 1974, p.31). Once again, however, such figures describe both retailers and wholesalers, though all the contemporary commentators expressed their strong conviction that retailers contributed most to the recorded increases. Between 1895 and 1907 the number of shops increased by 42 per cent while population only grew by 8 per cent, further cutting the number of customers per shop (Blackbourn, 1984, p.41). Furthermore, the number of retail outlets employing fewer than five people had reached almost 800,000 by 1907, this at a time when, as Blackbourn (1984, p.41) points out, shopkeepers were seen as victims of large-scale competition from multiples and department stores.

Behind these figures there appear to have been three different sectors of retail growth. The first was the very rapid increase in the number of very small, almost marginal retailers who worked alone without any paid employees. Numbers in this category increased from 293,339 in 1882 to 318,300 by 1907. For these small businesses the competition from large retail organisations was very often of little importance, although co-operative stores were of greater consequence. The second group concerned the established shopkeepers, those who, together with craftsmen, represented the *Mittelstand* proper. These competed with both the small marginal retailers and, more importantly, the large retail organisations. It was this group that felt most threatened by department stores, co-operatives and multiples, and it was these people that voiced most concern. Large-scale retail organisations represented the third sector, and although their numbers increased fourfold between 1882 and 1907 they accounted for only a small percentage of retail turnover even by 1914 (Gellately, 1974, p.33); Blackbourn, 1984, p.41). Indeed, estimates by the International Chamber of Commerce (1931, p.93) suggest that department stores in Germany, for example, only accounted for between 4 and 5 per cent of total retail turnover in 1930, compared with 7.5 per cent in Britain (Smith, 1937, pp.49–51).

At a broad level, therefore, the available statistical evidence does not suggest that the impact of large-scale retailers was leading to an absolute decline in the number of independent shopkeepers before 1914. However, as we have shown, the rhetoric of the shopkeepers and their supporters was very clear in highlighting the threat of large, capital-intensive retail firms. This discrepancy is accounted for by the fact that competition was variable, both by location and between different trades. Evidence from Leipzig, for example, shows that the very small retailers frequently went out of business, most without even declaring themselves bankrupt (Gellately, 1974, p.36). Overall the competition was felt in another way: the decline in turnover and the growing impoverishment of the independent retailer. Contemporaries all seemed to be agreed that newcomers within the independent shopkeeper category had much lower turnovers and incomes, less capital and displayed a greater propensity to bankruptcy than the older firms (Gellately, 1974, p.36). At the heart of this change was the demise of the independent *Mittelstand*, with the growth of 'proletarian-like' existence in retailing (Sombart, 1903, p.255). One survey of co-operative stores undertaken in the late 1890s, showed that they forced down the profit margins of the independents who were either forced out of business or driven into supplementing their incomes by taking part-time jobs (Gellately, 1974, p.47).

The established independent shopkeepers fought long and hard for government legislation against all types of large-scale retailing, with some 972 petitions being presented to the Reichstag in 1891 alone (Mataja, 1909). However, their main targets, and to a great extent their chief successes, were the department stores and co-operative societies. Unlke the situation in Britain, government in Germany did take up legislation against department stores, with the introduction in Bavaria during 1899 of a special tax on large shops, followed by similar legislation in Prussia in 1900, and other German states after that date. Most independent retailers attempted again and again to persuade state governments to adopt the broadest definition of department stores in an attempt to hit all large shops. In Prussia, for example, application of the special tax was directed at those stores with annual turnovers exceeding 400,000 marks.

Similar pressures faced the consumer co-operatives with the introduction of state legislation in 1889, which attempted to control the operations of co-operatives by restricting sales to only those who were members of a particular co-operative society. This law considered that sales to non-members were incompatible with the essential character of co-operation (Gide, 1921, pp.49–50); a character that was by and large formulated for central government by the *Zentralverband deutscher Kaufleute*. The *Zentralverband* (in its various forms) was the national federation of retail protection groups that put pressure on central government throughout the late 1880s and 1890s to control large-scale retailers. To these independent retailers, consumer co-operatives, they argued, should be viewed as merely self-help organisations with 'the procurement of cheaper food for the worker, as their only aim' (Gellately, 1974, p.123). Hence as self-help societies they should only retail to their own members. Anything more than this was seen as a direct attack on the *Mittelstand*; as was the attempt to form co-operatives by civil servants, who owed a direct loyalty to the state and hence the *Mittelstand* by virtue of their profession. The *Zentralverband* summed up the view very clearly, 'You are either an officer, a civil servant, or you are a retailer . . ., you are not permitted to be both' (quoted in Gellately, 1974, p.125).

More general legislation was introduced by the federal government in 1896 aimed at curbing unfair selling practices, prohibiting, for example, co-operatives and other stores from issuing tickets or counters redeemable only for goods (Gide, 1921, p.59). This legislation was further strengthened in 1909 when a new law was introduced on retail practices. In particular the 1909 law prevented abuses in advertising, and came to be used locally against the establishment of bazaars, which advertised themselves as '50 pfennig bazaars', even though they sold many goods above this price (Gellately, 1974, p.127).

It is not clear what impact this legislation had on the growth of large-scale retailers, although there are a few examples of limited local setbacks, as previously discussed in the case of department stores and co-operatives. In the long term the picture becomes clearer, since the development of large-scale retail organisations proceeded at a quickened pace during the immediate pre-war period. As the department store owners claimed, 'No law will prevent that development' (Messow, c.1900, p.4).

For many independent retailers and their champions the failure to halt these new forms of retailing was attributed to inadequate government help and legislation. In the face of this inadequacy the independents turned to self-help through the formation of new organisations, the main types of which are shown in Table 9.7. These range from the many and various retail protection groups (*Schutzerbände*), through to formally associated retail buying groups whose aims were to gain scale

Table 9.7 Types of retail organisations established by independent retailers

---

1. Retail protection groups (*Schutzverbände*), operating as political groups and economic pressure groups.

2. Discount savings unions: self-help groups (*Rabattsparvereine*), informal voluntary groups developed from 1870 onwards.

3. Retailer-purchasing co-operatives, retail buying groups (*Einkaufsgenossenschaften*), generally formal membership.

---

economies for the independent retailers. In Germany, more so than in Britain for example, these attempts by retailers produced new forms of retail organisations that were to become potent forces in the inter-war period. However, before focussing on the development of organisations such as retail buying groups some consideration should be given to the other more informal groups.

The retail protection groups (*Schutzverbände*) were mostly formed in response to the local difficulties faced by independent retailers, especially within large cities where pressure from large-scale retailing was often greatest. The main aims of these retailers' defence groups were to exert pressure on local, regional and federal government to enact legislation against co-operatives and department stores, as well as putting economic pressure on various factory owners not to sell goods to the large retailers. Most of these *Schutzverbände* were created after 1890, though the earliest regional society was established in 1884 (Table 9.8). In most cases the formation of local societies was followed by them joining together into regional groups as Gellately (1974) and Wein (1968) have shown. Within these organisations independent grocers and dry-goods retailers are particularly well represented, though some were even formed by independent wholesalers (Gellately, 1974, p.117). An examination of their primary aims by Gellately (1974) has shown that those established before 1895 were largely preoccupied with the threat of consumer co-operatives; while after 1895 the picture is more confused as *Schutzverbände* started to oppose the ideals of each other.

Of greater interest in this study are those attempts by independent retailers to fight the multiples, co-operatives and department stores with economic weapons. The earliest of these was the formation of retailer self-help groups in the form of discount savings unions (*Rabattsparvereine*) during the 1870s and the early 1880s. These *Rabattsparvereine* were based on the simple but effective marketing ploy of granting discounts to consumers in the form of eight coupons or stamps for cash purchases. Early attempts to create these discount unions were short lived, primarily because of the inability of the retailers to work together. The whole process intensified competition among retailers rather than producing an air of co-operation. Indeed many of the discount retailers were not part of any co-operative union but worked individually as so-called 'wild discount stores'. Furthermore, early progress was also hindered by the fact that in the traditional independent retailers there existed the spirit of *Händlerstolz*, which saw the granting of discounts as undignified (Gellately, 1974, p.73). It was only when independent retailers faced economic reality and accepted a changed relationship with their customers that these discount unions flourished. Such acceptance appears to have come during the late 1890s, with the successful formation of the Brema discount union in Bremen (1899). This grew from 862 member firms in 1900 to some 1,597 by 1910; while other large-scale unions were established at the same time in Hanover (1898). In 1903 a national organisation of discount unions was established representing by 1904 some 62 unions with a collective membership of 12,000 individual retail firms; by 1914 the figures had grown to 503 and 73,495 respectively (Gellately, 1974, p.76).

The economic and retail marketing strategy of these discount unions was based on breaking down the consumers' use of credit, particularly when they used the independent retailers. A common picture among the working classes was to use cash payments at the co-operative and multiple stores, which did not accept credit, and

Table 9.8 Regional level retail protection groups (*Schutzverbände*)

Date of foundation	Organisation	Location
1884	Verband Thüringischer Kaufleute	Headquarters in varying cities
1887	Verband von Kaufleuten der Provinz Hannover und der angrenzenden Länder	Hanover
	Verband Der Kaufleute der Provinz Sachsen, der Herzogtümer Anhalt und Braunschweig	Cöthen
1889	Verband der Vereine zum Schultz des Handels und Gewerbes für Schlesien	Breslau
	Verband Sächsischer Kaufleute und Gewerbetreibender	Leipzig
1891	Verband von Kaufleuten der Provinzen Rheinland und Westfalen und der angrenzenden Länder	At first with headquarters in varying cities. Later Barmen
1892	Württembergischer Schutzverein für Handel und Gewerbe	Stuttgart
1893	Verband selbständiger Kaufleute und Gewerbetreibender des Grossherzogtums Baden	Headquarters in varying cities
1894	Bayerischer Verband der Vereine zum Schultz für Handel und Gewerbe	Munich, until the end of 1894
	Detaillistenverband für Rheinland und Westfalen	Barmen
1895	Detaillistenverband für Hessen und Waldeck	Cassel
	Zentralausschuss Hamburg-Altonaer Detaillistenverbände	Hamburg
1898	Bund der Handel- und Gewerbetreibenden	Berlin
1900	Verband süd- und westdeutscher Detaillistenvereine	Frankfurt/M
1902	Kaufmännischer Provinzialverband zu Stettin	
1905	Zentralvereinigung preussischer Vereine für Handel und Gewerbe	Berlin
1906	Bayerischer Verband der Vereine zum Schutz für Handel und Gewerbe	Nuremberg
1907	Provinzialverband der Kolonial-warenhändler Ostpreussens	
	Verband der Detaillistenvereine im Grossherzogtum Hessen	Darmstadt
	Verband der selbständigen Kafleute und Gewerbetreibenden der Pfalz	Ludwigshafen

Table 9.8   (*Contd*)

Date of foundation	Organisation	Location
1908	Verband kaufmännischer und Detaillistenvereine von Elsass-Lothringen	Strasbourg
1909	Verband Mecklenburgischer Handelsvereine	Rostock

Source: Gellately, 1974

then, when they required goods on credit, to make use of the independent shop. This placed increasing burdens on the independents, while at the same time giving an economic boost to their major rivals. The idea of the discount unions was to cut through such entrenched problems by bringing independents together, offering collective support and the provision of cash-discount stamps. It was furthermore a good inducement to consumers that they were able to collect the same stamps from participating shops. Some contemporary commentators also saw the *Rabattsparvereine* as having a wider role in raising the political and collective consciousness of independent retailers (Beythien, 1913, p.29); a feature reflected in their original statutes, which were to:

1. induce cash payments and fight against credit trading,
2. unify the discount granted and fight against the misuses of retail discounts,
3. fight against unfair competition,
4. fight against consumer co-operatives and department stores,
5. recruit a definite group of steady and loyal customers,
6. raise the level of consciousness among retailers

(Gellately, 1974, pp.76–7).

These discount unions not only reflected a self-help response by independent retailers against large-scale retailing, but also in turn led to the formation of a new retail organisation in late nineteenth-century Germany. To this may also be added the establishment of another, and more formalised, retail organisation, the retail buying group or purchasing co-operative (*Einkaufsgenossenschaften*). The earliest one of these appears to be that established by textile retailers at Bamberg, Bavaria, in 1886, with a similar organisation for grocers opening at Frankfurt and Oder in 1888. Most retail buying groups, however, were established after 1890, and by 1893 there are records of at least 30 spread throughout Germany, with their numbers rising to 208 in 1906 (Dursthoff, 1903). According to Gellately (1974, pp.64–5) there was a direct correlation between the areas of strong consumer co-operative development and the growth of retail buying groups, as more and more retailers turned to self-help. Retail co-operation, an idea already used in the discount unions, was promoted on a more formal level in the *Einkaufsgenossenchaften*. In these organisations the co-operative strength of the independent retailers was focussed on centralised, bulk buying, aimed at achieving some of the scale economies so successfully gained by multiples, consumer co-operatives and department stores. These buying groups existed in all branches of the retail trade though the largest and most successful were among grocers. It was within this sector that competition tended to be at its most intensive, and self-help often became a last attempt at economic survival. By 1907 a national organisation was established at Leipzig: the *Vergand deutscher kaufmännischer Genossenschaften*, or *Edeka*. This was to become a major force in the inter-war period, but even by 1913 it covered some 6,400 grocers (Gellately, 1974, p.66).

Political in-fighting and disagreements appear to have kept the three main types of retail organisations (*Schutzverbände*, *Rabattsparvereine*, and *Einkaufsgenossenschaften*) divided. However, in the case of the latter two their development makes a distinct, though not unique, feature in the evolution of Germany's retail system. In numerical terms they may have been very small, and their impact on retailer co-operation most probably has more significance in the inter-war period, but they did provide an effective means of competing with highly capitalised, large-scale retailers. Furthermore their growth was as much a socio-political response to changes in the distribution system, as it was economic.

References

Adlmair, K. and Bahnbrecher, F.H., 1909, *Die Lage des bayerischen Kleinhandels*, München

Beythien, H., 1913, *Die Rabattsparvereine der Kaufleute und Gewerbetreibenden*, Bremen

Blackbourn, D., 1984, Between resignation and volatility: the German petite bourgeoisie in the nineteenth century, in J. Crossick, and M-G Haupt (eds.), *Shopkeepers and Master Artisans in Nineteenth-Century Europe*, Methuen, London

Cassau, T., 1925, *The Consumer's Co-operative Movement in Germany*, Co-operative Union, Manchester

Crossick, J. and Haupt. M-G. (eds.) 1984, *Shopkeepers and Master Artisans in Nineteenth Century Europe*, Methuen, London

Dursthoff, H.M., 1903, *Die Lage des Kleinhandels und die Begründung von Einkaufsgenossenschaften*, von Stalling, Oldenburg

Fuchs, V.K., 1988, Zur Geschichte Des Warenhaus-Konzerns: I. Schocken Söhne, *Zeitschrift Für Unternehmengeschichte*, 33 (4): 232–52

Gellately, R., 1974, *The Politics of Economic Despair: Shopkeepers and German Politics 1890–1914*, Sage, London

Gide, C., 1921, *Consumer's Co-operative Societies*, Co-operative Union, Manchester

Hesselbach, W., 1976, *Public, Trade Union and Cooperative Enterprise in Germany: The Commonweal Idea*, Frank Cass, London

Hirsch, J., 1925, Der moderne Handel, seine Organisation und Formen und die staatliche Binnenhandelspolitik, *Grundriss der Sozialökonomik* 11, Tübingen *Journal For Cooperative Affairs*, 1875

Lux, K., 1910, *Studien über die Entwicklung der Warenhäuser in Deutschland*, G. Fischer, Jena

Mataja, V., 1909, Kleinhandel, in J. Conrad (ed.) *Handwörterbuch der Staatswissenschaften*, Vol. 1, Fischer, Jena

Messow, P., c.1900, *Die Schäden im Detailhandel und die Warenhäuser*, Dresden

Mosse, W.E., 1987, *Jews in the German Economy: The German–Jewish Economic Elite 1820–1935*, Clarendon Press, Oxford

Pasdermadjian, H., 1954, *The Department Store: Its Origins, Evolution and Economics*, Newman, London

Pilbeam, P.M., 1990, *The Middle Classes in Europe, 1789–1914: France, Germany, Italy and Russia*, Macmillan, London

Plümer, E., 1982 *Das Versandhaus August Stukenbrok in Einbeck*, Plümer, Einbeck

Schmoller, G., 1919, *Grundriss der Allgemeinen Volkswirtschaftslehre* (2 vols), Duncker & Humblot, München

Smith, H., 1937, *Retail Distribution: A Critical Analysis*, Oxford University Press, London

Sombart, W., 1903, *Die deutsche Volkswirtschaft im 19. Jahrhundert*, G. Bondi, Berlin

Staudinger, F., 1908, *Die Konsumgenossenschaft*, B.G. Teubner, Leipzig

Wein, J., 1968, *Die Verbandsbildung im Einzelhandel Mittelstandsbewegung, Organisation der Grossbetriebe, Fachverbande, Genossenschaften und Spitzenverband*, Duncker & Humblot, Berlin

Wernicke, J., 1907, *Kapitalismus und Mittelstandspolitik*, Fischer, Jena (second edition, 1922)

Wiener, A., 1912, *Das Warenhaus*, E. Wasmuth, Berlin

Zimmermann, O., 1903, quoted and referenced in R. Gellately, 1974, *The Politics of Economic Despair* Chapter 5, p.125 and note 36

Chapter 10
Large-scale retailing in Canada
John Benson

10.1 Introduction: The Hudson's Bay Company

The study of nineteenth- and early twentieth-century Canadian retailing tends to be as deficient in its treatment of large-scale concerns as it is in its approach towards small-scale undertakings. In fact, of course, these deficiencies are closely connected. For in retailing, as in so many other spheres of economic life, it is the growth of large-scale enterprise that seems to monopolise popular and scholarly interest, and so to conceal the survival of smaller-scale forms of enterprise.

Indeed it is ironic that the power of the one long-established, large-scale undertaking engaged in retailing, the Hudson's Bay Company, declined rather than increased as the period progressed. The Company began the nineteenth century with exclusive rights to trade among the native peoples of Rupert's Land, the vast area of land drained by the rivers flowing into the Hudson's Bay; indeed the company's power was increased in 1821 when it absorbed the Northwest Company, and with it the trade in furs that was conducted out of Montreal (Bliss, 1987, p.196). For the following 50 years this giant colonial undertaking, with its 2,000–3,000 employees, dominated the fur trade across a huge swathe of Canada: from Lake Superior in the east, to Hudson's Bay in the north, and the Pacific Ocean in the west (Easterbrook and Aitken, 1961, pp.322–4).

Because the Hudson's Bay Company was primarily a fur-trading enterprise, it is not always easy to distinguish its role in bartering goods (in exchange for furs) from its role in selling goods (in exchange for cash). However, it seems clear that the Company engaged in many forms of retail activity. It organised fairs, it sent out pedlars, and of course it established the fur-trading posts cum general stores for which it is so well known. These, it has been pointed out, were the earliest form of fixed shop to be found in Canada (Lee, 1931, p.56). Indeed it has been discovered that in larger centres, such as Red River, there was a tendency for the company's general storekeeping business to expand along with the growth of settlement (Bliss, 1987, pp.204–5).

Nonetheless the Hudson's Bay Company was losing its monopolistic powers. For although it did not cede Rupert's Land to the Canadian government until 1870, its control over the fur trade – and thus its control over retailing – was beginning to break down long before then. The Company found it increasingly difficult to enforce its monopoly either against newcomers or against former employees who attempted to trade on their own account (Harris and Warentin, 1974, p.259; Gunn, 1910–11). The company's policy of undercutting these competitors proved only partially successful. 'It is astonishing', reported an exasperated company executive in 1824, 'to see the ruined depart annually, but still like the Hydra heads another succeeds' (Galbraith, 1957, pp.39–40, 169–70). Thirty years later there were said to be between 150 and 175 individuals trading on their own account at Red River alone. Norman Kittson was one of these independent traders. According to Michael Bliss, he

was almost driven out of business by renewed Company pressure and a host of whiskey-selling competitors at Pembina. 'Wish to God I was out [of] the infernal trade or rather that I had never embarked upon it,' he wrote early in 1851. Kittson held on, retrenched and reorganized, turned the corner and was soon making more money (a clear $10,000 in 1852) than he had thought possible. Scoffing at the Hudson's Bay Company, he opened a post within sight of its Fort Garry – you could get champagne at Mr. Kittson's store – and outfitted and grub-staked independent traders ranging north and west toward the centre of the Hudson's Bay Company's Kingdom (Bliss, 1987, p.201).

Such competition, and the other difficulties faced by the company must not be allowed to obscure its place in the history of Canadian retailing. The Hudson's Bay Company provides an early, if sometimes overlooked, example of the large-scale organisation of retail distribution. Indeed even the formal dismantling of the company's monopoly in 1870 preceded by several decades the attempts made by co-operative, multiple and departmental stores to achieve the economies of scale denied to small independent retailers.

10.2 Consumer co-operation

This is not to suggest that the efforts of co-operative, multiple and departmental stores were necessarily successful in the years before the First World War. The failure of the co-operative movement is particularly striking. It was not that consumer co-operation was unknown in Canada. In fact in the early years of the twentieth century there were repeated attempts to establish the movement in the industrial areas of the country. The Finns were active in Port Arthur, the Italians in parts of Alberta, and miners (of many nationalities) in the coalfields of Alberta, British Columbia and Nova Scotia (Michell, 1916, pp.333–4; O'Meara and Lalonde, 1941, p.9). Several initiatives were undertaken in Montreal, and in Ontario societies were organised in Guelph, Brantford, Hamilton and Toronto: by 1914 the Guelph Co-operative Association had 672 members, a share capital of over $5,000 and annual sales of more than $120,000 (Michell, 1916, pp.330–3, 336–7; *Eastern Labor News*, 20 February 1909; *Globe*, 2 February 1914; *Canadian Grocer*, 26 February 1915).

Nonetheless, nearly every attempt to establish consumer co-operation proved short-lived and unsuccessful. The societies in Brantford, Hamilton and Toronto succumbed very rapidly: in Toronto, for instance, the 'Householders' Co-operative

Stores' was formed in the summer of 1914, only to collapse six months later with liabilities of $10,000 (*Canadian Grocer*, 26 February 1915). In fact when the Co-operative Union of Canada was established in 1909, it could muster no more than 1,595 members in six societies – not all of which were even retail organisations (Dominion Bureau of Statistics, 1941, p.513).

The weakness of Canadian consumer co-operation is not easy to explain. It is well known that producer co-operation, in organisations such as the United Farmers of Alberta and the Saskatchewan Grain Growers' Association, was practised widely and with considerable success in the west of the country (Easterbrook and Aitken, 1961, pp.499–500). It has been seen too that by the end of the period the Dominion generally was displaying two of the demand-side features supposedly most conducive to the successful establishment of retail co-operation: a growing concentration of working-class settlement; and a generally rising level of working-class purchasing power.

How then is the weakness of Canadian consumer co-operation to be explained? Two possible solutions suggest themselves. It may be that the social geography of urban Canada was characterised less clearly by class divisions than proponents of the 'new' labour history would lead one to suppose. Such at least has been the view put forward by some of those engaged in the retail trade. Co-operation would not succeed in Canada, suggested the *Canadian Grocer* in 1935, because even at this late date working people were not 'massed in definite sections in large centres' (*Canadian Grocer*, 17 May 1935). In all events, the one consumer society with a long and successful history, the British-Canadian Co-operative Society, was based in Sydney, Nova Scotia, one of the most homogeneous working-class communities in the whole of the Dominion (O'Meara and Lalonde, 1941, p.9).

However it seems probable that the weakness of consumer co-operation is to be explained less by the social geography of urban Canada than by the nature of the Canadian retailing system. Established shopkeepers liked to believe that it was the efficiency and competitiveness of the independent sector that had inhibited the challenge of co-operation (*General Merchant*, 5 April 1929; *Canadian Grocer*, 17 May 1935). Less committed commentators might point to the collective organisation, as well as the economic competitiveness, of those engaged in the legitimate trade. Certainly established retailers and their representatives were vehement in their opposition to any sign of co-operative selling. In Saskatchewan the Retail Merchants' Association campaigned against the stirrings of co-operation (*The Retailer*, 1915–18, *passim.*). In Toronto the Retail Merchants took what steps they could to undermine the nascent Householders' Co-operative (*Canadian Grocer*, 16 February 1915). In Guelph the establishment of a co-operative bakery was 'met with very swift opposition both from the other bakers and also from the Retail Merchants' Association of the town, and a very great deal of suspicion of the motives of the organizers was engendered in the minds of the working people' (Michell, 1916, p.331; also Drummond, 1987, p.291).

The failure of consumer co-operation to take root in Canada is still not fully understood. However, because it is a failure which contrasts so sharply with the success of co-operation in countries such as Britain and Germany, it seems likely that the movement's difficulties in Canada will be understood best by the development of the comparative perspective that is propounded in this volume.

10.3 Chain stores

The chain (or multiple) store movement was a great deal more successful. However, with its centralised management, its large-scale purchasing and its high-volume turnover, this was a form of selling that depended, even more than consumer co-operation, upon the emergence of geographically concentrated and economically effective working-class demand. It is perhaps not surprising therefore that it was only during the second half of the 1920s that chain store retailing really came into its own (Royal Commission on Price Spreads, 1935, p.201; *General Merchant*, 5 April 1929). In fact, in so far as chain store selling did emerge before the First World War, it did so chiefly in the industrialised and urbanised areas of central Canada, and it did so overwhelmingly in just a few branches of the retail trade: clothing and furniture; groceries; and jewellery, drugs and novelties.

The movement developed first in the so-called 'dry-goods'. One of the pioneers was the Grafton chain which originated in 1853 as a single dry-goods store in Dundas, Ontario. By 1905 it had two stores in Dundas and branch stores, selling furnishing and men's clothing, in London, Hamilton, Brantford, Peterboro, Woodstock and Owen Sound (Royal Commission on Price Spreads, II, 1935, pp.1, 197; *Globe*, 12 January 1914; Wilson, 1965). The movement developed more widely in groceries, the two best-known chains being Loblaws and Carrolls, the latter firm alone controlling eleven stores in Hamilton and south-west Ontario by the end of the period (*Canadian Grocer*, 17 January 1930; White, 1931, pp.3–4).

The chain store movement developed most successfully of all in jewellery, novelties and drugs, with the early years of the new century seeing the foundation of several nationally known concerns. The Tamblyn drug store chain opened its first outlet in Toronto in 1904, and in the following year the Independent Druggists' Alliance was founded as a voluntary chain 'to help the independent druggist meet competition that was then developing' (White, 1931, p.9; Royal Commission on Price Spreads, 1935, p.213; II, p.1, 357). But of course the best known of all pre- (and post-) 1914 chains was that belonging to F.W. Woolworth. The firm's strategy was, and is, well known: 'the Chief coached his store managers to create a sales environment so pleasant to consumers that they would regard browsing and shopping at Woolworth as, in effect, going to a fair' (Nichols, 1973, p.122). It was a strategy that worked. The first Woolworth store in Canada was opened in 1908, and within four years the chain had 32 outlets, and was doing over three million dollars worth of business a year in the Dominion (Royal Commission on Price Spreads, 1935, I, pp.590–1; Lee, 1931, p.71; Nichols, 1973; Brough, 1982).

However, it was not until after the First World War that chain store retailing began to exert a major impact across the whole of Canada. In fact, even in 1930, at the end of five years of very rapid expansion – and a full decade and a half after the end of the period covered by this book – chain stores (including filling stations) accounted for fewer than one fifth of total retail sales in the Dominion (Royal Commission on Price Spreads, 1935, p.435; Census of Canada, 1931, xi, p.1, 169). For the historian of nineteenth- and early twentieth-century Canadian retailing, the chain store movement is significant as an indicator, less of contemporary change, than of forthcoming developments.

10.4 Department stores

A great deal more central to pre-1914 developments in Canada was the emergence and expansion of the department store. With its wide range of products, its fixed prices, its cash sales and its extensive range of customer services, the department store was of crucial, and novel, importance. Yet this, more than any other, form of distribution remains bedevilled by the biographical – not to say hagiographical – approach that seems to be adopted so often by those interested in retailing history.

Such an approach can be most misleading for, whatever the quality of individual entrepreneurship, department store selling could flourish only when technological change was capable of supplying the goods – and technological, demographic and economic change the demand – that this form of retailing required. For not only did department stores, like chain stores, depend upon the growth of working-class prosperity, they, much more than chain stores, were dependent upon the expansion of middle-class purchasing power. Moreover department store selling could succeed only by exploiting the technological changes which were occurring towards the end of the nineteenth century:

it is impossible to imagine a sizeable department store without elevators, or without good artificial light, whether gas or electric. Telephone ordering further increased the outreach of the stores, especially into middle-class families . . . Thanks to electric streetcars and radial railways, by 1900 central shopping districts could draw clients from an ever-increasing hinterland, and thanks to the big stores' efficient delivery systems, purchases could arrive almost as speedily as purchasers (Drummond, 1987, pp.281–2; also Hower, 1943, pp.145–56).

Nonetheless, the success of department stores is generally attributed not, as so often in retail history, to the impersonal growth of consumer demand, but to the personality, drive and commitment of the entrepreneurs who founded them. In Canada, two Toronto pioneers, Robert Simpson and Timothy Eaton, receive virtually all the plaudits. 'The retailing revolution, based on high volume, low prices, cash payment and the ability of entrepreneurial retailers to break the traditional horizontal and vertical divisions of trade, was an international phenomenon', explains Michael Bliss. 'Timothy Eaton was its Canadian prophet' (Bliss, 1987, p.290; also Santink, 1990).

Timothy Eaton opened his first store in Toronto in 1869, moved to a new four-storey building in 1883, and by 1890 'was employing upward of four hundred and fifty clerks (six hundred during the Christmas rush) . . . in a mammoth sixty-department store covering almost a whole city block' (Bliss, 1987, p.290). Fifteen years later the firm expanded to Winnipeg, opening a store that covered more than 5½ acres of floor space (Artibise, 1979, p.16). By the end of the First World War Eaton's owned factories in Toronto, Hamilton and Montreal, and had opened buying offices overseas in cities such as New York, Kobe, Yokohama, Belfast, Manchester and London (Drummond, 1987, p.280; Santink, 1990, pp.154–5). The stores in Toronto and Winnipeg strove hard to attract both working-class and middle-class customers (Santink, 1990, p.126). The latter were wooed with exhibitions, banking and restaurant facilities, tailoring and dressmaking services, and assistance in the form both of a 'Scribe' (who would advise customers about fashions, books, pictures and home decorations) and of a 'Shopper' (who would do the customers' shopping for them) (*Globe*, 24 June, 6, 8 July 1910; 2, 12, 24 January, 2 February 1914). 'Everything is looked to for your comfort in shopping, making it a pleasure rather than a drudgery', explained Eaton's 1887–8 catalogue: 'All modern conveniences known to establish your comfort . . . have been adopted throughout the building' (Santink, 1990, p.98; also p.146).

Robert Simpson followed where Timothy Eaton led. Simpson moved from Newmarket to Toronto in 1872, and opened new, and increasingly impressive, buildings in 1894 and 1895. By 1910 the company had an office in England and an agency in France; it was operating a factory in Toronto that employed 400 workers making women's clothing; and it had stabling sufficient to accommodate 50 wagons and 100 horses. The store itself provided middle-class customers with a wide range of services. It housed a telegraph office, a post office, a number of public telephones and 50 outside lines; it provided a check room, a ladies' waiting room and a restaurant. 'We have', it was claimed in the hot summer of 1910 'one of the largest, coolest and best appointed lunch rooms in Canada' (*Globe*, 6 July 1910; also 25 June 1910; Drummond, 1987, pp.280–4; Patterson, 1906, pp.432–4, 438). The store also sought to attract customers by organising art exhibitions, and by stressing that it should (and could) be 'a treat to take a morning for leisurely shopping' (*Globe*, 13 January 1914). It advertised many of its goods with the middle-class consumer particularly in mind: a purchase of gloves was described as 'Ideal Mitts for the Chauffeur'; a sale of underwear was announced with the reminder that 'It's by no means what is seen that stamps the gentlewoman, but rather the careful grooming that is the foundation' (*Globe*, 8, 9 January 1914).

The attention that has been lavished upon Eaton's and Simpson's makes it easy to overlook the existence of many other large and successful department stores. (Indeed as Ian Drummond and Joy Santink have pointed out, Eaton and Simpson were not even the first retailers in Toronto to adopt the departmental form of organisation (Drummond, 1987, p.280; Santink, 1990, p.51). Certainly by the turn of the century every major urban centre seems to have possessed at least one large department store. Montreal, for example, had Rea's, Almy's, Ogilvy's, Morgan's and Dupuis Frères; Hamilton had McKay's, 'The Arcade', 'The Right House' and Robinson's, which advertised itself as 'The Store of Many Departments' (*Cotton's Weekly*, 4 November 1909; 4 February 1910; *Hamilton Spectator*, 1, 8, 15, 17, 19–20 September 1900; Bliss, 1987, p.291).

Yet it would be a mistake to conclude that stores organised on departmental lines were confined to the industrialised and urbanised areas of central Canada. It has been discovered, for instance, that 'By 1911 most of the larger Western towns boasted at least one department store' (Bellan, 1978, p.109). Winnipeg had two, Robinson's and 'The Bay', both of which predated the arrival of Eaton's in 1905 (Shanks, 1970, p.10). Calgary had The Bay, Glanville's, Pryce Jones and Slingsby's, which was known as 'The Big Riverside Store'. By the end of the period, Pryce Jones, like Eaton's and Simpson's, was sending its buyers to Europe, had opened its own sub-post office, and was providing its customers with an extensive, and apparently sophisticated, range of catering facilities: the 'Royal Welsh Tea Rooms' were open on week days from 9 a.m. to 6 p.m., and on Saturdays from 9 a.m. to 9.30 p.m. (*Calgary Daily Herald*, 17, 21 April 1911; 22, 24–6 March, 8 April 1913).

It is no easy matter to assess the impact that these, and other department stores had upon the Canadian retailing system in the years before the First World War. There are a number of difficulties: the deficiencies of the contemporary evidence are not readily overcome; the popular and scholarly attention paid to Eaton and Simpson can lead easily to misunderstanding; while the generally underdeveloped state of Canadian retail history makes it difficult to compare the importance of department store selling with that of chain store selling, small-scale shopkeeping, and other forms of distribution.

There is no doubt of course that department store sales increased enormously in the years after 1880. It will come as no surprise to learn that Eaton's sales in particular grew prodigiously: from $1.6 million in 1891, to $125 million in 1921 (Drummond, 1987, p.284). Indeed it has been estimated that, in theory at least, Eaton's two stores in Toronto and Winnipeg were able to reach as many as 10 per cent of the Canadian population during the early 1920s (Psutka, 1976, p.26). There is no doubt either that, in the long run, the sales of department stores, together with those of other large organisations, came to represent a very significant proportion of Canadian retail trade. The compilers of the first Census of Merchandising and Service Establishments estimated that by 1930 'stores with sales of $200,000 or more formed slightly less than 1 per cent of the total number but handled 28.58 per cent of the trade' (Census of Merchandising and Service Establishments, 1931, X, p.xxv).

However the impact of department store selling cannot be captured by statistical indicators alone. Established retailers believed that the opening of a large department store was likely to constitute a major, if not terminal, threat to their livelihood. Thus it was claimed even before the end of the century that department stores in Toronto had 'succeeded in closing up hundreds of the smaller shops, which now stand empty' (*Dunnville Chronicle*, 6 November 1896). Consumers too believed that the opening of a large department store was likely to have a major impact upon the local system of retailing. Until 1905, recalls one Winnipeg resident 'we had to deal with a very few neighbourhood grocers and butchers scattered far apart, until Eaton's department store introduced a new pattern' (Shanks, 1970, p.39). This new pattern of retailing had far-reaching consequences, believes another Winnipeg consumer: 'The advent of Eaton's great store in Winnipeg brought about not only a revolution in the prices of the vendor, but in the ideas of the buyer; and two and a half years after my first visit to the city I found a marked improvement in the value for money displayed in shop-windows' (Santink, 1990, p.252). The attractions of city shopping appeared ever more compelling. In eastern Canada, it was complained in 1928, customers did their shopping in the cities 'because the stores are bigger, they are nicely decorated, a larger assortment of goods is to be found to choose from, and it is nice to tell the people at home that they got the merchandise in the bigger centre' (*General Merchant*, 5 January 1928; also 5 April 1929; *Canadian Grocer*, 7 July 1905).

Both the contemporary record and common sense observation confirm that the department store has exercised a profound effect upon the shopping habits of twentieth-century Canadian consumers. However this too has its dangers, for it makes it easy to exaggerate the role that department store selling played in the years before the First World War. It is not acceptable simply to extrapolate from the known to the unknown, to assume that because the department store was important in the 1920s and 1930s, it must have been very nearly as important during the first decade and a half of the century. In fact, even if it were possible to extrapolate from the known to the unknown, considerable caution would still be necessary. Department stores were remarkably slow to dominate; it has been calculated by one commentator, for instance, that even during the late 1920s department stores received no more than $7 dollars and 70 cents out of every $100 that were spent by Canadian consumers (Heywood, 1941, p.34).

Department store entrepreneurs did come to play a leading role in the development of late nineteenth- and early twentieth-century retailing. But they did so less by their opening of city-centre shops, than by their establishment of nation-wide systems of mail-order selling. For mail order was the one large-scale form of distribution that did undoubtedly attain a high level of market penetration in the decades preceding the First World War (cf. Emmet and Jeuck, 1950).

10.5 Mail order

Mail order was organised on a more heterogeneous basis than is sometimes supposed. For instance, several United Kingdom concerns participated, on a modest scale, in the growing Canadian market. Thus in early twentieth-century Toronto, firms from Edinburgh, Manchester, Belfast and London used the local press to advertise the sale of items such as books, men's clothing, Irish linen and Edison phonographs (*Globe*, January–July 1914, *passim.*). A much larger number of Canadian firms were involved, of course, with druggists, jewellers and fur-sellers particularly prominent. Drug company advertisements for patent medicines, with their catchy slogans (and unconvincing testimonials) will be familiar to even the most casual browser among the pages of contemporary newspapers and periodicals (Bliss, 1987, p.290). The advertisements by jewellers and fur retailers were less arresting than those of the drug companies, but a good deal more informative. Toronto's Gough Fur Company explained in 1914 that express charges would be prepaid to any town in Canada; and unwanted purchases, it was added, could be returned to Toronto at the firm's expense (*Globe*, 1 January 1914).

No doubt the trade done by such businesses was relatively modest. In all events, Canadian mail order, like Canadian department store selling, has become associated inextricably with the names of Timothy Eaton and Robert Simpson. Eaton produced his first mail-order catalogue in 1884, an initiative that was taken up by Simpson a decade later (Glazebrook, Brett and McErval, 1969, p.iv; Savitt, 1985, pp.1, 580; Hande, 1988, p.108). The business of both firms grew rapidly. During the second half of 1906 Simpson's mail order department received orders from 97,000 different people – a figure which, although it excluded both orders from within Toronto and multiple orders from the same person, represented purchases by 1.6 per cent of the entire population of the country (Patterson, 1906, p.428). Eaton was more successful still. 'Eatons' buying power, sales volume, breadth of offerings, and distribution system were so well developed', believes Michael Bliss, 'that few small retailers could compete with the catalogues. These fat, colourful, and free magazines became legendary as the most widely distributed publication in Canada next to the Bible, and perhaps the better read.' 'At the turn of the century', concludes

Bliss, 'Eaton's proudly advertised itself as "Canada's Greatest Store"' (Bliss, 1987, p.292).

The expansion of Canadian mail order, like the growth of its department store progenitors, does not seem difficult to explain. It has been seen already that, during the second half of the nineteenth century, consumer demand was growing in ways that were likely to encourage the expansion of large-scale retailing – and in ways, indeed, that seemed almost designed to stimulate the growth of mail-order distribution. 'In a country of great distances and scattered populations such an organization was an obvious way of bringing the department store into the homes of Canadians at points distant from the larger centres' (Bank of Montreal, 1956, p.49; also *Retailer*, August 1916). 'Obvious' or not, mail-order selling was able to expand only with the development, also during the late nineteenth century, of the freight and postal services capable of moving both goods and payments across the country with relative ease and at relatively low cost (Patterson, 1906, p.428; see also Emmet and Jeuck, 1950, pp.2–3).

Naturally the department stores organising mail order did their best to make shopping by post as pleasant and convenient as possible. The catalogue was the key to successful mail-order retailing. By early in the new century Simpson's fall and winter catalogues each contained 200 pages, and were sent free to anybody who had placed an order within the preceding six months – or to anybody indeed who took the trouble to apply for one (Patterson, 1906, p.428). Eaton's catalogue also ran to 200 pages, and it too was published twice a year: in 1904 the company published 1.3 million copies: one for every five men, women and children in the country (Santink, 1990, p.226). 'Format and contents developed from the uninspiring, if informative, price list of the eighties to the fat, glossy volume of the twentieth century' (Glazebrook, *et al.*, 1969, p.v). The Winnipeg store produced its own volumes, and supplementary editions were published to advertise special events or the sale of specialised products such as bicycles, Christmas goods, or house plans and builders' supplies. These volumes offered a wide, and growing, selection of products, so that by the turn of the century Eaton's regular half-yearly catalogue was advertising everything – in alphabetical order – from 'abdominal bands' to 'yarns' (Glazebrook, *et al.*, 1969, pp.v–vi; Davis, 1986, p.7; Santink, 1990, p.157). Such a selection shocked those involved in rural shopkeeping.

So Dad looked at the Eaton's catalogue and he said it would be the death of him. It looked that way. It had everything in it. Oh Lord, what was in it you could write down in a month of Sundays. Every dry goods you could imagine – ladies' shoes with instructions how to measure your foot to get the right size, kitchen pans and pets and cutlery and harness and grub hoes and axes and camps and boots for the men, overalls, jackets, bells to put on your cutters and pumps and guns and everything galore. The only thing as I remember that they didn't have was groceries, but there I could be wrong. Maybe they did have groceries. Of course, the very first catalogue didn't have all these things but they soon did (Broadfoot, 1976, p.278).

Simpson's and Eaton's stressed too that they offered low prices, speedy service and, by the end of the period, free delivery throughout the country on all orders amounting to $10 or more. They emphasised too that their generous exchange and/or refund policies meant that shopping from a catalogue was no more risky than purchasing from a local store: 'Money Refunded if Goods are Not Satisfactory', trumpeted Eaton's: 'We Prepay All Charges on Exchanges' (Stoddart, 1970, pp.155–9; *Globe*, 7 February 1914; Patterson, 1906, pp.428, 430; Bellan, 1978, p.76).

It is impossible to quantify in any statistical fashion the impact that mail-order selling had upon late nineteenth- and early twentieth-century retailing. Nonetheless, it was an impact which by the turn of the century was making itself felt upon a national scale – and not, as might be expected, only in the rural areas of the country. The mail-order catalogues of the great department stores of Canada (and the United States) enjoyed a nation-wide circulation; it was claimed soon after the turn of the century, for instance, that 'Almost every house in Canada contains a catalogue from Simpson's or from one or more of the large retail establishments in Toronto, New York and Chicago' (Patterson, 1906, p.428; also Glazebrook *et al.*, 1969, p.vii). In urban, suburban and rural areas alike, the catalogue was used for information, for comparison and, of course, for consumption. It was a boon to the sick, the elderly, the house-bound and to all those – no matter where they lived or what their circumstances – who enjoyed the anticipation of placing an order and waiting for their chosen goods to arrive (*Globe*, 26 December 1899; 23 June 1910; *Maritime Merchant*, 21 October 1915).

Nevertheless, it was in rural areas that mail order had its greatest impact. Its attractions to isolated country consumers appeared self-evident.

They could sit out there in their log houses, their shacks on the bald prairie with the wind whistling through the cracks, and they could look at the catalogue with every consarned thing in its that man could think up to make, all the good things and all the trashy frivolous things too. Let the wind blow. They just got out their pencil and marked in what they wanted. Bolts of cotton, hames straps, patent medicines, axe handles, anything you wanted. They filled in the slips and that was that. No waiting around. No taking a substitute for something that Dad or Carter didn't have. Carter was the other storekeeper in our little town (Broadfoot, 1976, pp.279–80).

The attractions of mail order were largely spurious, complained country storekeepers like 'Dad' and 'Carter'. Mail-order prices, they objected, were not necessarily lower than those in the general store: 'mail order houses successfully lead the people to believe that they sell all goods at cut prices when as a matter of fact they cut prices on a few lines to-day and put them up again to-morrow and make cuts on another list' (*Canadian Grocer*, 22 January 1915; also 5 February 1915; *Maritime Merchant*, 18 November 1915). When mail-order prices were lower, they protested, it was only because no credit was advanced. Indeed it was claimed that many customers manipulated the competition between mail-order houses and general stores to their own advantage: they shopped locally when they needed credit; and they shopped by catalogue when they had cash to spend (Glazebrook *et al.*, 1969, p.vii). Spurious or not, the attractions of mail-order selling proved difficult for country shopkeepers to withstand. Prairie retailers were one group that found the challenge particularly severe.

And Lord, I can remember when it first dawned on Dad what was happening. You see, you didn't send money through the mail to Eaton's. They didn't want money. Postal orders. That's what they wanted. It was down there in black and white. I think it said "Send No Cash". So these people would come in to Dad's store and he'd see them going down to the back to the wicket and he knew darn well that they were buying postal orders in his own store to send off to Winnipeg. To buy things that were on sale not 10 or 20 feet from them, right in Dad's general store. (Broadfoot, 1976, p.280; also Olson and Pybus, 1982, p.19; Burnet, 1951, pp.78–80).

It is difficult to distinguish the rhetoric from the reality. But there seems no doubt that by the early years of the twentieth century the mail-order departments of city department stores were affecting significantly the trade of many country general stores. Quebec, it is true, was little affected. Eaton's, for instance, made little effort to encourage potential francophone customers: 'Nous préférons que vous vous écriviez en Anglais,' it explained in 1904, 'mais si vous ne pouvez pas, alors veuillez écrire distinctment en Français. En envoyant vos ordres mentionnez toujours la page du Catalogue et le numero de l'article' (Santink, 1990, p.224). Indeed the company did not publish its first French-language catalogue until 1910, a quarter of a century after it had established its mail-order business. English-speaking Canada was affected much more profoundly, with southern Ontario, the prairie west and the Atlantic provinces providing the majority of customers for this new form of selling (*Cotton's Weekly*, 17 December 1908, 7 October 1909; Glazebrook *et al.*, 1969, pp.v–vi). A Nova Scotia resident recalls the impact of this new form of large-scale retailing:

Up until the early 1900s the local merchants had the field all to themselves and with no outside competition charged the natives all the traffic would bear. Then, along came Eaton's catalogue with its alluring bargains, bargains that is, compared to what the local people were forking over for the same grade merchandise. Naturally a howl arose from the outraged merchants [who] resented the invasion of outside competition and the threat of their overcharging (Santink 1990, p.253).

10.6 Conclusion

However, it is necessary once again to urge considerable caution in considering the changes that took place in Canadian retailing. Concentration upon the growth of department stores and the expansion of mail-order selling can lead easily to misunderstanding. For it tends to exaggerate the extent to which large-scale forms of retailing came to occupy a dominant position in the Canadian system of distribution in the years before the First World War. The Hudson's Bay Company lost its monopolistic powers; the co-operative societies made virtually no impact at all; the chain store movement did not exert real influence until well into the 1920s; and the department stores assumed major importance primarily as organisers of mail-order distribution. Changes there were, but not to the extent that is often assumed.

References

Artibise, 1979, *Gateway City: Documents on the City of Winnipeg 1873–1913*, Manitoba Record Society, Winnipeg

Bank of Montreal, 1956, *The Service Industries*, Royal Commission on Canada's Economic Prospects, Ottawa

Bliss, M., 1987, *Northern Enterprise: Five Centuries of Canadian Business*, McClelland and Stewart, Toronto

Bellan, R., 1978, *Winnipeg's First Century: An Economic History*, Queenston House Publishing, Winnipeg

Broadfoot, B., 1976, *The Pioneer Years 1895–1914: Memories of Settlers Who Opened the West*, Doubleday, Toronto

Brough, J., 1982, *The Woolworths*, McGraw-Hill, New York

Burnet, J., 1951, *Next-year Country: A Study of Rural Social Organization in Alberta*, University of Toronto Press, Toronto

Calgary Daily Herald, Calgary, 1911, 1913

Canadian Grocer, Toronto, 1905, 1915, 1930, 1935

Census of Canada, 1931

Census of Merchandising and Service Establishments, 1931

Cotton's Weekly, Cowansville, 1908–10

Davis, A.E., 1986, Brigden's and the Eaton's Catalogue: Business and Art in Winnipeg 1914–40, Canadian Historical Association, Winnipeg

Dominion Bureau of Statistics, 1941, *Canadian Year Book 1941*

Drummond, I.M., 1987, *Progress Without Planning: The Economic History of Ontario*, University of Toronto Press

Dunnville Chronicle, Dunnville, 1896

Easterbrook, W.T. and Aitken, H.G.J., 1961, *Canadian Economic History*, Macmillan of Canada, Toronto

Eastern Labour News, Moncton, 1909

Emmet, B. and Jeuck, J.E., 1950, *Catalogues & Counters: A History of Sears, Roebuck & Company*, University of Chicago Press

Galbraith, J.S., 1957 (1977), *The Hudson's Bay Company as an Imperial Factor 1821–1869*, Octagon Books, New York

General Merchant, Toronto?, 1929

Glazebrook, G.T., Brett, K.B. and McErval, J., 1969, *A Shopper's View of Canada's Past: Pages from Eaton's Catalogues: 1886–1930*, University of Toronto Press

Globe, Toronto, 1899, 1910, 1914

Golden Jubilee 1869–1919: A Book to Commemorate the Fiftieth Anniversary of the T. Eaton Co., Ltd., 1919, T. Eaton Co., Ltd, Toronto and Winnipeg

Gunn, H.G., 1910–11, The fight for free trade in Rupert's Land, *Proceedings of the Mississippi Valley Historical Association*, 4: 73–90

Hamilton Spectator, Hamilton, 1900, 1920

Hande, D.K., 1988, The Small Businessman in Saskatchewan 1919–1939, MA thesis, Saskatchewan University

Harris, R.C. and Warentin, J., 1974, *Canada Before Confederation: A Study in Historical Geography*, Oxford University Press, Toronto

Heywood, P.K., 1941, Tested retail selling policies, *Commerce Journal*, March: 33–9

Hower, R.M., 1943, *History of Macy's of New York 1858–1919: Chapters in the Evolution of the Department Store*, Harvard University Press, Cambridge

Lee, C.E., 1931, Recent developments in wholesale and retail distribution in Saskatchewan, MA thesis, University of Saskatchewan

Maritime Merchant and Commercial Review, Halifax, 1915

Michell, H., 1916, The co-operative store in Canada, *Queen's Quarterly*, 73: 317–38

Nichols, P., 1973, *Skyline Queen and the Merchant Prince: The Woolworth Story*, Trident Press, New York

Olson, G. and Pybus, V., 1982, *By the Old Mill Stream: A History of the Village of Holmfield*, Holmfield History Book Committee, Holmfield

O'Meara, J.E. and Lalonde, L.M., 1941, *Co-operation in Canada 1941*, Dominion of Canada Department of Agriculture, Ottawa

Patterson, N., 1906, Evolution of a department store, *Canadian Magazine of Politics, Science, Art and Literature*, 27 (5): 425–38

Psutka, S.V., 1976, Equalization of retail prices in Canada: the case of the T. Eaton company, 1869–1976, University of Toronto, Geography 1702X paper

The Retailer, Regina, 1915–18

Royal Commission on Price Spreads, Report, 1935

Santink, J.L., 1990, *Timothy Eaton and the Rise of his Department Store*, University of Toronto Press

Savitt, R., 1985, Retail trade, *The Canadian Encyclopedia*, Vol. 3, Hurtig Publishers, Edmonton

Shanks, G.L., 1970, Old Winnipeg as I knew it, Public Archives of Manitoba

Stoddart, J. (ed.), 1970, *The 1901 editions of the T. Eaton Co. Limited Catalogues for Spring & Summer, Fall and Winter*, Musson, Don Mills

White, W.E., 1931, The present status and future of the chain store, MA thesis, University of Western Ontario

Wilson, A., 1965, *John Northway: A Blue Serge Canadian*, Burns and MacEachern, Toronto

Chapter 11
Conclusion
John Benson and Gareth Shaw

The studies brought together in this volume raise a number of fundamental, and extremely complex, issues. Some, such as the influence of legislation on retail change and the reasons for the particular growth of large-scale retailers, have been addressed directly within individual chapters. Others have not. Accordingly it is the purpose of this brief conclusion to consider two of the most important, and most intractable, of the many problems with which the historian of retailing has to deal: the relationship between theory and evidence, and the relationship between small-scale and large-scale forms of distribution.

The problem of integrating theory and evidence is rarely resolved. Indeed, within the history of retailing the attempt has not often even been made. For while few historians, geographers or marketing experts would doubt the value of using some kind of descriptive and/or analytical framework when studying the history of retail change, many would entertain serious reservations about the particular theories and models that have been proposed, and which were discussed in the Introduction to the book. It seems, in fact, that these theories and models tend to suffer from two major limitations. The most obvious difficulty is that they lack both geographical and chronological perspective. For they are generally based upon, and attempt to extrapolate from, the particular experience of the United States. Moreover, they very often concentrate upon, and attempt to determine long-term trends from, the study of specific, and relatively short, periods of time. The danger is obvious and real. It is tempting – and probably misleading – to construct, to accept uncritically, and to assume universal validity for models of retail change which should be regarded, at least until shown otherwise, as being specific with regard both to place and to time. Thus it is clear that the three countries considered in this volume display variations both in the pace of their retail evolution and in the degrees to which different types of retail institution become important.

The other major limitation afflicting the theories of retail change is that they have been constructed by scholars who, whether students of history, geography or marketing, seem preoccupied with size, survival and success. Once again an obvious danger emerges. For it would be easy – and quite certainly misleading – to base any understanding of an economic activity characterised generally by small-scale organisation and business mortality upon the development of that part of it which was distinguished by large-scale organisation, and, often, by entrepreneurial longevity.

Moreover, the studies contained in this volume raise the problem, more generally, of understanding the relationship between large-scale and small-scale forms of retail organisation. It was shown in Part Two of the book that the resilience of 'traditional', small-scale retailing was an important feature of the distribution systems of each of the three countries under consideration. Indeed, the numerical evidence, such as it is, suggests the expansion, rather than the mere survival, of these forms of retailing. Market traders retained a role as suppliers of fresh food to the urban working class; itinerant retailers expanded the range of activities in which they engaged; while small shopkeepers underwent a substantial increase in numbers, becoming linked inextricably with the satisfaction of working-class demand.

The survival of these forms of selling raises, in its turn, the question of what constituted the factors affecting retail change. Previous discussions of retail evolution have drawn attention to demand-side factors such as population growth, urbanisation, and changes in real incomes, to explain the rise of large-scale organisations. However, in many circumstances these changes in demand acted in contradictory ways as dual controls, throwing up new opportunities for both large and small retail firms. In many cases, the former organisations responded to changed circumstances by offering new products and new ways of selling, so as to take advantage of scale economies. Small-scale retailers, by contrast, were becoming focussed more and more on servicing lower-income consumers, who very often could not take full advantage of department stores or many of the multiples. Indeed even the co-operatives, which in theory dealt only in cash sales, could not be used to any great extent by the vast majority of low-income households which had to buy many of their goods on credit.

There were, however, other important factors conditioning the survival of small-scale retailers. Not least of these was the acceptance of shopkeeping as a marginal way of life, by increasing numbers of people who could find no other employment. In many cases, especially at the turn of the century, this led to the growth in female shopkeepers, many of whom were attempting to supplement family income. In addition, in some countries (Germany being the best example) there were legal responses attempting to curb or control the impact of the growth of large-scale retailers. These were not successful and this lack of success (or in Britain and Canada the failure of governments to offer any protection to small-scale retailers) led to a high degree of retailer self-help. This self-help, especially among the more established independent retailers, created not only new organisations, as in Germany, but also introduced some small-scale retailers to more progressive forms of selling. Finally, increased government concern over urban food supply and public health created fresh opportunities for market trading as new market halls were opened in many towns and cities.

Thus the theories and models of retail evolution provide only one context, that of demand, for explaining change. While this is an important dimension for considering the growth of large, capital-intensive retail organisations, which did after all pioneer new and important ways of selling, it fails to offer an adequate explanation of why small-scale retailers expanded. Students of modern retail systems have attempted to overcome this by highlighting the so-called polarisation theory (Davies and Kirby, 1980, p.161; Kirby, 1986; Kirby, 1987), which sees small-scale retailing as an important corollary of large-scale organisations. Those exploring the long-term evolution of retailing may well wish to try to incorporate such concepts into their theories and models.

References

Davies, R.L. and Kirby, D.A., 1980, Retail organisation, in J.A. Dawson (ed.), *Retail Geography*, Croom Helm, London

Kirby, D.A., 1986, Convenience stores: the polarisation of British retailing, *Retail and Distribution Management*, March/April, 7–12

Kirby, D.A., 1987, Convenience stores, in E. McFadyen (ed.), *The Changing Face of British Retailing*, Newman Books, London

Index